VOLUME 471   JANUARY 1984

THE ANNALS

of The American Academy *of* Political
and Social Science

RICHARD D. LAMBERT, *Editor*
ALAN W. HESTON, *Associate Editor*
THOMAS FOGARTY and DAVID LUDDEN,
Acting Associate Editors

PAYING FOR CULTURE

Special Editor of this Volume

PATRICIA A. McFATE

President
The American-Scandinavian Foundation
New York City

SAGE PUBLICATIONS   *BEVERLY HILLS   LONDON   NEW DELHI*

THE ANNALS

© 1984 *by* The American Academy *of* Political *and* Social Science

ERICA GINSBURG, *Assistant Editor*

Editorial Office: 3937 Chestnut Street, Philadelphia, Pennsylvania 19104.

For information about membership* (Individuals only) and subscriptions (institutions), address:

SAGE PUBLICATIONS, INC.
275 South Beverly Drive
Beverly Hills, CA 90212 USA

From India and South Asia, write to:	From the UK, Europe, the Middle East and Africa, write to:
SAGE PUBLICATIONS INDIA Pvt. Ltd. P.O. Box 3605 New Delhi 110 024 INDIA	SAGE PUBLICATIONS LTD 28 Banner Street London EC1Y 8QE ENGLAND

*Please note that members of The Academy receive THE ANNALS with their membership.

Library of Congress Catalog Card Number 83-051274
International Standard Serial Number ISSN 0002-7162
International Standard Book Number ISBN 0-8039-2189-6 (Vol. 471, 1984 paper)
International Standard Book Number ISBN 0-8039-2188-8 (Vol. 471, 1984 cloth)
Manufactured in the United States of America. First printing, January 1984.

The articles appearing in THE ANNALS are indexed in *Book Review Index; Public Affairs Information Service Bulletin; Social Sciences Index; Monthly Periodical Index; Current Contents; Behavioral, Social Management Sciences;* and *Combined Retrospective Index Sets.* They are also abstracted and indexed in *ABC Pol Sci, Historical Abstracts, Human Resources Abstracts, Social Sciences Citation Index, United States Political Science Documents, Social Work Research & Abstracts, Peace Research Reviews, Sage Urban Studies Abstracts, International Political Science Abstracts,* and/or *America: History and Life.*

Information about membership rates, institutional subscriptions, and back issue prices may be found on the facing page.

Advertising. Current rates and specifications may be obtained by writing to THE ANNALS Advertising and Promotion Manager at the Beverly Hills office (address above).

Claims. Claims for undelivered copies must be made no later than three months following month of publication. The publisher will supply missing copies when losses have been sustained in transit and when the reserve stock will permit.

Change of Address. Six weeks' advance notice must be given when notifying of change of address to ensure proper identification. Please specify name of journal. POSTMASTER: Send address changes to THE ANNALS, c/o Sage Publications, Inc., 275 South Beverly Drive, Beverly Hills, CA 90212.

Origin and Purpose. The Academy was organized December 14, 1889, to promote the progress of political and social science, especially through publications and meetings. The Academy does not take sides in controverted questions, but seeks to gather and present reliable information to assist the public in forming an intelligent and accurate judgment.

Meetings. The Academy holds an annual meeting in the spring extending over two days.

Publications. THE ANNALS is the bimonthly publication of The Academy. Each issue contains articles on some prominent social or political problem, written at the invitation of the editors. Also, monographs are published from time to time, numbers of which are distributed to pertinent professional organizations. These volumes constitute important reference works on the topics with which they deal, and they are extensively cited by authorities through-out the United States and abroad. The papers presented at the meetings of The Academy are included in THE ANNALS.

Membership. Each member of The Academy receives THE ANNALS and may attend the meetings of The Academy. Membership is open only to individuals. Annual dues: $26.00 for the regular paperbound edition (clothbound, $39.00). Add $6.00 per year for membership outside the U.S.A. Members may also purchase single issues of THE ANNALS for $6.95 each (clothbound, $10.00).

Subscriptions. THE ANNALS (ISSN 0002-7162) is published six times annually—in January, March, May, July, September, and November. Institutions may subscribe to THE ANNALS at the annual rate: $45.00 (clothbound, $60.00). Add $6.00 per year for subscriptions outside the U.S.A. Institutional rates for single issues: $10.00 each (clothbound, $15.00).

Second class postage paid at Philadelphia, Pennsylvania, and at additional mailing offices.

Single issues of THE ANNALS may be obtained by individuals who are not members of The Academy for $7.95 each (clothbound, $15.00). Single issues of THE ANNALS have proven to be excellent supplementary texts for classroom use. Direct inquiries regarding adoptions to THE ANNALS c/o Sage Publications (address below).

All correspondence concerning membership in The Academy, dues renewals, inquiries about membership status, and/or purchase of single issues of THE ANNALS should be sent to THE ANNALS c/o Sage Publications, Inc., 275 South Beverly Drive, Beverly Hills, CA 90212. *Please note that orders under $20 must be prepaid.* Sage affiliates in London and India will assist institutional subscribers abroad with regard to orders, claims, and inquiries for both subscriptions and single issues.

THE EIGHTY-SEVENTH
ANNUAL MEETING OF
THE AMERICAN ACADEMY
OF POLITICAL AND SOCIAL SCIENCE

APRIL 27 AND 28, 1984
THE BELLEVUE STRATFORD HOTEL
PHILADELPHIA, PENNSYLVANIA

The annual meeting of The Academy is attended by hundreds of distinguished scholars, statesmen, authors, and professionals in diverse fields, including representatives of many embassies, academic institutions, and cultural, civic, and scientific organizations.

This 87th Annual Meeting will be addressed at each session by prominent scholars and officials and will be devoted to the topic of

CHINA IN TRANSITION

Members of the Academy are cordially invited to attend and will receive full information. Information on Academy membership can be found in each volume of THE ANNALS.

- Proceedings of the 87th Annual Meeting will be published in the November 1984 volume of THE ANNALS.

- FOR DETAILS WRITE TO: THE AMERICAN ACADEMY OF POLITICAL AND SOCIAL SCIENCE • BUSINESS OFFICE • 3937 CHESTNUT STREET PHILADELPHIA, PENNSYLVANIA 19104

CONTENTS

BOOK DEPARTMENT CONTENTS

INTERNATIONAL RELATIONS AND POLITICS

AFRICA, ASIA, AND LATIN AMERICA

EUROPE

UNITED STATES

SOCIOLOGY

ECONOMICS

Publisher's Note: The following information is printed in accordance with U.S. postal regulations: Statement of Ownership, Management and Circulation (required by 39 U.S.C. 3685). 1A. Title of Publication: THE ANNALS OF THE AMERICAN ACADEMY OF POLITICAL AND SOCIAL SCIENCE. 1B. Publication No.: 026060. 2. Date of Filing: September 30, 1983. 3. Frequency of Issue: Bi-monthly. 3A. No. of Issues Published Annually: 6. 3B. Annual Subscription Price: paper-inst., $45.00, cloth-inst., $60.00; paper-ind., $26.00, cloth-ind., $39.00. 4. Location of Known Office of Publication: 3937 Chestnut Street, Philadelphia, PA 19104. 5. Location of the Headquarters or General Business Offices of the Publishers: 3937 Chestnut Street, Philadelphia, PA 19104. 6. Names and Complete Addresses of Publisher, Editor, and Managing Editor: Publisher: The American Academy of Political and Social Science, 3937 Chestnut Street, Philadelphia, PA 19104; Editor: Richard D. Lambert, 3937 Chestnut Street, Philadelphia, PA 19104. Managing Editor: None. 7. Owner (if owned by a corporation, its name and address must be stated and also immediately thereunder the names and addresses of stockholders owning or holding 1% or more of total amount of stock. If not owned by a corporation, the names and addresses of the individual owners must be given. If owned by a partnership or other unincorporated firm, its name and address, as well as that of each individual must be given.): The American Academy of Political and Social Science, 3937 Chestnut Street, Philadelphia, PA 19104. 8. Known Bondholders, Mortgagees, and Other Security Holders Owning or Holding 1% or More of Total Amount of Bonds, Mortgages or Other Securities: None. 9. For Completion by Nonprofit Organizations Authorized to Mail at Special Rates (Section 423.12, DMM only): Has not changed during preceding 12 months.

	Av. No. Copies Each Issue During Preceding 12 Months	Actual No. of Copies of Single Issue Published Nearest to Filing Date
10. Extent and Nature of Circulation		
A. Total no. copies printed (net press run)	12233	8168
B. Paid circulation:		
1. Sales through dealers and carriers, street vendors and counter sales	0	0
2. Mail subscription	6773	6712
C. Total paid circulation (sum of 10B1 and 10B2)	6773	6712
D. Free distribution by mail, carrier or other means: samples, complimentary, and other free copies	125	127
E. Total distribution (sum of C and D)	6898	6839
F. Copies not distributed:		
1. Office use, left over, unaccounted, spoiled after printing	5335	1329
2. Return from news agents	0	0
G. Total (sum of E, F1 and 2—should equal net press run shown in A)	12233	8168

11. I certify that the statements made by me above are correct and complete. (Signed) Ingeborg Hessler, Business Manager.

PREFACE

For the issue of *The Annals* dated July 1981, I wrote an article, "The Effects of Inflation on the Arts." At that time, it was apparent that inflation had been taking its toll upon a field that has always been people-intensive and program-expansive.

If there was any doubt about my gloomy conclusions, a recent study undertaken by eight major museums—the Metropolitan Museum of Art, Cleveland Museum of Art, Museum of Fine Arts-Boston, Art Institute of Chicago, Toledo Museum of Art, Museum of Modern Art, Philadelphia Museum of Art, and Los Angeles County Museum of Art—reveals that the impact of inflation has been severe. Despite a 17 percent increase in dollars in a six-year period, the purchasing power of the museums' endowments in 1981 was $122 million less than in 1975.

As the inflationary rate slows, there are still signs that the cultural world remains fragile fiscally. The establishment institutions are having their share of troubles. The 1980 operating deficit of the Metropolitan Museum of Art was $686,557; the deficit for 1982 was $2,102,450. The Art Institute of Chicago, Museum of Fine Arts-Boston, Museum of Modern Art, Philadelphia Museum of Art, and Metropolitan Museum have estimated deficits for 1983 ranging from $49 thousand to $1.5 million. The New York City Opera's deficit is more than $2 million, and a debilitating strike, begun on the opening night of its summer-fall 1983 season, did not bode well for the company's future. The Civic Opera of Atlanta and the Central City Opera in Colorado canceled their 1982-83 seasons for lack of operating funds. Channel 13, the 20-year-old public television station, announced a deficit of $6 million in November 1982 due, according to its president John Jay Iselin, to a lack of reserve cash. Public television station KCET has been forced to sell its studio and stop production of several television programs. The estimated deficit for 1983 for National Public Radio has undergone revision upward almost weekly: in June 1983 it was $8.5 million; 140 staff members had been laid off; and the chairman and president had resigned.

Cuts in the budgets of two federal agencies, the National Endowment for the Arts and the National Endowment for the Humanities, and reductions in city and state governmental support have been causes for concern. President Ronald Reagan has called upon the private sector to meet "those needs of society that the government has not, cannot, or will never be able to fill"; but hard times dictate tough choices, and the arts can hardly expect to be on top of a list that includes human services, community health programs, institutions of higher education, and other areas hit by the recession, unemployment, and federal budgetary cuts. The Exxon Corporation has shifted more than $3 million of its 1983 budget from arts and public television to health and social welfare. The BankAmerica Foundation now is concentrating its funds on health and human services. Urgent appeals from social service agencies are expected to affect other companies' patterns of giving as well.

Not only arts institutions but individual artists are complaining. The boom in art sales is apparently over. The New York market—which includes 300-500 dealers in the area—is no longer thriving. Fewer artists are being shown, less work is being sold, and cash-flow problems are cropping up as buyers not only pay more slowly, but do not always meet their commitments. The concept of art as investment seems to have vanished. The only part of the market that is still thriving is the area of old master paintings, and the work of established modern artists such as Cézanne and Picasso.

In the book field, serious authors are in despair and independent bookstores are in trouble. Four major publishing houses have closed down in the past two years, and several others are expected to fold by the end of 1983. Discount bookstore chains are forcing the smaller stores out of business. Even the prestigious stores may suffer; the closing of Brentano's Fifth Avenue store in New York City, for example, was not unrelated to the proximity of a Dalton's discount store. The discount book chains have an impact on quality, according to Joan Riley, past president of the American Booksellers Association: "when the name of the game is volume for volume's sake, you can't expect works of lasting merit."[1]

But it would be wrong to say that the last two years have held only bad news. Cultural funding has always had its sunny side. Americans gave an estimated $2.6 billion to arts organizations in 1981; corporate contributions to the arts were estimated to be over $300 million for the same period. Edward Broida, a West Coast real estate developer, is opening a contemporary art museum in SoHo. Dallas is building a 60-acre arts district. Art museums in Atlanta, Richmond, Portland (Maine), and Hanover (New Hampshire) are undergoing enlargement or new construction. Chicago's Lyric Opera is operating in the black, and has a $1.1 million bank account.

While Exxon has recently shifted some of its support from public television, it continues to fund "Great Performances," a showcase for American regional theater and other entertainment. Philip Morris contributed about $7 million to the arts in 1982. A new National Arts Stabilization Fund, organized by the Ford Foundation and funded by the Ford, Mellon, and Rockefeller Foundations, was established in July 1983 in order to provide grants to arts organizations seeking to achieve better fiscal management. The National Endowment for the Humanities awarded a $2 million matching grant to the New York Public Library in December 1982—the largest matching grant ever given by the Endowment to a single institution—and the library's president, Dr. Vartan Gregorian, did not doubt his ability to raise the matching funds of $6 million from the private sector. Nine public television stations have participated in a congressionally mandated test of a restricted use of commercials. While the prospect of the commercialization of public television might fall into the category of what Pogo calls "insurmountable opportunities," the consciousness-raising aspects of cooperating with companies have not been entirely lost upon the television station managements.

Creativity seems to be inspiring creative thinking in the area of funding. The owners of Sports Etcetera, a professional promoting organization, have begun using their packaging techniques to pioneer ways in which they can put arts organizations in need of financial backing for an event together with backers in the

---

1. Quoted by Donald Dewey in "Red Ink," *Review* (May 1983), p. 46.

corporate world; the first such deal involved the Pittsburgh Symphony and Merrill Lynch. Other matches have been made between the securities and investment banking company and The Guthrie Theater, the Cleveland Play House, Chicago's Lyric Opera, the Milwaukee Repertory Theater, and several other symphonic orchestras.

Cultural institutions, hard pressed by decreasing operating funds, have continued to find novel, if sometimes controversial, ways to find money. The Museum of Modern Art has sold its air rights to a developer for $17 million and participated in the development of a 52-story residential tower over its galleries. The Museum of American Folk Art has followed suit, with plans for an office tower above its midtown site; the Whitney Museum, with an addition that includes stores along Madison Avenue; and the Jewish Museum, despite protests, with a 19-story residential building on Fifth Avenue. The Metropolitan Museum is seeking endowments to pay for the salaries of department chairmen and promising to add the donors' names to the chairmen's titles.

Federal and local governmental officials have been doing their part to encourage private sector support. Last May President Reagan called for the establishment of a national medal to honor artists and patrons of the arts. At an awards ceremony at the White House, Mr. Reagan cited the Texaco Foundation, Philip Morris, the Cleveland Foundation, and the Dayton-Hudson Foundation along with a roster of artists including Frederica von Stade, James Michener, Frank Stella, and Pinchas Zukerman. Bess Myerson, the latest appointee to the position of Cultural Affairs Commissioner for New York City, has announced a major campaign aimed at winning support for the arts from small businesses, a hitherto untapped source. Public gambling in a state-run game entitled "Megabucks" netted $10 million for the arts in Massachusetts in the first six months of 1983.

Even the criminal justice system seems to have entered into the spirit of things. When Frank Lloyd, one of the world's best known art dealers, was convicted in January 1983 of tampering with evidence in a lawsuit over the estate of Mark Rothko, the late abstract-expressionist painter, Mr. Lloyd's sentence was to develop a scholarship fund for young artists and an art appreciation program for New York City high school students.

All the attention paid to the arts in America leaves little doubt about their importance even in a period of changing values and shrinking resources. However, although cultural workers have written and spoken on a number of issues related to their field—for example, developing new audiences, expanding sources of funds, and paying attention to newly emerging community interests—too often the urgent has driven out the important. Very little coherent argumentation has come from the field on the subject of who should pay for culture.

This volume of *The Annals* looks at paying for culture from various, and varying, points of view. Kathleen McCarthy explores the realities of private sector funding. Michael Joyce raises some provocative questions about the public sector and the price of culture. Edward Keller, Kitty Carlisle Hart, and David Finn give their own and others' estimations of what the public wants. Donald Platten explains his corporation's approach. Sheldon Hackney presents the thinking of an institution that both supports and seeks support for culture. Frank Hodsoll and Livingston Biddle offer differing views on the National Endowment for the Arts. Claiborne Pell and Barnabas McHenry recall their roles in the history of the federal response to the needs of cultural institutions. An international perspective is offered, with articles by Christopher Price and Hans Dahl on England and Norway. Finally, Michael O'Hare and Alan L. Feld, and Kenneth Goody provide excerpts from their reports to the Twentieth Century Fund and the Rockefeller Foundation.

The authors have not had an easy assignment. The topic rouses strong and contradictory feelings. Data are misleading or difficult to find. Projections of funding are linked to the economic climate, and that climate is subject to wide fluctuations over time. As Niels Bohr said, "It's hard to predict—especially the future."

Whatever the conclusions of their arguments, the tone of these essays remains sympathetic: the writers have truly performed labors of love. And if the articles serve as a dialogue in the national interest, then love's labors will not be lost.

PATRICIA A. McFATE

ANNALS, *AAPSS*, **471**, January 1984

American Cultural Philanthropy:
Past, Present, and Future

By KATHLEEN D. McCARTHY

ABSTRACT: Many observers fear that the 1980s will usher in a cultural depression. In the face of governmental cutbacks, economic duress, and rising social-welfare needs, arts organizations may be less competitive for limited private support, and the less established, more experimental groups would be particularly in danger of falling by the wayside. Despite the widespread belief that major portions of the funding community have slashed their arts spending, data reveal that only limited cuts have actually occurred. The commitment to long-term cultural philanthropy seems undiminished. The coming decade may witness a sharper emphasis on strengthening management practices among cultural grantees; the creation of consortia to share technology, physical resources, or fund-raising costs; and audience development to increase the pool of individual donors. Should the economy worsen, the anticipated cuts may, indeed, become a reality. But for the present, individual, foundation, and corporate philanthrophy is holding strong. Rather than an era of retrenchment, the 1980s promise to be a decade of cultural reassessment, stabilization and reform.

Kathleen D. McCarthy received her Ph.D. from the University of Chicago in 1980, after which she served as a Rockefeller Foundation Visiting Research Fellow until 1982. She is the author of Noblesse Oblige: Charity and Cultural Philanthropy in Chicago, 1849-1929 *and editor of a forthcoming volume,* International Philanthropy and the Humanities: The Foundation Perspective. *Ms. McCarthy has served as a consultant to the Donors Forum of Chicago, the Continental Bank Foundation, and the Office of Planning and Policy Assessment of the National Endowment for the Humanities.*

T HE great American writer Mark Twain once observed that "history does not repeat itself, but it often rhymes." Twain's witticism seems to have taken on a poignant significance in the faltering economic climate of the 1980s. In city after city across the nation the unemployed fill the streets, businesses are declaring bankruptcy in increasing numbers, and the voice from the White House is once again urging an economically pressed citizenry to shoulder responsibility for private welfare and cultural services. Many cultural agencies perished in the bleak days after the crash of 1929, and many seem in danger of doing so now. Current thought is that in the face of governmental cutbacks, economic duress, and rising social-welfare needs, cultural organizations will be less able to compete for limited private support, and that the less established, more experimental groups are particularly in danger of falling by the wayside—in effect, that the 1980s will usher in a cultural depression.

These notions have gained wide currency not only among arts spokesmen, but among a broad swath of foundation and corporate contributions personnel. Yet, if one separates rhetoric from reality, a more encouraging pattern appears. Despite the widespread belief that major portions of the funding community have significantly slashed their arts spending, only limited cuts have actually occurred, and the commitment to long-term cultural philanthropy seems undiminished. Arts giving, which grew spectacularly during the last two decades, may slow in the 1980s, and if the economic downturn continues, the anticipated cuts may indeed become reality. For the moment, however, the most striking changes have consisted of minor calibrations in budgetary allotments for the arts, and a growing insistence on better management practices among cultural grantees.

HISTORICAL BACKGROUND

In the 1950s, as in the 1850s, the arts became the province of the many. Run primarily as profit-making ventures, most pre-Civil War arts groups sought broadly based audiences as a means of maintaining their economic survival. From rustic troupes of thespians performing Shakespeare in makeshift frontier theaters to P. T. Barnum's spectacular showcasing of the great Swedish soprano, Jenny Lind, the emphasis was democratic: their doors were open to all. After the Civil War, the constituency narrowed as high culture became the pleasure and the prerogative of the well-to-do. Although efforts were often made to cultivate more heterogeneous audiences within the controlled setting of the museum or the symphony hall, the arts took on a decidedly aristocratic cast, which continued to envelop them to varying degrees until World War II. In the process, they came to be regarded as a luxury for the rich, rather than an imperative for the country as a whole.[1]

This state of affairs changed dramatically in the 1950s. Postwar Americans lived longer, worked shorter hours, and retired earlier than previous generations. The democratization of leisure raised intense fears about how this free time would be spent, whether it would be-

1. For a more detailed account of some of these trends, see Neil Harris, "Four Stages of Cultural Growth," in *History and the Role of the City in American Life,* ed. Arthur Mann, Neil Harris, and Samuel Bass Warner, Jr. (Indianapolis: Indiana Historical Society, 1972), pp. 24-40; and Kathleen D. McCarthy, *Noblesse Oblige: Charity and Cultural Philanthropy in Chicago, 1849-1929* (Chicago: University of Chicago Press, 1982).

come a "peril" or "the opportunity to gain the inner satisfaction, the spiritual and mental balance we need in an anxious age."[2]

Patriotic considerations meshed with the drive to improve Americans' use of their leisure time. Cold War rivalries made Americans increasingly aware that the United States would be judged for its culture as well as its economic and military prowess. Yet the nation's contributions to the arts paled beside governmental outlays in France, Germany, and the Soviet Union; America, it seemed, was falling behind in the competition for the minds of men. In a report to President Kennedy, cultural spokesman August Heckscher underscored the need to send "the best examples of America's artistic achievements abroad" and "to ask whether we have in fact cultivated deeply enough the fields of creativity."[3]

Ironically, as the arts gained in public stature, a plethora of new problems arose. The 1965 Rockefeller Panel report, *The Performing Arts: Problems and Prospects,*[4] listed a litany of artistic woes: although companies expanded tremendously to meet increased demands in the 1950s and early 1960s, few could afford to employ dancers, musicians, and choreographers full-time. Revenues no longer covered expenses. Salaries were notoriously low, spaces for performance limited and woefully inadequate, and financing was strung precariously from one crisis to the next. Clearly arts organizations needed a broader base of support. Box office receipts and the generosity of a few prominent patrons were no longer adequate to the task of supporting the nation's artistic development unaided.

Even as these considerations were being voiced, a new, more sophisticated framework for cultural support was taking shape. In addition to the patronage of wealthy individuals, mass fund-raising techniques increased the number of small donors, middle-class subscribers, and guild members. Foundations and corporate donors, both of which began to proliferate after 1950, would soon play an increasingly important role, spearheaded by the spectacular generosity of the Ford Foundation. Government, too, was about to enter the scene. Indeed, President Lyndon Baines Johnson signed the National Endowment for the Arts into existence shortly after the trustees of the Ford Foundation approved a staggering $80 million appropriation for the nation's symphony orchestras. By the late 1960s a fully articulated system of individual, foundation, corporate, and governmental support was firmly in place. American cultural patronage had come of age.

INDIVIDUALS

Both then and now individuals accounted for the bulk of cultural giving. According to the American Association of Fund-Raising Counsel, individuals provided approximately 60 percent of symphony revenues in 1981, affording major leverage for the nation's theaters as well. As a Filer Commission report noted in the 1970s, individual giving to the arts "is still greater than all govern-

2. U.S., Congress, Senate, *Hearings before the Special Subcommittee on the Arts,* testimony of John D. Rockefeller 3rd, 88th Cong., 1st sess., 1963, p. 198.

3. U.S., Congress, Senate, August Heckscher, *The Arts and the National Government: Report to the President,* 88th Cong., 1st sess., 1963, Document No. 28, p. 1.

4. *The Performing Arts, Problems and Prospects,* A Rockefeller Panel Report on the Future of Theater, Dance, and Music in America (New York: McGraw-Hill, 1965).

ment and national foundation giving combined."[5]

Wealthy individuals such as Henry Lee Higginson and Otto Kahn traditionally played a prominent role in the promotion of the fine arts. With the advent of the Great Depression, however, the possessive stewardship that marked the efforts of many patrons became a luxury few could afford. Otto Kahn reportedly turned down a grant to the Metropolitan Opera from the Juilliard Foundation in 1924, but a decade later the energetic Mrs. August Belmont was developing the Metropolitan Opera Guild to keep the institution alive. Ravinia had darkened its lights; and Samuel Insull's hubristic operatic monument lay in ruins.

Although wealthy individuals often still support cultural endeavors on a grand scale—witness Harold D. Uris's munificent $10 million donation to the Metropolitan Museum of Art in 1981, and the Segerstrom family's $5 million windfall for the Orange County Music Center—an increasing share of cultural funding comes from the more anonymous middle class. As Waldemar A. Nielsen noted in a provocative *New York Times* essay, "the patron of the arts—once so important in the cultural life of the country—has now been replaced by professional strategists and mass fund-raising campaigns. . . . Because of the growth in the number and scale of arts organizations it is now almost impossible for any benefactor single-handedly to make a major difference."[6]

The Rockefeller Panel report stressed the need for arts organizations to broaden their base of support and publicize their needs to the public at large. During the 1950s increased popular interest in culture combined with rising income and inheritance tax rates to make charitable giving more attractive to the middle- and upper-middle classes. This trend was capitalized upon by Ford Foundation matching grants, which encouraged arts organizations to raise millions of dollars in new funds. In the process, a growing pool of middle-class consumers "who respond to the modern merchandising techniques of the houses of culture" were drawn into the cultural fold as donors, subscribers, and members of the arts organizations.[7]

The rate of individual giving may slow somewhat in the 1980s, due to changes in the tax laws under the recently passed Economic Recovery Tax Act, which many fear will reduce the incentives for individual largess. But as of 1981 this sector of the funding triad remained strong. According to figures compiled by the Theater Communications Group, over 76 percent of theater expenses were met by individuals, either in the form of box office receipts or contributions. The American Symphony Orchestra League estimated that individual giving had risen by 42.3 percent in 1981; and $15.6 million in new revenues was raised for public television through auctions and subscription drives. Individual giving has been, and will continue to be, the backbone of cul-

5. Caroline Hightower, "A Report on the Arts," in *Research Papers Sponsored by the Commission on Private Philanthropy and Public Needs* (Washington, DC: Department of the Treasury, 1977), 2: 713.

6. "Needy Arts: Where Have All the Patrons Gone?" *New York Times,* 26 Oct. 1980.

7. Ibid., p. 26. Other important early reports on the state of the arts include William J. Baumol and William G. Bowen, *Performing Arts: The Economic Dilemma* (New York: Twentieth Century Fund, 1966), and *The Finances of the Performing Arts* (New York: Ford Foundation, 1974).

tural philanthropy. It is the area that has the greatest potential for growth, or for disaster, should the ranks of individual donors be significantly thinned.[8]

FOUNDATIONS

Prior to the 1950s foundation and corporate support of the arts had been haphazard at best. Indeed, the great triumphs of foundation philanthropy—the transformation of American medical education, the eradication of a variety of endemic diseases in the United States and abroad, the Green Revolution—were rooted in the sciences, not the arts. By the 1960s, however, John D. Rockefeller 3rd detected a growing sensitivity to cultural needs. In the era of the organization man and the lonely crowd, observers such as Rockefeller felt that foundation support of creative fulfillment would maintain the quest for cultural excellence in a mechanized age.

Although specialized arts foundations such as the Juilliard Foundation began to appear in small numbers in the 1920s, their ranks remained limited throughout the ensuing decades. The Carnegie Corporation was one of the first major, national multipurpose foundations to enter the cultural arena. Under the stewardship of Frederick Keppel, who was himself the son of a prominent New York print dealer, Carnegie launched an art education program between 1925 and 1938 for college art history and art appreciation courses, cura-

torial and teacher training, and adult education.

Founded by the progeny of John D. Rockefeller, Jr., several of whom were noted art collectors in their own right, the Rockefeller Brothers Fund regularly funded New York's cultural instituitons after its inception in 1940, and underwrote the famed Rockefeller report on the state of the arts. Individual support is generally expended close to home. This fund, like many family foundations, institutionalized that support.

Most national foundations, on the other hand, operate within a broader field, and often with more specific aims. Rather than proffering ongoing operating support, they are likely to provide seed money for time-limited pilot projects.

In a particularly thoughtful essay, the president of the Andrew W. Mellon Foundation, John E. Sawyer, outlined the nuances between foundation, government, and individual support. Unlike governmental agencies, foundations can act rapidly, anticipate emerging needs, and undertake sensitive, value-laden, and esoteric projects that might be inappropriate for public support. By the same token, they can underwrite programs, institutions, or causes that are beyond the scope of individual largess, and can afford the kind of decades-long research projects that individuals or government might not. "To purposes such as these," concludes Mr. Sawyer, "an endowed foundation can bring professional evaluation, early response, and a long view of the future."[9]

Foundation giving has risen steadily in all arts categories since the 1950s and

8. Cited in *Giving USA: 1982 Annual Report* (New York: American Association of Fund-Raising Counsel, 1982), pp. 69, 71; Joy Beaton, *A Report of the Executive Committee of the Chicago Community Trust on the Arts in Chicago* (Chicago: Chicago Community Trust, 1983), p. 29.

9. Quoted in the *Report of the Andrew W. Mellon Foundation* (New York: Andrew W. Mellon Foundation, 1980), p. 10.

early 1960s. According to a Foundation Center survey of 369 major foundations, total gifts for culture rose from 13.5 percent of all grants in 1980 to 15.3 percent in 1981. However, it is feared that several factors may begin to slow the growth of foundation giving to the arts in the coming decade—particularly, declining assets, changes in the tax laws, and the competing demands of social welfare organizations.[10]

A survey published by the Rockefeller Foundation recently tested these hypotheses. Approximately 50 percent of the foundations that responded specifically stated that they expected to increase their arts budgets for 1983, or keep their giving at the same level. A Chicago Community Trust survey of community foundations found somewhat the same results: ten of the twelve respondents did not anticipate changes in their priorities as a result of federal cutbacks, one intended to place greater emphasis on information gathering, and one planned to devote greater attention to the needs of mid-sized arts organizations. Several also planned to stress financial or managerial improvements among grantees.[11]

In many instances, the prevailing attitude is one of pragmatism rather than permanent change. As one president of a mid-sized Texas foundation pointed out, although greater attention would be paid to local social-welfare needs, good arts projects would continue to hold their own. Because foundations are bound by guidelines, charters, and the decisions of their trustees, their programs are less vulnerable to economic and social vicissitudes and will continue to be shaped by the perceptions and commitments of their donors, staffs, and trustees.

The Rockefeller Foundation, for example, remained relatively aloof from the exigencies of the Great Depression, cleaving to the course of experimentation, pioneering, and fundamental research. Rockefeller was the first major foundation to fund dance, donating over $350,000 to various organizations between 1953 and 1959; it also generously promoted the cause of contemporary music though a ten-year, $400,000 grant to the Louisville Orchestra for the commissioning, performance, and recording of new works. Other early Rockefeller efforts incuded a domestic program for the development of community, university, and regional theaters throughout the United States, and international donations to individuals and institutions active in music and drama.

After 1963, when the new Arts Division was formed under the direction of composer Norman Lloyd, the foundation focused its attention on the support of artistic development in the United

10. *Foundations Today* (New York: Foundation Center, 1982), p. 15.

11. For the results of the Rockefeller Foundation survey, see Kenneth L. Goody, *The Funding of the Arts in the United States* (New York: Rockefeller Foundation, 1983). In the course of researching this article, interviews were also conducted with representatives from the Rockefeller, Mellon, Ford, MacArthur, Meadows, Northwest Area, Mobil, Atlantic Richfield, Dayton Hudson, and Metropolitan Life Foundations; the Carnegie Corporation, Rockefeller Brothers Fund, and Pew Memorial Trust; the National Endowment for the Arts; the Exxon and Philip Morris Corporations; the Donors Forum, Foundation Center Library, Chicago Community Trust, and Business Committee for the Arts; Lincoln Center, Kennedy Center, the Theater Communications Group, Lyric

Opera, New York City Opera, and Museum of Modern Art; and W. McNeil Lowry. For information on community foundations, see Beaton, *A Report,* chart 6.

States, helping to lengthen symphony seasons; underwriting the performance of works by American composers; developing showcases for contemporary opera; fostering acting, directing, and playwrighting through major universities; and funding experimental ventures in theater, opera, dance, and video art. By the 1980s the program had achieved a threefold focus under the stewardship of former *New York Times* music critic Howard Klein: aid to creative individuals, international cultural exchange, and exploration of issues bearing on the place of the arts in American society.

However imaginatively conceived, the program has not significantly expanded over the course of the past two decades. Rockefeller's allocations for the arts rested at $3 million in 1964, where they remain today. Nor are prospects for future expansion particularly bright. Like many of the big foundations, Rockefeller's portfolio failed to prosper in the inflationary 1970s. As part of a general move toward consolidation, the Arts and Humanities Divisions have once again been combined and are currently awaiting trustee review. Thus, while it is probable that the foundation will retain its commitment to support for creative individuals, greater emphasis may also be placed on points of convergence between the arts and humanities in the future.

Ironically, three of the grandes dames of the foundation world—Rockefeller, Carnegie, and Ford—have acquired new presidents since 1979, leaving their future courses of action unclear. Ford was an early leader in the arts, donating over $350 million to American cultural organizations since the program's inception in 1957, when the foundation became the first major national patron of the arts since the government's brief flir-

tation with cultural support under the auspices of the Works Progress Administration in the 1930s.

The chronology of Ford's commitment is well known. In 1957 the foundation began spending a modest—for them—$2 million in arts grants each year, coupled with a full-scale national inquiry into the social and financial state of the nation's artistic resources. Five years later the trustees designated the arts as one of the five areas in which the foundation would concentrate its giving over the next decade, a program which rapidly expanded under the inspired stewardship of W. McNeil Lowry.

In 1963, for example, Ford inaugurated "the most ambitious program ever conceived for dance," donating $7,756,000 to strengthen professional ballet companies thoughout the United States: over $35 million was ultimately expended.[12] The artist-in-residence program was developed to aid creative individuals and enable small museums to purchase their works, thus whetting the public's appetite for contemporary art. The biggest windfall was granted in 1966, when $80 million was allocated for symphony orchestras. These grants reverberated throughout the musical community, more than doubling symphony endowments through matching provisions, helping to broaden the base of popular support, lengthening seasons, increasing audiences, and helping to raise musicians' salaries. In the process, Ford's initiatives helped to publicize the value—and the problems—of artistic endeavor in American society.

12. Anatole Chujoy, "Philanthropic Foundations and the Dance," in *U.S. Philanthropic Foundations,* ed. Warren Weaver (New York: Harper & Row, 1967), p. 316.

Unfortunately allocations for the program so brilliantly conceived under Lowry diminished after his departure. In 1974 Howard Klein noted that Ford had donated more to the arts "than all other foundations and the National Endowment put together."[13] Three years later Ford's shrinking portfolio had halved the foundation's budget and reduced the arts budget by four-fifths, to a mere $4 million.

Ford's current commitment to the arts has been clouded by the foundation's abrupt reorganization in 1980 and the slow evolution of new guidelines in the Education and Culture Division. Recently, however, several areas of interest have crystallized, including the examination of public policy issues affecting the arts, the development of talent, strengthening of cultural resources, cultural preservation, and a continuing commitment to the financial stabilization program initiated under Mr. Lowry in 1971. Briefly, the latter program is designed to strengthen the financial and managerial capabilities of professional performing arts companies through two methods. If a group is able to reduce its net current liabilities by 50 percent within a given year, Ford will eliminate the remaining 50 percent; and should the group continue in the black, the foundation will provide access to a revolving reserve fund to tide it over the temporary cash flow crises that habitually plague organizations dependent upon box office receipts. Thus, although cultural philanthropy is no longer the central priority it was during Mr. Lowry's administration, it still has a place in the foundation's agenda.

Despite their historic significance, the combined contributions of Rockefeller and Ford are presently well below those of the Mellon Foundation. Interest in the arts is deeply rooted in Mellon's history. Andrew W. Mellon, for whom the foundation is named, founded the National Gallery of Art in Washington during the Great Depression. Between 1937 and 1942 the family spent an estimated $71 million in construction costs as part of an ongoing commitment to cultural philanthropy.

Mellon's giving is strongly focused, and like some of the work at Rockefeller and Ford, many of its grants are superb. The foundation's commitment to "activities of enduring value" has been uncompromisingly articulated by its president, John E. Sawyer, who underscores "the value of maintaining highly qualified organizations that can set their own agendas and bring their own talents, initiatives, and independent judgments to bear on important needs and questions. It is imperative that we sustain this capacity in strength—and protect the fullest opportunities for its private support—against vicissitudes of funding and vagaries of government policies."[14]

As a result Mellon has funded programs to foster art conservation techniques, laboratories, and research; established artistic directors' discretionary funds to assist and stimulate creative activity; promoted theatrical revivals; helped to strengthen the endowments and managerial capacities of leading arts organizations; and worked to build new audiences by partially underwriting

13. "Private Philanthropy," *The New Republic,* 171:20(16 Nov. 1974).

14. Quoted in the *Report of the Andrew W. Mellon Foundation* (New York: Andrew W. Mellon Foundation, 1981), pp. 16-17.

the *Live from Lincoln Center* series on public television.

Unlike Rockefeller and Ford, Mellon's portfolio prospered during the 1970s, providing substantial sums for the continuation of these programs. As program officer David Saltonstall explains, the foundation's interest in the arts, inherited from the founders, has remained strong. Thus the cultural budget is expected to remain at about the same level as last year, around $11 million.

Nor are Rockefeller, Ford, and Mellon the only giants on the arts funding scene. Chicago's MacArthur Foundation has made local cultural philanthropy a focus of its giving programs since 1979, when 16 Chicago organizations received the first arts grants. By 1981 the number of recipients had grown to 39, including small, off-Loop theaters, community arts groups, and cultural activities in the city's schools. These recipients represent grants totaling over $1 million, making MacArthur the third-largest private donor on the city's cultural scene. Similarly, the newly formed Getty Foundation in California promises to pour millions into art conservation and research through the development of a string of self-created, self-operated institutes in the 1980s.

The foundation scenario is, therefore, mixed, but not as bleak as is generally feared. Across the broad spectrum, more organizations appear to be increasing or stabilizing their arts budgets than cutting back. Although the situation at some of the major foundations has been colored by internal reorganization and declining revenues, Mellon's commitment is undiminished, as is that of some of the other largest donors, such as the Pew Foundation, and new leaders— MacArthur and Getty—have recently entered the field. Although the torch of foundation leadership may have been passed, there is a good chance that it will continue to burn brightly in the 1980s.

CORPORATIONS

Corporate support was the *wunderkind* of the funding community in the 1970s. By 1979 over 600 corporations had developed foundations, and business giving surpassed foundation largess for the first time. Cultural agencies were among the primary beneficiaries of this growth. In 1959 business donors allotted a sparse 3 percent of their donations to arts groups; by 1980 this figure had reached almost 11 percent, fueled by a spectacular 33 percent rise in corporate cultural patronage between 1979 and 1980. Estimates for 1981 place the total figure as high as 12 percent, and in-kind donations may account for as much as another $75 million in donated exhibition space, publicity, and loaned expertise. Employee matching gifts are also on the rise. In 1975 only 4 companies matched employee donations to cultural grantees; by 1981 the number had risen to 168, a trend that constitutes "one of the more constructive and promising developments on the cultural scene."[15]

The flow of corporate gifts into cultural coffers was sparked by a growing realization that association with the arts might enhance company concerns. Healthy arts organizations enrich the quality of community life in areas of company operations—so the argument

15. Nielsen, "Needy Arts." For a more detailed analysis of corporate giving, see the *Annual Survey of Corporate Contributions* (New York: Conference Board, issued annually) and the publications of the Business Committee for the Arts.

ran—thus helping to retain valued employees; they tend to be noncontroversial, and highly visible as well, burnishing the image of businesses that support them. Moreover, strong centers of artistic activity promised to supply the imaginative talent needed to improve advertising, product, and office design.[16]

Recently, however, changes in the economy and competition from social-welfare services threatened to disrupt the corporate-cultural honeymoon of the 1970s. The crisis mentality was genuine. The majority of corporate respondents to the Rockefeller Foundation survey felt that federal cutbacks and the general economic malaise had placed significant constraints on cultural largess and that smaller, less established organizations would bear the brunt of retrenchment. As one corporate contributions official explained, "It's hard to justify supporting modern dance groups, contemporary chamber music, and similar activities when employees are being laid off."

Equally ominous, in the minds of some, was the press's lukewarm response to "The Vatican Collections," an exhibition that had been underwritten by a $3 million grant from Philip Morris, Incorporated. As Metropolitan director Philippe de Montebello explained, "The Philip Morris contribution is the most generous ever made to an art exhibition by any corporation."[17] When coupled with an estimated $2 million in additional advertising and promotional fees, it quickly becomes clear that the company's investment was staggering.

The rationale for sponsorship of such an exhibition, or the King Tut exhibit, which was jointly funded by Exxon and the National Endowment for the Humanities, is that the corporation will benefit from the resulting publicity, enhanced visibility, and association in the public's mind with a product of indisputable quality. The Vatican show may have challenged some of these assumptions. Some of the publicity has been negative. For local sponsors, such as Merrill Lynch in New York and the Continental Bank in Chicago, it has been almost nonexistent. And the sheer expense of such an undertaking makes it difficult for a corporation to do anything else. In the words of the former head of Philip Morris's corporate contributions program, Barbara Reuter, the company's "arts budget isn't going to grow as fast as it has been" as a result of the Vatican show grant.[18] Museum directors especially have begun nervously to test the wind for the corporate community's response.

However, only a few corporations sponsor blockbusters of this genre. The majority have been content to till their own gardens, providing support for the continued activity of local arts institutions in headquarters and factory areas, and the Rockefeller Foundation data suggest that these activities may not have been as stringently circumscribed

---

16. For a thoughtful analysis of one corporation's philosophy, see C. C. Garvin, "Exxon and the Arts," *The Lamp*, 60(4):1 (Winter 1978).

17. Quoted in Business Committee for the Arts, *News*, 59: 6 (Oct. 1982).

18. Quoted in Sandra Salmans, "Big Business Tightens Its Arts Budget," *New York Times*, 20 Feb. 1983. Nevertheless, Philip Morris has continued to experiment with innovative programs in the visual arts, such as the recently opened branch of the Whitney Museum on the first floor of the corporation's midtown New York headquarters. For a discussion of the company's ongoing commitment to the arts, see *Philip Morris and the Arts: 25 Year Report* (New York: Philip Morris, 1983).

as is popularly believed. Very few corporate contributions respondents reported cuts in their arts budget: approximately 75 percent predicted increased giving for the arts in the coming decade. Only a few recorded qualitative changes in their priorities, but their answers are revealing. Several stressed better administrative practices among grantees, a greater emphasis on outreach, and in some instances, attention to smaller, more locally based organizations.

The Rockefeller data provide a useful cross section of corporate largess spanning the spectrum from small programs of only a few hundred thousand dollars to giants in the corporate field. The largest corporate cultural patrons—according to the Business Committee for the Arts—include Atlantic Richfield, Exxon, and Mobil, and here again the picture is not as bleak as it might seem.

The Exxon Corporation has supported the arts for over 35 years, and has to its credit sponsorship of the King Tut show and some of the most significant and best-loved programming on public television. Exxon's domestic contributions budget skyrocketed in recent years, reaching $52 million in 1982, a figure that placed it on a par with the contributions of the Mellon Foundation. Moreover, because the company determines its contributions budget by a set percentage of pretax net income averaged over three years, its philanthropic activities have been shielded somewhat from violent vicissitudes in world economic markets and oil consumption. As a result Exxon spokesmen expect that the company's total contributions budget will remain at about the same level in 1983. As Leonard Fleischer, who directs its arts contributions explained, "Exxon is

still heavily involved with public television, it is still focusing on cultural activities, and we anticipate that it will continue to do so."[19]

Similarly the Mobil Foundation will continue to fund the arts at approximately the same level in 1983 as in 1982, including substantial gifts to smaller, community-based organizations. Although best known for its work with public television, Mobil also has a flourishing community-based cultural program, which currently underwrites organizations in 80 communities, including over 100 small organizations in New York City. Now in its eighth year of operations, the community program was augmented in 1979 with the inclusion of employee matching gifts to cultural agencies.

Nor is the Atlantic Richfield Foundation predicting cutbacks in its cultural support. In fact Atlantic Richfield increased both its total budget and donations to the arts and humanities, which currently constitute approximately 14 to 16 percent of the foundation's $33 million budget. However, in addition to funding a diverse range of cultural activities, such as residencies for prize-winning chamber music orchestras and a traveling exhibit of Indian art, Atlantic Richfield is now exploring programs to mesh cultural and social-welfare concerns, such as a series of "Strings and Beans" concerts by the Denver Symphony Orchestra, to which the price of admission will be canned goods for the poor. In the process Atlantic Richfield is trying to devise creative ways of fostering cooperation rather than competition among the various components of the nonprofit sector.

19. Interview, 28 Feb. 1983.

THE GRANTEE PERSPECTIVE

The crisis mentality so prevalent among foundations and corporate donors has tinged the perceptions of the grantee community as well. As is the case among donors, the general perception is that one's own organization is faring well, while others are bearing the brunt of the cuts. After noting his own good luck with fund raising, the director of a major New York cultural institution admitted that corporate project support had waned slightly and predicted that, should reductions become more apparent, "certain things won't be done": short-term, experimental, and public outreach ventures. The development director of another major New York cultural landmark suggested that it is becoming increasingly difficult to elicit first-time grants from foundations, but noted that the biggest drop had occurred in contributions from small donors— the ordinary guy whose contributions run in the $35-to-$100 range.[20]

While some Chicago institutions raised ticket prices and shortened hours in response to reduced public support, others reported record levels of private giving. The Lyric Opera, for example, just completed its most successful fundraising year in history, with 92 percent of the tickets sold and 100 percent of its $4.6 million funding goal raised. Similarly, as this article was being written, corporate contributions to Lincoln Center were running well ahead of previous years. Organizations such as the Lyric are working harder than they once had to in order to raise these revenues, occasionally even drawing in outside profes-

sional assistance, but they are managing to meet their campaign goals.[21]

Some smaller organizations are forming consortia to raise funds, share physical properties and computers, or sharpen their fund-raising or managerial skills— a trend encouraged by both private foundations and corporations. Donor consortia are less common, although a few have appeared in recent years. Joint funding ventures are frequently devised informally among foundations with similar programmatic or geographical interests as a means of maximizing contributions and ensuring that programs will be adequately funded. Thus the Exxon Corporation, the Rockefeller Foundation, and the National Endowment for the Arts collectively underwrote the composers-in-residency program; Lincoln Center benefited from a Consolidated Corporate Fund Drive; and Chicagoans recently launched City Arts II to create a safety net for small inner-city arts organizations. However, the problems inhibiting the creation of formal funding consortia are manifold. Smaller corporations run the risk of being buried by major corporate donors in jointly funded exhibitions such as the Vatican show; and many grantee and donor institutions see membership in formal consortia as a threat to their autonomy.[22]

A more marked trend is a growing awareness of and sympathy for the

20. Interview, 28 Feb. 1983.

21. For a strongly dissenting view, see *Theater Facts '82* (New York: Theater Communications Group, 1983).

22. Many of those interviewed spoke of the difficulties entailed in assembling and maintaining consortia, particularly among grantees. However, there appear to be some regional variations. While New Yorkers and Philadelphians noted a certain resistance to consortial undertakings, respondents from Minneapolis and Texas pointed to a number of such ventures in their regions.

plight of smaller, less established institutions. These institutions often fail to attract funds because of their limited audiences, or because of their lack of visibility. New organizations often fail to attract prominent trustees who could open the door to private fortunes and corporate funds, and thus lack adequate endowments to tide them over hard times. While many operate with shoestring budgets and highly committed volunteers, even those with the most dedicated staffs can seem of marginal importance in times of economic duress.

Nevertheless the desire to sustain these organizations appears to be strong. Over half of the corporate and foundation respondents to the Rockefeller Foundation survey noted an ongoing commitment to promising but less established professional arts organizations, a trend verified by spokesmen for the major corporate foundations.

In order to ensure the continued viability of these organizations, foundations and corporations have underwritten a variety of programs to strengthen arts management skills. This subject has been of concern to the private sector since the Ford Foundation first embarked on its princely campaign to build orchestral endowments in the 1960s. More recent efforts have included Dayton Hudson's $100,000 grant to a Minneapolis arts organization to develop new means of generating revenue; Exxon's support of the American Business Council's skills bank and Business Volunteers for the Arts; a flurry of Mellon Foundation grants to help arts companies increase their earned and contributed income; and the formation of the Dallas Center for Nonprofit Management, which includes a substantial percentage of arts groups among its constituency.

CONCLUSION

"When do performing artists prove their quality enough to stop rattling the tin cup?" queried Robert Brustein in the *New York Times* six years ago. Unfortunately in the current economic climate, arts organizations will not only have to rattle their cups more vociferously but more ingeniously as well if they are to be heard, for as John Sawyer and countless others have explained, "There is no way that corporate or private philanthropy, already facing requests that far exceed available funds, can make up the difference" in the face of substantial federal cutbacks.[23]

Corporate support may change markedly in the 1980s. A keener emphasis on better grantee management practices will almost certainly be coupled with a greater insistence on audience development to ensure the continued survival of the nation's cultural institutions. As one corporate executive pointed out, "The overwhelming percentage of private funding for the arts has traditionally come from individuals, and arts organizations will have to continue to cultivate and widen this constituency."[24] Recent events have underscored the precarious dependency of corporations and foundations on portfolios and economic shifts, and the linkages between public support and political vicissitudes. Audience development and increased ranks of individual donors, large and small, is still perceived as the soundest means of providing a stable base on which arts

23. Robert Brustein, "Can the Show Go On?" *New York Times Magazine* (7 July 1977), p. 57, and the *Report of the Andrew W. Mellon Foundation* (1981), p. 10.

24. Interview, 28 Feb. 1983.

organizations can grow. There may also be a greater emphasis on grantee consortia, information sharing, and time-limited grants. The 1960s and 1970s were marked by the rapid proliferation of both funders and grantees; the 1980s will be a time of reassessment, stabilization, and reform.

Yet, despite the widespread belief among donors, the press, and grantees that social-welfare demands are eclipsing cultural concerns, artistic ventures have remained competitive for private funds. The majority of foundations and corporations polled in the course of this study are currently planning to increase or at least maintain previous levels of arts support, to continue that support through the long term, and to ensure that both new and established organizations will receive a fair hearing. Arts groups may have to work harder for private dollars, they may have to focus more on management and less on special projects, they may even have to band together to lure additional funds. Should the economy worsen they, like all nonprofits, will feel the sting of shrinking revenues; but they are presently holding strong. To paraphrase Franklin Roosevelt's inimitable phrase, for the moment there is little to fear but fear itself.

Government Funding of Culture:
What Price the Arts?

By MICHAEL S. JOYCE

ABSTRACT: The immediate challenge to the National Endowments for the Arts and the Humanities is not financial but philosophical. Government responsibility for culture must include an explicit statement of policy based upon a careful consideration of essential questions concerning the nature of and relationship between the state and culture. In the past the Endowments have been reluctant to enunciate a cultural policy lest it be objected that talk of a cultural policy sounds like a call for an autocratic ministry of culture. But grants cannot be made in a vacuum, and some cultural policy, however incoherent, inevitably informs decisions about grants. The issue is whether such a policy is to be made explicit, so that it may be studied and criticized, or whether such a policy is tacit, in which case it is likely to be enforced with little public scrutiny or evaluation. The federal government—responsible to both the individual and the nation, to the present and the future—has a unique role to play in American culture. What the role is can be defined only through the political process, in open debate.

Michael S. Joyce is executive director and a trustee of the John M. Olin Foundation. He is a trustee of the Foundation for Cultural Review, which publishes The New Criterion, *a monthly cultural review. He was a member of the President's Task Force on Private Sector Initiatives. In addition to his involvement with other organizations, he was chairman of the Heritage Foundation's Task Force on the National Endowment for the Arts and the National Endowment for the Humanities.*

27

"Because of the arts," I said, "Because our government finally decided to support the arts."

> —Michael Straight, in September 1964, explaining to Anthony Blunt why he had decided to expose to the Federal Bureau of Investigation the Soviet spy ring in which he had been a participant, however unwittingly.[1]

The history of the governmentalization of support for culture in the modern era has yet to be written, and the reasons for this are easy enough to understand. On the one hand the mind of the advocates of public spending for culture has been so deeply affected by the process of the politicization of the arts that it cannot view that process in an objective historical manner; while on the other hand defenders of a private sphere for culture have been forced into an attitude of negative opposition, which rarely results in dispassionate study. Yet some preliminary political analysis might be possible and desirable.

THE POLITICIZATION OF GOVERNMENT SUPPORT FOR CULTURE

Advocacy of government support for certain kinds of cultural activities is a political enthusiasm that appears to be in the ascendancy in the United States today. At present the Congressional Arts Caucus is the largest and perhaps the most powerful special interest caucus in the U.S. Congress. "Artistic endeavor in America is endangered by the insensitivity that the Reagan Administration continues to show toward federally funded arts programs," said Congressman Thomas J. Downey, speaking before a gathering of mayors at the 1983 midwinter meeting of the U.S. Conference of Mayors. Downey, chairman of the Congressional Arts Caucus, stressed that the arts have "an important economic and social impact" on the cities. But the congressman also displayed an interesting, if not advanced, aesthetic taste and curious notion of the nature of the creative act when he explained to his audience that "making more cuts in arts programs is equivalent to tying da Vinci's hands behind his back and then telling him to paint the Mona Lisa."[2]

To understand a political position of this kind one must study not only its real characteristics as they appear to reasonable men and women in public debate; one must also examine the distortions produced, it appears, by the passions and interests of the advocates themselves. In politics it is not enough to consider the actual; it is necessary also to consider the imaginary, for in politics we deal not only with real things but with extreme, exaggerated, and distorted opinions about these things. Considerations of the imagination are essential to our understanding of politics.

In 1869 Matthew Arnold defined culture as being "a pursuit of our total perfection by means of getting to know, on all the matters which concern us, the best which has been thought and said in the world."[3] Even the most charitable critic would find it difficult to reconcile the overall performance of the two fed-

---

1. Michael Straight, *After Long Silence* (New York: W. W. Norton, 1983), p. 326.

2. Remarks before the Midwinter Committee Meeting of the U.S. Conference of Mayors (Washington, DC, 27 Jan. 1983).

3. Matthew Arnold, *Culture and Anarchy: An Essay in Political and Social Criticism,* ed. J. Dover Wilson (Cambridge: Cambridge University Press, 1932), p. 37.

eral departments officially established to support culture with this definition. Nonetheless it must be said that the National Endowment for the Arts and the National Endowment for the Humanities have supported some good work both interesting and lacking a wide audience.

Yet, since they were founded in 1965, the Endowments' appropriations have grown from $2.5 million each to $162 million for the Arts and $140 million for the Humanities in fiscal year 1984— dollars which have played such a very large role in the expansion of the cultural amusements of some Americans at public expense. The Arts Endowment spends millions of dollars each year to subsidize programs and events unconcerned in any way with enduring artistic accomplishment, but with the aid of sophisticated marketing and advertising techniques capable of producing sizable audiences. To some arts advocates such a calculus of social and economic impact is sufficient reason for maintaining the federal endowments and even for substantially increasing their budgets. Yet such policies ought to occasion deep misgivings among true friends of culture and of democratic politics; for they are at bottom policies whose practical results are to provide programs of entertainment for some at the expense of all.

CULTURAL POLICY

In the spring of 1980, under the auspices of the Heritage Foundation, I organized a committee charged with producing a study of the National Endowments for the Arts and for the Humanities. Upon the study's completion—at the beginning of 1980—it was to be made a part of a governmentwide study of the executive branch that would be made available to the winner of the November election and published in 1981.[4]

We began our work by considering the assumption that the federal government could be involved in support of culture at the level of hundreds of millions of dollars without a cultural policy. We concluded that if democratic governments were to be involved in spending public funds on culture, there was no choice about whether or not to have an official cultural policy. Where the spending of millions of dollars of public monies was taking place, there was no doubt that some policy was being observed, however incoherent. Grants cannot be made in a vacuum. The only real choice is whether such a policy is made explicit, open, and public, in which case it can be studied— criticized, defended, improved upon or modified; or whether such a policy is tacit or implied, in which case it is likely to be uncritically accepted and enforced without public debate and with little opportunity for evaluation or reform.

It might be objected that talk of an explicit cultural policy sounds like a call for an autocratic ministry of culture. What is objectionable about a ministry of culture, of course, is that it aims at stamping out diversity by governmentalizing the whole of cultural activity. It's exactly for this reason that the role and policies of the Endowments must be made clear in a country where we assign a limited role to government. The implied or tacit cultural policy that we found to be the custom at both of the National Endowments helped to explain,

4. Charles L. Heatherly, ed., *Mandate for Leadership: Policy Management in a Conservative Administration* (Washington, DC: Heritage Foundation, 1981).

in our view, the presence of programs supported for political and social reasons rather than for artistic or scholarly reasons. It was for this reason that our committee saw the challenge to the federal cultural Endowments' future as "not financial but rather philosophical; it is recognition of the need to redefine its missions as support of art and artists, nothing less, and nothing else."[5] We sought an understanding of the interests of the federal government and the American people in perpetuating the Endowments; an articulated strategy for the fufillment of their mandates.

We made the assumption that any official cultural policy, whether or not such policy provides or precludes support for cultural activities, must be based upon a careful consideration of essential questions concerning the nature of and relationships between the state and culture. For the purpose of our work these questions included

1. Should the national government support culture?

2. Should distinctions between cultural endeavor and programs of entertainment be made?

3. Should official support of the culture be expected to accomplish particular social and economic goals, however desirable they may be?

Over the summer and into the fall of 1980, the committee members read reams of public documents from the two Endowments, conducted many interviews with officials and grantees of the Endowments, and worked out the arguments among themselves.

Two opposed positions about the future of the two Endowments existed

among the committee members from the outset. One urged drastic cuts to put an end to the funding of what was seen as nonsense: vague notions of entitlement and concern with the promotion of social causes to replace traditional standards in the arts and humanities; a tendency to confuse the spirit of the humanities with an expansive humanitarian enthusiasm; the support of entertainment over art and artists, of consumption rather than creation. Drastic cuts, some committee members felt, perhaps would close down the Endowments eventually.

The other initial position agreed with the economic arguments and with ending grants for nonsense, but still wished to continue federal support for quality programs. This position proposed directing funds away from individuals and toward prestigious and well-established institutions.

Whatever the merits of abolishing the Arts and Humanities Endowments might be, such an outcome came to be seen as highly unlikely in the course of our work on the Heritage Foundation report. Terminating any federal agency is well nigh impossible, and the Endowments have created powerful constituencies with their largess, while influential members of the establishment are often counted on to champion government support for the performances and exhibitions sponsored by the famous cultural institutions. Some members of Congress can regularly be seen to display generous philanthropic habits when spending public monies. Calls for the disestablishment of the federal Endowments are likely to be seen by members of the Congressional Arts Caucus as attacks on certain of their own most cherished virtues.

5. Michael S. Joyce, "The National Endowments for the Humanities and the Arts," in ibid., p. 1056.

The second approach—restricting sub-sidies to established institutions—held some appeal initially. But funding the large institutions would only accelerate a tendency of the Arts Endowment since its inception: a preference for perfor-mance and exhibition of past art works rather than support for the creation of the new. It was also clear that support for these institutions often amounted to little more than a public subsidy for the entertainment of those most able to afford the true costs of particular exhi-bitions or performances.

We asked ourselves, Is there another policy that could take account of the political and fiscal realities and at the same time be of benefit to our nation's cultural life?

The Heritage Foundation report on the Endowments set forth an alternative policy for cultural support. The general thrust was a policy based on support of arts and artists rather than entertain-ment and advocacy groups, an emphasis on education and scholarship, and sup-port for creation rather than for con-sumption.

Arguing for an official policy of limited scope implemented in a low pro-file style, the Heritage Foundation report emphasized art for art's sake.

Because art does not move in obedience to social dictates, because it cannot be planned in advance, and because it grows acording to its own (mostly unarticulated) rules, it must be granted an existence independent from the proclaimed social goals of the state; accordingly, it must be funded for its own sake, rather than for any presumed eco-nomic or propaganda benefits. . . .

the NEA [National Endowment for the Arts] must accept the proposition that official support can have only limited goals. It can ease to some extent the birth pangs of new art. It cannot determine the exact part of the past which is preserved, nor can it dictate the manner of its presentation to a contempor-ary public; these are artistic questions which must be decided anew by each successive generation of artists. The NEA cannot de-cide, either directly or indirectly, the course of new art or devise a schedule for its pro-gress; at most, it can modestly support the individual efforts of artists who are serious, highly competent, and large of vision.[6]

At this writing, despite news reports to the contrary, it would seem that the recommendations contained in the Her-itage Foundation report have little or no effect on the official policy of the Arts Endowment. While the Arts Endow-ment under the Reagan administration has reduced the overall budget from what the Carter administration had pro-posed, there is little discernible differ-ence in the policies being implemented.

PUBLIC/PRIVATE PARTNERSHIP

One new emphasis is distinctive in the present administration. The Arts En-dowment seeks to arrange private sup-port for the arts in partnership with the federal government. Chairman Francis S.M. Hodsoll told the *New York Times* as reported on 10 April 1983 that "a principal role of the Arts Endowment is to confer a stamp of approval," an "imprimatur" that will have the effect of giving organizations receiving federal grants not only money but also a creden-tial that gives them an advantage in the competition for private funds. More recently, Mr. Hodsoll said in a speech to the New York Chapter of the National Society of Fundraising Executives that the Endowment is

encouraging greater private support (includ-ing efforts of the President's Committee on

6. Ibid., p. 1055.

the Arts and the Humanities; greater leverage from our grants; and a variety of specific projects designed to recognize, inform, assist and advocate new private support for the arts).[7]

It is easy to understand the appeal of such an arrangement to the current Arts Endowment adminstration. The old establishment of official cultural policy, as expressed in the National Endowments for the Arts and for the Humanities, supported the bad along with the good, the ephemeral along with the eternal, the national treasures of pure art and learning along with the use of culture for the achievement of dubious—and, from the standpoint of many, distasteful—social and political ends. A safer emphasis for the new administration might sweep out the objectionable programs wholesale, leaving a clear field to the well-established and the widely approved. In any case, the Reagan administration won an election on the basis of a political philosophy that clearly prefers the private to the public, the individual initiative to the bureaucratic edict.

One must also assume that the chairman of the National Endowment for the Arts came under pressure for both patronage and preferment from important segments of the entertainment and cultural community. These segments, which include celebrities, arts advocacy organizations, and the major performing and exhibiting institutions, have demanded their right to be heard. The combination of a policy of continued support for the large, established institutions together with an aggressive policy aiming to influence the size and direction of private support for culture would seem to provide a method for satisfying the most powerful constituencies while at the

7. New York, 20 Jan. 1983.

same time ostensibly accommodating the political philosophy advocated by the Reagan administration.

What can be said about a policy that bids to accomplish so many agreeable purposes in so comfortable a way? At the outset there may be a flaw in the very device of shifting governmental responsibility from the state itself to a private sector initiative or partnership coordinated by the federal government. The essence of our political system is political accountability for the expenditure of government funds. Here is the meaning of no taxation without representation; here is the necessary function of elected legislatures. For the federal Endowments to attempt to influence the flow of private funds for the support of culture is to remove policy, spending, and staff from public scrutiny. To do so is to short-circuit the proper process of open discussion and presentation of alternatives. No one will deny that the problems of cultural policy fit clumsily into the world of political controversy. The same, however, can also be said of every other aspect of our public life.

The use of government money to influence the spending of private money constrains private decisions. A reliance on the governmental imprimatur for the arts by establishing de facto governmental standards of taste results in an erosion of private responsibility. In addition, because the amount of private funds is limited, those applicants who have been rejected for government matching grants will likely be deprived of equal access to private funding.

What about the more basic problem of the ending of a federal role in culture and its replacement by private patronage? If we are true to our heritage of freedom and private initiative, the conclusion we reach must never involve a culture controlled and directed by government. But this is not to say that government has no responsibility for culture. It is rather to favor a maximum of individual and voluntary group activity in the realm of culture, setting private requirements and conditions without direction by the federal government.

Cultural patronage by government in a democratic society is invariably going to be bureaucratic, and a policy of patronage based on bureaucratic tastes tends to fossilize the culture it supports. Thus we must allow for as much diversity in patronage as possible. The more diversity, the more alternatives for the artist and the scholar, and the more likely we are not to have an ossified culture. Private donors must be guided by their own tastes, by their own judgments about the good and the beautiful, not by reliance on the herding effect induced by government jawboning for culture.

THE UNIQUE ROLE OF
FEDERAL CULTURAL PATRONAGE

In support of culture, our national government has a role that by definition differs from that of the private sector. The private role should be that of patron of first resort. What can be funded in this manner should be. But there is much that private philanthropy, whether from individuals or corporations, seems to have difficulty in doing to a sufficient extent: the support of esoteric scholarship, of individual artists, of the preservation of unfashionable but nonetheless great art. All these tasks demand that the federal government—because it is responsible to both the individual and the nation and to the past and the future—be a patron of last resort.

Here, perhaps, is the crux of the matter. The private sector has to support what it will; the public sector has to support what it must. What that "must" is can be defined only through the political process. Both those who believe that federal cultural policy should be directed toward support of art and of scholarship and those who wish to provide public entertainment and produce social and economic impact have a duty to make their respective cases cogently and straightforwardly in the political arena, rather than place an illusory faith in yet another manipulation of institutional arrangements. The American people, regardless of their economic or social condition, deserve a fair and open argument.

ANNALS, *AAPSS,* **471,** January 1984

The Public and the Arts

By EDWARD B. KELLER

ABSTRACT: The tremendous growth in public involvement with the arts and public funding of the arts, which the United States witnessed in the 1960s and 1970s, took place during a unique period in American history. During that period the social values of the nation shifted radically. In the 1980s, we are again undergoing fundamental change in our social, economic, and political environment. A more restrictive economy is causing the American people to rethink many of the assumptions that engendered the social-values revolution of the last two decades. The watchword of the 1980s can best be described as adaptation, as the nation seeks to blend social and economic goals. In this climate almost all assumptions are being reexamined, including those about the arts and funding of the arts. This article reviews the social and political climate of the 1960s and 1970s, in which culture and the arts exploded, and the changes that have taken place in the 1980s; it then analyzes current public attitudes toward funding of the arts; finally, it identifies some key social and public-policy trends that are emerging in the eighties and are likely to influence the future of funding of the arts.

Edward B. Keller is a vice-president of Yankelovich, Skelly and White, the national survey and marketing research firm. His primary responsibilities are in the firm's Policy Planning Group, where he works with organizations to help define their public policy objectives and develop strategies to achieve those objectives. He is a graduate of the University of Pennsylvania, where he also earned his M.A. in Communications from the Annenberg School of Communications.

A S art critic Hilton Kramer has observed, "In several important respects, the art scene as we know it today owes its essential features—and most especially, the scale of its operations—to the cultural world that came into existence in the 1960s. It was then that the two National Endowments [for the Arts and for the Humanities] were created and the role of the Federal Government in the art life of the country began to gather momentum."[1]

The arts, of course were not alone. In a wide variety of spheres—from health, education, and welfare to the work place to consumerism and the environment—the sixties and seventies saw a new and expanded role for the federal government, a role that the American public strongly endorsed.

The 1960s also produced a significant expansion of public interest in the visual arts, what Kramer calls a cultural "explosion": "Before you could have the 'blockbuster' exhibitions of the 1970's, you had to have a blockbuster public, and this was one of the things the 1960's gave us for the first time."[2]

Here, too, the trend is completely in sync with a broader shift in social values —some have called it a cultural revolution—that swept the country in the 1960s and 1970s. The Protestant ethic, with its emphasis on self-denial and future rewards, was rejected in favor of values that stressed the pursuit of self-fulfillment, immediate gratification, individualism, and personal involvement. The American public went in search of the full, rich life, and the arts were a part of that life.

The 1980s, however, are shaping up to be very different from the 1960s and the 1970s. We are again undergoing fundamental change in our social, economic, and political environment. The economy has grown more restrictive, and social and political values are adapting as a result. In the words of Daniel Yankelovich, "In a matter of a few years we have moved from an uptight culture set in a dynamic economy to a dynamic culture set in an uptight economy. . . . The world we live in has been turned upside down."[3]

This article reviews the social and political climate of the 1960s and 1970s, in which culture and the arts exploded, and the changes that have taken place in the 1980s; it then analyzes current public attitudes toward funding of the arts; finally, it identifies some key social and public policy themes that are emerging in the eighties and are likely to influence the future of funding for the arts.

THE SOCIOPOLITICAL CLIMATE

In the aftermath of World War II the United States enjoyed a period of unparalleled economic growth. The country industrialized rapidly, and American technology, developed in response to the necessities of war, became preeminent. Domestically scores of Americans, by virtue of their increased access to affluence and higher education, began to realize the American dream. Upward mobility and middle-class lifestyles became the norm and, by the end of the 1950s, nearly 70 percent of the population had attained middle-class status.

---

1. "When Modernism Becomes Orthodoxy," *New York Times,* 28 March 1982.

2. Ibid.

3. *New Rules: Searching for Self-fulfillment in a World Turned Upside Down* (New York: Random House, 1981), p. 22.

Overseas, America's military and economic power were unmatched.

The psychology of affluence

With this rapid economic growth came unprecedented optimism; in fact, by the end of the 1950s the prevalent opinion was that the nation was capable of nearly unlimited economic growth. With the optimism also came a new social phenomenon: the psychology of affluence. As depression-bred economic insecurities gave way to an expectation of affluence, the nation's traditional social values—the Protestant ethic, with its emphasis on self-denial and rigid moral standards—were replaced by a new set of values that emphasized a focus on self, creativity, self-expression, and freedom from moral and financial constraints.

Many Americans had come to believe that affluence was no longer something that had to be struggled for; instead it was considered the logical by-product of America's endlessly expanding economy. With affluence and economic growth now taken for granted, the economic agenda of the forties and fifties was supplemented in the 1960s by a social agenda that sought to fix the perceived inequities of American society and improve the quality and style of American life.[4]

To help advance the social agenda the public turned to the government, which was ready and willing to heed the call. The public sector rapidly increased its investment in social welfare programs that served not only the poor, but also the middle class. The government was also quick to take on the task of regulating business to assure that business did not put the pursuit of profit ahead of the new agenda, which demanded greater corporate attention to such matters as health and safety, environmental protection, and corporate responsibility to society.

This was the climate in which funding for the arts—both public and private—soared. The funding level of the National Endowment for the Arts increased from approximately $2.5 million in 1966 to more than $150 million by 1981; the American Association of Fund-Raising Counsel estimates that philanthropic contributions to cultural institutions increased from $376 million to $3.35 billion during the same period.[5]

The new realities

In a few short years, as the 1970s ended and the 1980s began, the social and political climate suddenly shifted again as the assumption of affluence that had given rise to the social agenda was called into question. The assumptions that had engendered the fix-everything trend were weakening.

At home the shocks of seemingly incurable double-digit inflation and a second energy crisis led the public to believe that the economy was out of control, while events taking place abroad—the Soviet invasion of Afghanistan, the seizure of the American embassy in Iran, and increasing competition in the international marketplace—caused the nation to wonder whether the United States was losing its position as a world economic and military power.

4. For a more thorough discussion of the shift in social values that took place in the 1960s and 1970s, see ibid.

5. *Giving USA: 1982 Annual Report* (New York: American Association of Fund-Raising Counsel, 1982), p. 36.

New economic realities had developed, and both business and the public began to doubt the idea of unlimited economic growth. By 1980 over 60 percent of the population had come to believe that "Americans should get used to the fact that our wealth is limited, and most of us are not likely to become better off than we now are," and that "our current standard of living may be the highest we can hope for."[6] The classic American optimism is eroding; the psychology of affluence is giving way to a psychology of limits and lowered expectations.

The response to the new realities has not been a return to the past, as some observers had predicted. Rather, if the keynote of the 1950s was self-denial, a future orientation, and a belief in the power of hard work in order to get ahead in a climate of economic growth; and if the keynote of the 1960s and 1970s was a zeal to fix the quality of American life, and a trend toward focus on self, less rigidness, self-fulfillment, and social responsibility, all based on the assumption that economic plenty was assured; then the keynote of the 1980s can best be described as adaptation.

Signs of adaptation can be seen in our political fabric, as the foundation of the public policy process in the 1970s—big government—has been rejected as too costly and inefficient. A new public policy foundation is emerging, which is predicated upon a realization that no single institution in society will solve the problems confronting us, but rather that responsibility for solutions will have to be shared. Thus we are seeing a reassigning of institutional responsibility: both business and individuals are gaining

6. *The Yankelovich Monitor* (New York: Yankelovich, Skelly and White, 1980).

responsibility, while the government's role is inreasingly defined as one of oversight. The federal government is not likely to be shut out of the policy process, but neither is it likely to dominate the process again as it had in the 1970s, regardless of which political party is in power.

The social fabric is adapting as well. The new values of the sixties and seventies are becoming tempered as Americans attempt to reconcile personal expectations that developed over the last two decades with the economic realities of the 1980s.

A component of this adaptation has been a rethinking of our national priorities. The emergence of the new economic realities has caused a shift away from the overarching focus on the social agenda of the sixties and seventies. Americans have not retreated from their commitment to health and safety, a cleaner environment, or fairness and openness on the part of our institutions—the core components of the social agenda. Yet survey after survey indicates that the economy has become—and is likely to remain—a dominant issue of the eighties. No longer is the traditional economic agenda of economic growth, job creation, technological development, and international competitiveness taken for granted.

In short the eighties are seeing a blending of the social and economic agendas. Americans are attempting—as painlessly as possible, using strategic planning, competitiveness, and a greater emphasis on personal skill and self-reliance—to meet the new, more constricted economic outlook. At the same time, they attempt to retain the gains made by the social agenda of the 1960s.

Within this context—particularly concerning the recognition of new economic realities and the reemergence of an economic agenda—attitudes toward funding of the arts in the 1980s can now be explored.

ATTITUDES TOWARD FUNDING OF THE ARTS

There has been very little research conducted on attitudes toward the arts. One major study, conducted in 1980 by Louis Harris and Associates for the American Council for the Arts (ACA),[7] paints an extremely optimistic picture of Americans' attitudes toward the arts: "it is apparent from these results that the arts strike a warm and highly positive response in people. It is evident from this study that the arts are now earning a special place in the lives and consciousness of the majority of the people in this country."[8] It concludes that "the arts are becoming important in the mainstream of American life, and even in the face of deeply troubled times, they do not decline in perceived value and importance."[9]

Some of the study's major findings and the conclusions it draws are as follows:

1. Attendance at the arts is on an upward curve.

2. There is a growing desire to experience the arts. Two in three among the public (64 percent, up from 54 percent in 1975) feel that "if there were more theater and concert events in this community, I would attend more frequently." A similar percentage (62 percent) says that "if there were more showings in art museums in this community, I would attend more frequently."

3. No longer does the public believe that the arts are for the nation's elite only. By 59 percent to 39 percent, a majority rejects the claim that "the arts can only be enjoyed by a privileged few who have the financial means to attend arts events"; a more narrow 48 percent to 46 percent plurality rejected this view in 1975.

4. Personal involvement in the arts is sharply on the rise. As many as 44 percent of all members of the public now say they are involved with photography (up from 19 percent in 1975), while 30 percent say they play a musical instrument (up from 18 percent), 22 percent say they write creatively (up from 13 percent), and 20 percent say they dance (up from 9 percent).

5. There is strong public support for arts education as part of the regular school curriculum. A 56 percent to 39 percent majority says that school-age children do not have enough opportunities to be exposed to the arts.

In his forward to the ACA study, George Weissman—chairman of the board of Philip Morris Incorporated, the study's co-sponsor along with the National Endowment for the Arts—remarks that

what is significant [about the findings], to my mind, is not the ability of art to maintain, or even strengthen its hold upon the mass of American people, but to do so in the face of inflation, higher taxes, rising unemployment, cuts in services, high interest rates, and decreased leisure time.[10]

7. National Research Center for the Arts, *Americans and the Arts: Highlights from a 1980 Nationwide Survey of Public Opinion* (New York: American Council for the Arts, 1981). The National Research Center for the Arts is an affiliate of Louis Harris and Associates, Inc. Earlier studies were conducted for the American Council by the Harris organization in 1973 and 1975.

8. Ibid., p. 4.

9. Ibid., p. 10.

10. Ibid., p. i.

Yet it is evident from the ACA study, as well as other survey data, that the nation's economic troubles are taking a toll on the arts, particularly with regard to the critical question of funding. In the more restrictive economy of the 1980s, the arts are finding themselves in fierce competititon for scarce financial resources.

Government funding of the arts

In a period when federal funds are being cut back in virtually every area, the ACA study finds, "The arts are perceived as being more self-supporting, more dependent on private contributions and less dependent on government" than other nonprofit institutions. The study concludes,

This is significant, for it means that as much as arts funding from government might have increased in recent years, public perception that the arts are overfunded by government is certainly hard to find. Indeed, the reverse can be concluded: most people in America feel the arts have not been dependent on government at all.[11]

This finding is essentially confirmed by a 1981 Roper study for the American Enterprise Institute (AEI),[12] which found that a 37 percent plurality of the public is satisfied by the current mixture of public and private efforts to foster the arts. The remainder of the public is evenly split, with 25 percent in favor of a greater public role and 26 percent in favor of a greater private role.

Focusing specifically on the role of government, the AEI study found that a 66 percent majority of the public believes that the government has a role to play in fostering the arts. Most of these people (46 percent) feel the government's role should be "minor," while 20 percent feels the government should play a "major role," and only 27 percent of the public feels that the government has "no role at all." Asking more directly about government funding for the arts, a 1981 survey by the Los Angeles Times[13] found that a 54 percent to 34 percent majority of the American public approves of government funding for the arts.

On the question of the role of the federal government versus state and local government, both the AEI and ACA studies found that the public is more in favor of funding for the arts by state and local governments than by the federal government. AEI, for example, finds that 24 percent of the public thinks that the arts are best fostered by local government and 19 percent thinks they are best fostered by state government, while only 14 percent thinks they are best fostered by the federal government.

Making the same point somewhat differently, the ACA study found that a clear 64-to-31 percent majority of the public feels that local governments should provide financial assistance to arts institutions, and a 60-to-37 percent majority feels similarly about state governments. However, support for federal funding to arts institutions is expressed by a more narrow 50-to-46 percent majority.

11. Ibid., p. 17.

12. Roper Center for Public Opinion Research/Roper Organization, "Private Initiatives and Public Values" (Survey conducted for the American Enterprise Institute for Public Policy Research, Washington, DC, 1981).

13. Los Angeles Times, Poll No. 43 (April 1981).

Despite this sentiment, and reflecting, perhaps, the ACA study finding that the arts are not generally thought to be very dependent on government funding, a 1981 CBS/*New York Times* poll[14] found that only 37 percent of the public feels that federal spending on the arts should be decreased, while 49 percent feels that spending should be kept about the same.

The role of the private sector

As efforts have been made to reduce the rate of growth in the federal budget, increased attention has been paid to the role of private sector funding for many programs. In particular, there has been mounting pressure on corporations to step in and help fill the gap left by shrinking government budgets. For example the President's Task Force on Private Sector Initiatives, created in 1981 to encourage private sector activity in the social arena, in its 1982 report to the president called for corporations to double cash giving to charitable causes within four years, a goal that would raise the U.S. average for all corporations to 2 percent of pretax income.[15]

In fact total corporate giving increased almost fourfold from $797 million in 1970 to a record high of nearly $3 billion in 1981.[16] Looking to the future, a 1982 corporate survey conducted for the Council on Foundations by Yankelovich, Skelly and White found that about two-thirds of the chief executives interviewed expect their philanthropic contributions to increase by about 25 percent over the next four years.[17]

Corporate contributions to arts and cultural organizations have risen sharply as well. An annual Conference Board survey of corporate contributions has found that as a percentage of total corporate giving, contributions to art and culture have risen steadily from 5.3 percent in 1970 to 11.9 percent in 1981, making it the largest growth area in corporate philanthropy since the mid-1970s.[18]

This increase in corporate giving to cultural and arts organizations is consistent with the findings of another 1982 Yankelovich, Skelly and White survey, which found that corporate executives see the arts and culture as one of the top priority areas for business to help fill gaps left by shrinking government budgets. Mentioned by 50 percent of the respondents, only job training and retraining (76 percent), loaning executives to the public sector (61 percent), and aid to education (57 percent) were identified as higher priorities.[19]

While this view may be encouraging to supporters of the arts, it is completely at odds with the attitudes expressed by the general public when asked the same question in a concurrent Yankelovich, Skelly and White survey. The American public agrees with corporate executives that job training and retraining programs and education are important areas for corporate gap-filling; giving assistance to cultural organizations, however,

14. Conducted in April 1981.

15. E. B. Knauft, "A Case for Giving 2% of Pretax Income," *New York Times,* 17 Oct. 1982.

16. *Annual Survey of Corporate Contributions, 1983 Edition* (New York: Conference Board, 1983), p. 16.

17. Yankelovich, Skelly and White, Inc., "Corporate Giving: The Views of Chief Executive Officers of Major American Corporations" (May 1982).

18. Ibid., p. 10; *Annual Survey of Corporate Contributions, 1982 Edition* (New York: Conference Board, 1982), pp. 30-31.

19. *Corporate Priorities* (New York: Yankelovich, Skelly and White, 1982).

falls virtually at the bottom of the public's list of priorities.[20]

Why should the arts and culture fall so low on the public's list of gap-filling priorities when the ACA study found that the arts strike such a positive response in people? In a restrictive economy, when the public perceives the nation's economic pie to be shrinking, it is an emerging reality of the 1980s that the arts increasingly will be forced into competition with other worthwhile pursuits as the nation debates spending priorities.

In the first round of the debate, in the early years of the Reagan administration, the AEI study found that a 43 percent plurality of the public feels that total spending for the arts—from all sources, governmental and non-governmental—is "about right," while 22 percent feels that spending is "too high" and 17 percent feels that spending is "too low." In contrast, however, majorities of the public believe that spending in such competing areas as social services for the elderly, education, and job training is too low.

Similarly, the AEI study found that 40 percent of the public feels that private support for the arts will not make up for cutbacks in government spending in this area, while 37 percent expects that the private sector will be able to fill the gap. Again in contrast, 65 percent worries that cutbacks in social services for the elderly will not be offset by increases in private support, and a 54 percent majority does not think that cutbacks in either educational or job training programs will be offset, either.

Thus it may be true, as the ACA study concluded, that "the arts are becoming more important in the mainstream of American life" and that "even

in the face of deeply troubled times, they do not decline in perceived value and importance,"[21] but when forced to weigh one valued goal against another, the public—for now, at least—sees other areas as more in need of scarce funds than the arts.

IMPLICATIONS FOR THE FUTURE

As stated earlier, the public's response to the new economic realities has not been a return to the life-styles and values of the past, nor has it been to seek revolutionary social change. Rather our research reveals a pattern of adaptation. Americans are reacting to the new conditions by adopting a strategic, problem-solving approach to compensate for a static economy.

The art historian and critic John Caneday has observed that the so-called artistic boom has become "a deep-rooted critical growth that has yet to come to full flower."[22] While the arts might find themselves in increasingly greater competition for scarce funds, it is unlikely that the nation will turn its back on the artistic seeds that were planted in the 1960s and that blossomed in the 1970s. But if they are to come to full flower in the 1980s, arts and cultural institutions will have to adapt to the new realities along with the rest of the nation.

There are four broad social and political themes, or trends, that are emerging in the 1980s and are likely to influence the future of funding for the arts. While some might be antithetical to the traditions of fund raising for the arts, they represent the new climate to which the arts must adapt if they are to thrive in these more difficult times.

20. Ibid.

21. National Research Center for the Arts, *Americans and the Arts,* p. 10.

22. Ibid., p. i.

A strategic approach

Perhaps the most important of these themes is a new emphasis on strategic, or entrepreneurial, thinking. Manifestations of this new approach are increasingly evident in the marketplace, where traditional retail outlets are being bypassed by consumers in favor of undersellers; paraprofessionals are being consulted instead of professionals; buying in the underground economy is becoming an increasingly legitimate way to shop; and barter is now perceived as both respectable and feasible.

It is also evident in the work place, where the professional manager is coming under increased scrutiny and efforts are being made to restore enterpreneurial thinking. It is evident, as well, in the political arena, where activists, for example, have responded to their shrinking influence in Washington, D.C., by adopting a broad array of tactics, including boycotts, referenda, political action committees, litigation, and stockholder initiatives.

Arts organizations have already begun to adopt new strategies to meet the financial challenges they now face.[23] Perhaps the boldest example was the Museum of Modern Art's (MOMA's) decision in 1979 to sell its air rights to a real estate developer for $17 million. The museum will derive ongoing benefits from the luxury apartment tower that is being built due to a legislative

23. See, for example, Leslie Benetts, "Arts Groups Seek New Strategies As They Vie for Shrinking Funds," *New York Times,* 4 Dec. 1982; Cynthia Saltzman, "Recession Impact Hits Arts Organizations Hard, Forcing Cutbacks and Limiting Any Innovation," *Wall Street Journal,* 7 Dec. 1982; Howard Blum, "Museums Turning to Air Rights for Revenues," *New York Times,* 7 Jan. 1983.

program, developed by New York State to aid museums, which channels real estate taxes into a trust fund that benefits the museum. Other New York cultural institutions are now following MOMA's lead and are exploring ways to raise funds through real estate development.

Other strategies that arts and cultural institutions are applying include the hiring of professional fund raisers, direct selling, more aggressive marketing and advertising, new efforts to attract small donors, and more merchandising of products. There are new political strategies, as well, including the formation of a Congressional Arts Caucus in 1981 to argue for a greater federal role in financing of the arts, and ArtPac, a political action committee formed to help elect pro-arts candidates.

In this new climate there will be increasing pressure on the arts, in general, and individual arts organizations, specifically, to develop new and innovative strategies to find a niche and prove that they can win in a competitive environment.

The new meritocracy

An important element of the values revolution of the 1960s and 1970s, stemming from the psychology of affluence, was the rise of an egalitarian ethos, rooted in the conviction that in an era of unbounded economic vitality, economic and social well-being should be accessible to all segments of society. While most of the new values were able to weather the recession of 1973-74, the egalitarian ethos began to show signs of erosion; now, with the recognition of new economic realities in the 1980s, egalitarianism is giving way to an emerging meritocracy orientation, a values perspective that rewards competence and achievement, and—rather than seeking to equalize all groups in society—allows those who have earned, or feel they have earned, a certain status and position to actively seek mechanisms that distinguish themselves from others.

The arts explosion of the 1960s and 1970s—in which, according to the National Endowment for the Arts, the number of dance companies and resident theaters grew approximately tenfold and the number of orchestras more than doubled—was fostered by the spirit of egalitarianism and pluralism, in which there was a desire to broaden exposure to and involvement in the arts.

The new meritocracy orientation will probably broaden the schism between the largest and most renowned arts organizations, which are feeling the financial pinch but are managing, and less well-established groups, many of which are threatened with bankruptcy.

At the same time, the smaller arts organizations—the ones that are of high quality—can perhaps tap into this new meritocracy by positioning themselves as a vehicle for those who perceive themselves as elite and want to distinguish themselves from the rest of the public. Together with an emerging regionalism (described next), this suggests that small arts organizations may be able to survive in the new economic climate by positioning themselves to appeal to the new local elites, many of whom may be the so-called baby boomers who grew up with the new values of the sixties and have now grown into their thirties, started families, and moved into positions of prominence in their local communities.

Regionalism

Underlying the appeal of President Reagan's new federalism is a growing sense of regionalism. The public has reacted to the shrinking economic pie not by a return to national values, but by taking a more parochial view of the world. For example surveys by my firm have found that a significant minority of the public now believe that it is more important to worry about one's own part of the country than to worry about the nation as a whole.

Experts predict that the blockbuster exhibitions of the 1960s and 1970s will probably become less common in the future. For example Robert Montgomery Scott, president of the Philadelphia Museum of Art, believes that financial pressures will force museums "to plan exhibitions of a smaller scale [that are] more local in nature."[24] Such a trend might have a positive side effect, given the rise in regionalism, in that it may foster greater community identification with local cultural institutions across the country, thereby providing a more solid base of support as cultural institutions are forced to rely increasingly on local sources of funding.

An economic agenda

As has been repeated throughout this article the economy has become, and is likely to remain, the key issue of the eighties. Scarce funds—both public and private—are most likely to be developed in areas that are seen as contributing to economic revitalization. Congressman

24. Saltzman, "Recession Impact Hits Arts Organizations Hard."

Sidney Yates has argued, "The arts make an enormous contribution to the prosperity of the country as well as enhancing the quality of life of the American people."[25] New York's Mayor Edward Koch agrees:

That cultural institutions work out ways to raise funds to survive is extremely important to the future of this city. The vitality of these institutions is not just a question of the quality of life but of economic necessity.[26]

To compete effectively for funds it will become increasingly important for cultural institutions to document the economic contribution of the arts and culture, and to argue their case persuasively to government officials at all levels, to foundations and other private benefactors, and, perhaps most important, to the public.

25. Irwin Molotsky, "Chicago and the Arts: Merging Constituencies," *New York Times,* 28 Dec. 1982.

26. Blum, "Museums Turning to Air Rights for Revenues."

ANNALS, *AAPSS,* **471,** January 1984

Changing Public Attitudes
Toward Funding of the Arts

By KITTY CARLISLE HART

ABSTRACT: Throughout this nation's relatively brief history, a tradition of pluralistic funding of the arts has evolved. The partners in this pluralistic system are individuals, the federal government, state, county and local governments, foundations, businesses, and corporations. With all of these partners participating, the system prevents an unhealthy dependence on any one source and keeps any one source from dominating. An increasing number of Americans view the arts in a positive manner. Nationwide studies and the 1980 census indicate that more Americans are participating, actively and passively, in the arts than ever before in the nation's history. However, the typical American does not seem to understand the pluralistic funding process, especially the role government should play in the funding partnership. The public needs to understand the benefits of government funding of the arts for our society. The funds that taxpayers invest in the arts provide essential tools for economic development and social stability. Public funds spent on the arts multiply in the economy at large, attract tourists, and generate the need for related goods and services. Thus the public needs to be educated to comprehend that government participation is a vital ingredient in our American system of pluralistic support for our cultural endeavors.

Kitty Carlisle Hart was appointed chairman of the New York State Council on the Arts in 1976. A native of New Orleans, she was educated in Switzerland, France, and England, where she studied both at the London School of Economics and the Royal Academy of Dramatic Arts. An accomplished actress and singer, she made her Metropolitan Opera debut in 1967. Mrs. Hart was married to the late Moss Hart, the Pulitzer Prize-winning playwright and director.

NOTE: The author wishes to thank Joseph Wells, director of public relations of the New York State Council on the Arts, for his assistance with this article.

45

CHANGES in public attitudes are essential for any society that hopes to prosper in today's complex world. Over the years we Americans have changed our attitudes about a whole range of matters from how we dress to how we react to global concerns. However, attempts to predict or influence public attitudes often prove elusive. Social scientists remind us,

The proliferation of market research agencies and public opinion polling in America attests to the problematic nature of the individual's response in a mass society. . . . A new brand of automobile is launched with fanfare, only to die a year later; a party plays an issue hard and long, only to find at the polls that it took the wrong path; pharmaceutical houses manufacture vast quantities of a new vaccine, then discard it some months later after the public has stood pat.[1]

Throughout history only a precious few concepts have remained stable in a relative sense. The arts, and the role they play in a society, are one of those stable concepts, even if they themselves are constantly in flux.

Since the dawn of man the arts have led the way in how we think about ourselves and the world around us. The arts have been, and always will be, at the forefront of a changing society. Katherine Anne Porter's analysis illustrates this point most succinctly:

The arts live continuously . . . they outlive governments and creeds and societies, even the very civilizations that produced them. They cannot be destroyed altogether because they represent the substance of faith and the

only reality. They are what we find again when the ruins are cleared away.[2]

Given these few hypotheses and observations, how do we gauge the attitudes of Americans about funding the arts in our nation? Indeed should these public attitudes be changed; and, if so, how? In order to understand current attitudes on this subject it is necessary to comprehend where we are today and how we arrived at this juncture.

OUR PRESENT SYSTEM OF ARTS FUNDING

Most thoughtful persons would agree that the arts keep our souls nourished; but they keep dancers, painters, shoe salesmen, carpenters, and electricians nourished as well. From what wellspring do the funds for this nourishment come? They come from our American tradition of pluralistic funding for the arts. This system reflects our basic American ingenuity.

Like a lake fed by many streams, pluralism means support for the arts flowing from a variety of sources. It means funding from private patrons and other concerned individuals. It also means funding from the federal, state, county, and local governments. And it means funding derived from foundations, corporations, and businesses. The former commissioner of New York City's Department of Cultural Affairs, Henry Geldzahler, often compared the pluralistic system to an accordian, which emits its best sound when all of its compartments work in unison.

1. James C. Coleman, Elihu Katz, and Herbert Menzel, *Medical Innovation: A Diffusion Study* (New York: The Bobbs-Merrill Company, Inc., 1966), pp. 4-5.

2. Katherine Anne Porter, *Flowering Judas and Other Stories* (New York: Random House, Inc., 1940), introduction.

The individual partner:
  John Q. Public and the
  private patron

Art could not exist without individuals, both those who create it and those who purchase, collect, or merely enjoy it. By definition the nonprofit arts world does not make money. Funds for that prolific sector of the arts, much like Blanche DuBois, Tennessee Williams's heroine, "depend upon the kindness of strangers."

These strangers range from those nameless individuals who purchase tickets to performances and exhibits to the countless Americans who buy season subscriptions and who answer the endless fund-raising appeals from arts organizations from coast to coast. In addition there are those individuals, called private patrons, who have made it their goal not to be strangers to one or more arts organizations.

Indeed, from the beginning of the Republic until the Great Depression, funding of the arts in America was the sacrosanct domain of the privileged few. Some of this tradition remains, to be sure. In July 1981 Harold and Ruth Uris donated a landmark gift of $10 million to the Metropolitan Museum of Art for that institution's educational programs.[3] However, much to the chagrin of arts administrators, such large gifts are the exception rather than the rule.

Gone are the days of the reign of the private patron at their zenith. Benefactors such as Andrew Carnegie, J. Pierpont Morgan, and Mrs. August Belmont, to name but a few, saw to it personally that their favorite arts organizations kept their heads above water.

The preeminent position of the private patron has been greatly diminished over the years. In today's system of pluralistic support for the arts, the individual contributor has become a partner in the process, rather than the only source.

The federal government:
  emergence, retreat, reentry

One of the major accomplishments of President Franklin Roosevelt's efforts to deal with the Great Depression was the impetus to get the unemployed off the soup kitchen lines and back into the work force. A curious side effect of these initiatives was the concomitant entry by the federal government into the arts funding process.

Roosevelt's administration left its mark upon the arts and the public funding of them, the likes of which have never been seen before or since his presidency in this nation. Out of his public jobs programs flowed a generation of artists whose imprimatur would be stamped upon all those artists who followed.

Painters, poets, photographers, playwrights, writers, musicians, and other artists emerged from that collective experience and left the nation a rich and vibrant artistic legacy. To name but a few, their ranks included the artists Ben Shahn, Jackson Pollock, and Mark Rothko; the writers Saul Bellow and John Cheever; the photographer Walker Evans; and the theatrical giants, Orson Welles and John Houseman. The images those artists left behind reminded us of where we were as a nation and what we had become.

Even today the art of the Depression years lives on. It lives in James Brooks's

3. John Russell, "Met Museum Opens 5-Year Drive for $150 Million," *New York Times,* 26 Oct. 1982.

murals, in the photographs of Russell Lee, in the writings of James Agee, in the paintings of Thomas Hart Benton, in the music of Virgil Thompson and Aaron Copeland, and in the words of Archibald MacLeish.

The well-to-do private patrons found themselves in the strange position of working toward a common goal with the not-so-well-to-do artists of the Depression. Together they were forming a partnership to help the arts flourish and grow in this nation. America's entry into World War II would sound a retreat for federal funding of the arts.

Following the war the nation turned its energies to the education and employment of its returning heroes. Funding of the arts was not high on the American agenda of recovery. In addition the McCarthy hearings painted many artists, writers, actors, and actresses as being, at the very least, unsympathetic to the American goals of besting our adversaries in the Cold War. Under these circumstances, the arts were not exactly flourishing with federal encouragement.

Some thirty years after the Depression, the federal government reentered the arts funding process. In 1965, as part of President Lyndon Johnson's Great Society, the National Endowments for the Arts and the Humanities were established. Other federal agencies and departments began efforts to provide assistance to arts organizations and institutions. The Institute of Museum Services was established. The Departments of Labor, Housing and Urban Development, and Education and other agencies began to make grants to artistic institutions across the land. Federal funds for the arts continued to grow until the beginning of the Reagan administration.

After initially proposing to halve the National Endowments, the Reagan ad-

ministration retreated to the safe ground of the status quo following bipartisan opposition to the proposed cuts in Congress. Indeed during 1981 slightly more than $314 million for the arts came from the federal government, about half of that from the National Endowment for the Arts alone.[4] Thus the federal government remains a full-fledged partner in the pluralistic system of funding the arts in this nation.

The role of the states: from Utah to New York

Five years prior to the establishment of the National Endowment for the Arts, Governor Nelson A. Rockefeller of New York State created an emergency ad hoc commission on the arts in this state. He did so both in response to his own deeply held convictions about the arts and based upon his knowledge of the workings of the Arts Council of Great Britain.

The emergency never went away, and in 1965 the New York State Council on the Arts (N.Y.S.C.A.) became a permanent agency in the state's executive branch. Rockefeller's interest in the arts was matched by his ability to get things accomplished that he felt needed to be done. In retrospect, Robert H. Connery wrote of the Rockefeller-dominated years in Albany:

Since most programs originated in the governor's office, one might say the governor proposed and the legislature disposed. Many of the major undertakings of the Rockefeller years—expansion of the State University, the Pure Waters Program, the Metropolitan

4. John S. Friedman, "Who Funds the Arts?" The Grantsmanship Center News, 10(6): 21 (November/December 1982).

Transportation Authority, the Council on the Arts, and the Urban Development Corporation—were initiated by the governor and accepted with few changes by the legislature.[5]

Not all artists were thrilled that government was becoming increasingly involved in the arts funding process. The painter John Sloan spoke for many of his colleagues at the time: "Sure it would be good to have a Ministry of Fine Arts. Then we'd know where the enemy is."[6] The skeptics may have been a bit too skeptical. It was never the intention of Governor Rockefeller to establish a ministry for the arts. He envisioned N.Y.S.C.A. as a way of encouraging participation in and appreciation of the arts by all of the citizens of his state.

Today, some 24 years later, Rockefeller's concept lives on as N.Y.S.C.A. continues to have the largest budget of any state arts agency in the nation. During the 1984 fiscal year the council will disperse $32 million amongst its 1845 applicants composed of nonprofit organizations and institutions in each of the state's 62 counties.

Since the establishment of New York's arts agency, every state in the union has created an arts agency. It should be acknowledged here that although New York State has the largest state arts council, it was not the first. In 1899 the state of Utah created the Utah Art Institute, the forerunner of today's Utah Arts

Council. It was the first state-created arts council in the nation.[7]

During the 1983 fiscal year the 50 states and 6 jurisdictions—American Samoa, the District of Columbia, Guam, the Northern Marianas, Puerto Rico, and the Virgin Islands—appropriated over $125 million to their arts agencies, for a 3.2 percent increase over appropriations for the previous year.[8] State arts agencies today stand alongside the federal government and private citizens as meaningful partners in the American system of pluralistic support for the arts.

*Counties, municipalities,
and other localities:
little-known partners*

Throughout this century, and in many instances, even before, counties, municipalities, and other local government entities have been involved in funding the arts. Often this involvement has centered around the upkeep of museums, historical societies, and other cultural ventures. Unfortunately, outside their own borders, these funding partners do not receive the recognition they justly deserve.

For example, during the 1983 fiscal year the Department of Cultural Affairs of the city of New York had a budget in excess of $45 million.[9] This places it second, only behind the National Endowment for the Arts, as a source of government support for the arts. The

5. Robert H. Connery, "Nelson A. Rockefeller as Governor," in *Governing New York State: The Rockefeller Years,* ed. Robert H. Connery and Gerald Benjamin (New York: Academy of Political Science, May 1974), p. 10.

6. Waldemar A. Nielsen, "Needy Arts: Where Have All the Patrons Gone?" *New York Times,* 26 Oct. 1980.

7. *Laws of the State of Utah,* "State Institute of Art," chap. 29, secs. 1-19, approved 9 Mar. 1899.

8. "News Release" (Washington, DC: National Assembly of State Arts Agencies, 15 Apr. 1983).

9. *Annual Report* (New York: Department of Cultural Affairs, 1982), p. 27.

New York State Council on the Arts ranks third.

Despite great demands upon their limited resources, cities, counties, and other localities across the country have become quite deeply involved in arts funding. Metropolitan Dade (Florida), Milwaukee, and San Diego counties rank high among the 50 leading donors to the arts in the nation in one listing.[10] So do the cities of Philadelphia, San Francisco, Chicago, Houston, Baltimore, Portland (Washington), San Diego, Dallas, and Los Angeles, in addition to New York City.[11] Considering that many of these localities give more to the arts than their respective states and that they rank alongside major corporations, such as IBM, Mobil, and Exxon, their involvement and participation becomes all the more meaningful.

A recent examination of county expenditures for the arts in New York State, excluding New York City, found that 38 counties appropriated amounts from a modest thousand dollars for a rural, upstate county to over $2.6 million in Erie County.[12] All of these figures combined illustrate the growing importance of counties, cities, and other localities as important partners in the pluralistic funding system in this nation.

Foundations:
a tradition of giving

Private foundations have existed in America since the late 1700s. However, it was not until the late nineteenth and

early twentieth centuries that foundations began to fully develop, with the establishment of some of today's largest foundations. In the decade following World War II, the number of private foundations greatly increased due to the emergence of company-sponsored foundations, family foundations with living donors, and other factors related to taxation matters.[13]

In keeping with the spirit of giving by private patrons, the postwar era spawned many family-controlled, or family-established, foundations. Some—most notably the Ford Foundation, which distributed more than $300 million to American orchestras, theaters, and ballet companies—became deeply involved in arts funding.[14] With the rise of the corporate foundation, private foundations were not able to keep up with the growth of their new partners in the funding process, although pockets of leadership remain. In compiling a list of major donors to the arts in America, one writer noted,

Among foundations, the most generous to the arts turned out not to be Ford or Rockefeller but the Pew Charitable Trusts of Philadelphia, a group of 10 trusts administered by the Glenmede Trust Company. . . . Like many other foundations and corporations, the Pew Charitable Trusts gives the bulk of its arts money to local organizations.[15]

In large and small communities across the country, private foundations play a unique and important role in funding the arts at the local level. But their role appears to be somewhat stabilized due

---

10. Friedman, "Who Funds the Arts?" p. 22.
11. Ibid.
12. "Guidelines for the Local Incentive Funding Test (L.I.F.T.)," mimeographed (New York: New York State Council on the Arts, 1983), p. 5.

13. *The Foundation Directory, 8th Edition* (New York: Foundation Center, 1981), p. xiv.
14. Nielsen, "Needy Arts."
15. Friedman, "Who Funds the Arts?" pp. 21, 23.

to changes in the nation's tax laws. The new laws allow foundations to reduce their total spending, repealing earlier laws that forced foundations to spend either their total income or 5 percent of their assets, whichever was greater. Today they must spend only 5 percent of their assets. Nonetheless the private foundation remains a strong partner in the pluralistic system of funding the arts in this nation, and its impact will continue to be felt in the years ahead. Future changes in tax laws may allow foundations to become even stronger partners.

Corporations and businesses: friends or foes?

The newest member of the funding partnership for the arts in this nation has been the corporation. In 1978 corporations surpassed foundations in the percentage of their contributions to philanthropic causes, not the least of which have been the arts. There are of course some corporations that have been supporting the arts for decades, for example, Texaco's radio broadcasts of Metropolitan Opera performances to all corners of the nation. By and large, however, corporate involvement in funding the arts is a relatively recent concept. It offers hope for many, and also a sense of wariness. Nonetheless it would appear that this involvement is here to stay.

Just as the skeptics were wrong about government support of the arts, it would appear that corporate support of the arts has not turned out to be the boogeyman that some thought it might become. Critics feared that oil and tobacco companies, in becoming the Medicis of modern culture, would impose their personal tastes upon the arts world. To date these fears are without justifica-

tion. Indeed one of the wonderful things about our pluralistic system of funding the arts in this nation is the fact that with all partners participating, the system prevents an unhealthy dependence on any one source and keeps any one source from dominating.

During the 1970s, as the arts became more accessible to and accepted by Americans, corporations began to recognize these factors and greatly increased their involvement in funding of the arts. A new breed of managers believed that it was the responsibility of businesses and corporations to return some of their profits to society. They felt that such involvement was good for their employees and the communities in which their headquarters and plants were located. In addition they felt this was a significant way of informing their customers and shareholders that their moneys were being put to good use.

Viewed now as a matter of corporate policy and responsibility, funding for the arts began to take on various forms. The most common way in which corporations felt they could assist the arts was to make direct cash contributions to the operating costs of artistic groups. In addition, corporations offered in-kind services, such as donations of company products, equipment, and the expertise of their key employees. Some key staff members served on boards of arts groups, while others gave pro bono assistance in other ways to these groups, which were not always known for their business acumen. Other corporations took great pride in hiring the best architects available to make their corporate buildings aesthetically pleasing, while others purchased significant artwork to place inside and around their corporate structures. Programs to encourage participation by employees in arts-related activities have increased with each passing year. These efforts range from encouraging in-house exhibits of works of art of the employees to matching employees' contributions to the arts organizations of their choice.

Actions speak louder than words, as Edward M. Strauss, Jr., the president of the Business Committee for the Arts, points out:

In 1979, U.S. business support of the arts totalled $436 million, according to a survey conducted for the Business Committee for the Arts (BCA) by Touche Ross & Company. In comparison, for the same year private foundations gave an estimated $188 million to the arts and humanities, and the budget for the National Endowment for the Arts was slightly more than $154 million.[16]

The only group that gave more to the arts during the period of that study were private individuals, taken as one large entity. Although these figures are indeed positive, it must be noted that almost half of all business support for the arts came from 970 large corporations, which constitute only 1 percent of the companies in the nation.[17]

One of the immediate tasks for the future is to encourage small and medium-sized businesses to join in the arts funding partnership. Suffice it to say that businesses and corporations have joined the pluralistic funding process in a most significant manner and, despite economic trends, this involvement will continue to increase in the future.

Thus, historically, funding of the arts in America has grown to include the following partners: the individual and private patron, foundations, businesses and corporations, and all levels of government—federal, state, county, and local. We have arrived at our present juncture more by chance than by design. One writer has summarized our current situation as follows:

Finally, on the other hand, there is cause for rejoicing as well as for chagrin. The American system for financing the arts through patchwork (and this in the end may be its primary virtue) meets the most fundamental tests—freedom, diversity, excellence and vigorous new creative growth.[18]

With this historical perspective in mind, what are the attitudes of Americans about the arts and funding of the arts?

PUBLIC ATTITUDES ABOUT THE ARTS

American public attitudes about the arts have become increasingly positive during the past decade. Indeed culture in America has come a long way since the time when Henry James let it be known that he felt that the typical American viewed culture as the special concern of only "women, foreigners and other impractical persons." Such thoughts are now a thing of the past.

In 1980 the National Research Center for the Arts, an affiliate of Louis Harris and Associates, conducted a nationwide survey of public opinions for the American Council on the Arts, a private, non-profit organization. The survey, entitled *Americans and the Arts,* was the third such analysis of American public attitudes toward the arts.[19] The findings of the 1980 survey are quite illuminating.

16. "Introduction," in *Guide to Corporate Giving in the Arts-2,* ed. Robert A. Porter (New York: American Council for the Arts, 1981), p. 4.

17. Ibid., p. 5.

18. Nielsen, "Needy Arts."

19. National Research Center of the Arts, *Americans and the Arts: Highlights from a 1980 Nationwide Survey of Public Opinion* (New York: American Council for the Arts, 1981).

Attendance at motion pictures by Americans rose from 70 percent in 1975 to 75 percent in 1980. Likewise attendance at live theatrical performances rose from 41 percent to 59 percent during the five-year period. The number of Americans visiting art museums climbed from 44 percent in 1975 to 60 percent in 1980. Attendance at concerts of classical or symphonic music rose from 18 percent to 26 percent. In 1980, 26 percent of all Americans reported going to at least one opera or musical theater event during the preceding year. Finally dance performances climbed progressively from 9 percent in 1973 to 16 percent in 1975 to 25 percent in 1980.[20]

In addition, the survey found that more Americans were themselves participating in the arts than ever before. A dramatic increase was found in the number of Americans who were engaged in photography, both as a profession and as an avocation. Increases in participation were also found in the more traditional art forms as well. Music, writing, dance, painting, theater, crafts, and other forms of artistic expression showed increases. Significantly, when asked how they felt courses in the arts should be financed in our schools, a substantial 75 percent to 20 percent of the Americans surveyed stated that they believed the arts "should be paid for by the school system as part of the regular school budget."[21]

Clearly the survey demonstrates that Americans are growing increasingly aware that the arts are something they enjoy attending, participating in, and something they believe to be profoundly worthwhile.

The U.S. Census: another indicator of public attitudes

In April 1983 the Research Division of the National Endowment for the Arts issued a report based upon the 1980 U.S. census. Again the facts and figures of this analysis were illuminating.

The report found that between 1970 and 1980 there was a dramatic 81 percent increase in the number of artists in the United States.[22] Every state in the nation and the District of Columbia experienced a growth in its artistic population. In 1970 some 600,000 Americans identified themselves in the census as artists. By 1980 that number rose to 1 million, which represents 1 percent of the nation's civilian work force.[23]

In New York State 1.73 percent of its total civilian work force consists of artists, the highest proportion of any state. In 1970 there were 94,068 artists in New York State. By 1980 that number rose to 138,422.[24] These figures indicate an increase in this nation's creative population. Today's growing number of artists is another indicator of the American public's acceptance of the arts and artists. In contemporary America artists are respected as they never have been before, and many of them have earned that respect though hard work and dedication. Not long ago it was not always respectable to identify oneself as an artist. Public attitudes toward artists are changing rapidly.

Today's increasing number of artists, coupled with their fellow Americans

20. Ibid., pp. 11-12.
21. Ibid., p. 24.

22. "News" (Washington, DC: National Endowment for the Arts, 27 Apr. 1983), p. 1.
23. Ibid., pp. 1-2.
24. "Research Division Note #3" (Washington, DC: National Endowment for the Arts, 27 Apr. 1983), p. 1.

who have demonstrated that they too care about the arts, indicates that positive change has taken place in the way Americans view the arts. The question remains, How do Americans feel about funding of the arts?

ARTS FUNDING:
PUBLIC ATTITUDES

The Harris survey examined the question of how Americans view funding of the arts. "The results show that the public believes by and large that the arts are more self-supporting, more dependent on private contributions, and less dependent on government than most other nonprofit activities."[25] Given this conclusion it would appear that Americans do not fully comprehend their own tradition of pluralistic support of the arts. If, as stated previously, we must not allow any one source to dominate the funding process and thus create an unhealthy dependence, it becomes imperative that the public's misconceptions be clarified.

First, the nonprofit arts world never has been, and never will be, self-supporting. The Harris survey illustrates the public's lack of understanding of this concept: "large numbers of Americans hold the view that theatre groups (34%), ballet or modern dance troupes (34%), opera companies (31%), and symphony orchestras (29%) are mainly self-supporting; only 13% believe this of art museums."[26] A glance at the annual reports of opera companies, symphonies, dance troupes, and theatrical organizations would quickly dispel this misconception on the part of the public.

The second part of the response is a bit more accurate. Regarding dependence on private contributions, the study found that "the perception of a good portion of the public is that theatre groups (42%), symphony orchestras (41%), opera companies (39%), and art museums (37%) depend on private contributions for support."[27] Here the public perception is closer to the truth if in fact they realize that this private support encompasses individuals, foundations, businesses, and corporations.

The third and final part of the public's response to the survey is the most disturbing. When asked about government support of the arts, the respondents indicated that, "apart from art museums (24%), Americans do not generally believe that arts activities depend on government support; thus theatre groups are believed to be dependent on government financial assistance by only 5% of the adult population, followed by ballet or modern dance groups and opera companies (6%), and symphony orchestras (8%)."[28]

A breakdown of the survey's analysis of the responses of the public to financing by the various levels of government may shed some light on the matter. Only by 50 percent to 46 percent did those surveyed feel that the federal government should provide financial assistance to arts institutions. However, by 60 percent to 37 percent, they felt that their states should provide such assistance; and by a 64 percent to 31 percent, they felt that their local governments should be financially involved in arts funding.[29] Thus the public's attitude toward government funding of the arts becomes a

25. National Research Center for the Arts, "Americans and the Arts," p. 20.

26. Ibid., pp. 20-21.

27. Ibid., p. 21.

28. Ibid.

29. Ibid., p. 22.

matter of great concern to those who espouse the pluralistic system of support of the arts.

Interestingly, when the respondents were reminded that the federal government spends $600 per capita on defense each year, and another $130 for education but only $.70 on the arts, their opinions changed drastically. By an overwhelming 70 percent to 28 percent—compared to 58 percent to 37 percent in 1975—those adult Americans surveyed said that they would be willing to pay $5 more in federal taxes for support of the arts.[30]

CHANGING PUBLIC ATTITUDES ABOUT PUBLIC ARTS FUNDING

The problematic nature of the individual's response in a mass society vis-à-vis public-opinion polling in America was noted at the outset. Thus the remaining hypotheses and conclusions are not based upon empirical data, but rather upon common sense.

The main hypothesis is a simple one. Americans do not understand their own tradition of pluralistic support for the arts. They appear to believe in the worth of the arts for themselves and their children, but they do not comprehend who pays the bills. Americans are participating in the arts, both actively and passively, more than ever before. They understand the importance of museums and their funding, probably because most Americans live near one or, at the very least, have visited them during their years of formal schooling. Likewise, they seem to believe more in government support at the local level than they do at the state and federal levels, perhaps because they are more capable of

understanding how their tax dollars are spent closer to home. This is somewhat understandable.

In reviewing our American tradition of pluralistic support for the arts, it seems clear that American public attitudes toward funding of the arts, especially government support, need to be changed.

CONCLUSION: WHAT THE PUBLIC NEEDS TO KNOW TO CHANGE ITS ATTITUDES

Government support for the arts in this nation is a healthy concept that merits public acceptance. Time and time again it has been demonstrated that government support of the arts helps leverage private support. The private donor—be it an individual, foundation, business, or corporation—is often more inclined to give to an arts organization if that group has received a seal of approval from an impartial source. A grant from the National Endowment, or from a state or local arts agency, is one of the most useful tools available for arts groups when they are seeking out new sources of private support.

In addition, the funds that taxpayers invest in the arts provide essential tools for economic development and social stability in communities across the land. Money spent on the arts multiplies in the economy at large. Economists have determined that for every dollar spent on the arts, at least four dollars are generated in the local economy. This multiplier effect accounts for billions of dollars of economic activity each year. Arts dollars buy cleaning, maintenance, security, rentals, advertising, public relations, legal and accounting services, and mailing and postage. Then there are also the paper, lumber, liability insurance, costumes, cosmetics, even nails from the

30. Ibid., pp. 22-23.

local hardware store to build scenery for a community theater production. In the final analysis this means more jobs for more people than just those involved in the arts.

The arts also create revenues for localities and states through tourism. In New York State alone, tourism is an $8 billion a year industry, and the arts are one of the primary attractions for tourists. As one writer pointed out after attending a function at the Metropolitan Museum of Art, "The guests were also told that the museum was New York City's No. 1 tourist attraction, that it has 3.5 million visitors a year."[31] In fact, one respected pollster credits the arts for 48 percent of New York State's total tourism. Thus almost half of that state's tourists are drawn to its borders due to opportunities in the arts that exist there.

31. Russell, "Met Museum Opens 5-Year Drive."

The arts are also one of the most stable foundations for downtown and neighborhood redevelopment. Time and time again, in cities and towns across America, artists have moved into run-down, older neighborhoods, bringing new life to warehouses, vaudeville theaters, factories, and storefronts.

Americans need to understand that government participation is a vital ingredient in our American system of pluralistic support for our cultural endeavors. Only through a productive mix of funding partners can this system flourish and grow.

It is time we Americans change our attitudes about funding of the arts, especially the role government must play in the pluralistic funding partnership. In doing so we will better understand what an ingenious system of arts funding we have, and we can move forward together in making it the best arts funding mechanism ever created.

ANNALS, *AAPSS,* **471,** January 1984

Is There a Legitimate Role
for Public Relations in the Arts?

By DAVID FINN

ABSTRACT: Public relations is often considered a function of fund raising by arts institutions. This is particularly true in the United States, where the tax laws encourage both individual and corporate contributions to nonprofit institutions. Through a variety of techniques, public relations has helped arts institutions gain visibility for their programs and stimulate community and corporate interest in specific projects. In recent years there has been concern about the introduction of hype into the art world. There is little evidence that either the practice of public relations or the increasing financial support from corporations is creating an overpromoted environment in the arts. Public interest in blockbuster exhibitions and other special events has developed spontaneously. There is also no evidence that arts institutions are compromising their integrity in seeking support from business. Corporate support of the arts can help achieve marketing results or be aimed exclusively at helping the community. Whatever the motivations, they provide opportunities for business people to demonstrate leadership in our society. Public relations can play the important role of helping to find common ground on which both business and the arts can seek to achieve their objectives.

David Finn is chairman and chief executive officer of Ruder Finn & Rotman, Inc., the largest independent public-relations organization in the United States. The company's Arts and Communications Division works with arts institutions and with corporations that sponsor cultural programs. A photographer, Mr. Finn has published books on leading sculptors, including Michelangelo and Henry Moore. His photographs and paintings have been exhibited at the Metropolitan Museum of Art in New York, L'Orangerie in Paris, and elsewhere. He is a graduate of the City College of New York.

THE European tradition of government support for culture minimizes the need to develop a public relations program as an aid to raising money. Rarely does a European institution have to turn to individuals or corporations for contributions or sponsorship. The situation is quite different in the United States, where dependence on philanthropy and corporate support has made public relations an increasingly important function.

The tax structure of countries in which governments support cultural institutions discourages benefactions to museums from private individuals, since no deduction is allowed for such contributions. The theory is that the taxpaying public contributes to the national budget for its cultural enrichment and that funds should be allocated at the discretion of public officials.

Although government support for museums is attractive for many obvious reasons, the inability to appeal to the private sector deprives the public of potentially significant benefits. Works of art belonging to private owners are not donated, because they are assets that ought to bring some financial return.

There is, for example, a group of large Henry Moore reliefs on the facade of the Time-Life building on Bond Street in London. These were carved in the 1950s when Moore was a young sculptor, but because they are situated fairly high up on a narrow street, they cannot adequately be seen. They have never been able to pivot as originally intended because authorities have feared that they might fall out of their sockets to the street below. Moreover they are suffering from pollution in the London atmosphere. In the United States the owner of the building could not only gain public recognition but also make money by giving the reliefs to a major museum where they could be installed properly. The company would receive a tax deduction for its current value, which would be well over $1 million, and arrange for comparatively inexpensive casts to be made for the building.

I actually suggested such a plan some years ago. I discovered that a British insurance company owned the building, and the plan would not work since no tax deduction for such a gift was possible under British law. The result was that the sculpture must remain in its present unfortunate spot and suffer both inaccessability and deterioration.

Let us be honest about the fact that federal tax laws have enabled wealthy collectors to make money by giving works of art away in America. One of the most tempting tax shelters allows a taxpayer to deduct the current value of a work of art even though he or she may have managed to acquire it at a much lower price two or three years earlier. The key to this strategy is acquiring works of art that are rapidly appreciating in value. Thus one might acquire a painting by Picasso for a price of $50,000 and find that in a few years it is valued at $300,000. If the collector is in the 50 percent tax bracket he or she can give the painting to a museum and save $150,000. The taxpayer therefore makes $100,000 by the contribution.

This aspect of American tax law may not be too high a price to pay for the initiative it encourages among individuals who have a genuine interest in contributing to the cultural life of their communities. This is true both for private collectors who donate works of art to museums and for corporations that can obtain a tax deduction for grants to museums. Corporations may also deduct their art-sponsorship expenses as part of their operating public-relations budget, a deduction that is not easily made in European countries.

For the system to work effectively, organized efforts must be made by museums and other cultural institutions to attract the interest of potential donors and patrons. Public relations has been playing an increasing role in this regard—helping management and directors by creating events that draw the attention of business and community leaders to the activities of the institution, publishing materials for members and friends of the institution, and obtaining press coverage for museum activities.

When seeking help from public-relations professionals, cultural institutions in the United States are almost always looking for new sources of financial support. A director who has a flair for publicity may use it to help gain new friends or build a sense of pride among those already committed to help the institutions. But a systematic program of keeping the institution in the public eye is the best means of securing a steady source of support.

Experienced museum officials know that fund raising is a different field from public relations: public relations helps to establish the context in which moneys can be raised by achieving visibility for the institutions; fund raising involves the steps taken in order for the museum staff and trustees to ask for contributions. Institutional public relations can also lay the groundwork for corporate sponsorship by helping to make the business community aware of the important role the museum is playing for the public.

The occasions that prompt an institution to employ public-relations professionals vary. Sometimes there is a new building that must be funded. Or an institution may celebrate an important anniversary and use that occasion as a means of making new friends. Or there may be a new director or board chairman who is determined to take new initiatives for the institution. Or a special exhibition may be in the offing for which funding is needed. Or a threatened deficit may make it necessary to look for new sources of financial assistance.

To be sure there are routine public-relations functions that are handled by museum staffs who are not necessarily oriented toward raising money. As a matter of course, information is provided on exhibitions, staff appointments, acquisitions, and other news about the institution. Critics are invited to review exhibitions. Museum officials are encouraged to speak to the press or to important local groups. Guides, annual reports, and bulletins are produced. Community activities are organized around particular exhibitions. Posters are distributed around the city.

But it is the fund-raising aspect of public relations that distinguishes American museums from those in Europe and elsewhere. And it is the pressure created by the need to raise money that leads some to wonder whether the increasing tendency to develop public-relations programs may be producing some negative side effects.

THE IMAGINED
DANGERS OF HYPE

In recent years the involvement of public relations specialists in major exhibitions—particularly those sponsored by corporations that hope to achieve public-relations benefits—has been worrisome to some observers. When museums have turned to public-relations consultants to help obtain corporate sponsorship, observers have raised the question of whether this can be accomplished without sacrificing the integrity of the museum. One of the dangers implicit in the introduction of public-relations activity in the art world could be an incentive for museum curators to plan exhibitions that have more corporate public-relations values than genuine cultural values.

When a corporation makes a grant to an institution as sponsor, it is obviously in the interest of the company to achieve as much visibility as possible. Indeed when public-relations specialists recommend a project to a potential corporate sponsor, they do so because they feel that it will achieve widespread media attention. Publicity is a fairly standard measure of the value of a corporate public-relations project; but it is not the measure of the value of a museum exhibition. Therein lies the potential conflict between public relations and curatorial objectives.

The public-relations activities involved in drawing attention to certain exhibitions have recently come to be described as "hype." Although there are those who feel hype in connection with cultural events is a benefit because it helps attract the interest of a wide audience, the connotation of the word is negative. "Hype" is a new word, which only recently reached the dictionary, where it is still described as slang. It is clearly derived from "hyper" which means "excessive" as in "hypersensitive" or "hyperactive." It is defined as "intensifying by ingenuous or questionable claims." When applied to exhibitions it presumably means exaggerated values or overpromotion. Compared to the enjoyment that comes from looking at a nonhyped collection in a museum, a hyped response to a special exhibition is one that is thought to be inflated out of proportion to the worthiness of the works being shown. The implication is that something mediocre is being made to appear more important than it is. The result is a sham—a fake that deceives the public.

Yet if one examines closely what actually happens when a corporation puts its public-relations resources behind an exhibition, the dangers of hype seem to be more illusory than real. Extensive publicity occurs because the exhibition is newsworthy whether or not public-relations people are promoting it. The public-relations people merely facilitate the efforts of critics to report about an exhibition that genuinely interests them. And curators choose such exhibitions not because they are likely to appeal to corporations but because they are likely to appeal to the public.

Time, Incorporated's sponsorship of "The Search for Alexander" provides an excellent case history to show how the process works. The only special circumstance of Alexander was that the idea originated with a company executive rather than a museum curator. It was an imaginative concept developed by Zachary Morfogen, who at that time was director of the Books and Arts Division of Time, Incorporated. Acting as the company's public-relations counsel on this project, Ruder and Finn queried Carter Brown—director of the National Gallery—about the idea, and to Morfogen's delight, Brown's reaction was extremely positive.

What followed were several years of negotiations and planning with the Ministry of Culture and Archaeology in Greece—spanning the administration of three successive ministers—and with a variety of museum directors and archaeologists in the United States. The prime minister of Greece was involved in some of the negotiations, as were officials of the Foreign Tourism and Trade Ministries, and finally the National Bank of Greece, which became a cosponsor along with Time, Incorporated. In the United States there were discussions with over a dozen museums that wanted to show the Alexander exhibition; several institutions made elaborate presentations to submit to the minister of culture, who reserved the right to make the final choice. During all this time Ruder and Finn, as public-relations consultants to Time, Incorporated, played a coordinating role to help overcome the myriad obstacles that threatened to block the project.

The background for the exhibition was a discovery of extraordinary objects in the Vergina Tomb, believed by the archaeologist Manolis Andronicos to be that of Philip, father of Alexander, and the decision to permit these objects to leave Greece and be shown in the United States. No archaeological objects of equal value had been sent out of Greece in modern times. Moreover the story of Alexander, which is a source of great pride to every Greek citizen, was being told to the people of America in a dramatic and compelling manner. As a result of Time, Incorporated's initiative and support by the National Bank of Greece, there was to be a public television series on Alexander as well as a major new biography, which appeared at the time the exhibition opened in Washington in the fall of 1980.

Because of the significance of the entire project, the Greek government erected a new addition to the Salonica Museum where the objects could be exhibited before coming to the United States. Over 100 editors and museum officials were invited by the government

to the Salonica opening, a major undertaking that our public relations firm also helped coordinate. About three months later the exhibition opened at the National Gallery in Washington, D.C., with several gala affairs involving the Greek embassy, Time, Incorporated, and Mobil, which sponsored both the audiovisual component of the exhibition and the television series, and subsequently cosponsored the exhibition when it arrived at the Metropolitan Museum two years later.

The media coverage of the exhibition was enormous. Feature articles appeared in *Art News, Arts, Art in America, Museum, Portfolio, Apollo, Smithsonian, Time, Life,* and many other national magazines. Wire services covered the exhibition extensively, as did television and radio. Added to this editorial coverage were a series of Time, Incorporated advertisements in several of their own publications, which would have cost well over $1 million. These advertisements did not make excessive claims for the exhibition, but merely told what it was and where it could be seen. The exhibition was extremely well attended during its entire tour, which included the National Gallery, the Boston Museum of Fine Arts, the Art Institute of Chicago, the San Francisco Museum of Fine Art, the New Orleans Museum of Art, and the Metropolitan Museum of Art in New York.

It was during the two-year period when Alexander toured the United States that the world "hype" came into popular usage. As one of several exhibitions receiving extensive attention in the press during that time, it was occasionally cited in the art press as an example of hype. No critic questioned the extraordinary beauty and significance of the objects in the exhibition, or the importance of Alexander as a major factor in shaping the cultural life of the ancient world, or the unique opportunity offered to the American public to see these works of art at first hand. But some thought the word "Search" in the name of the exhibition, "The Search for Alexander," was pretentious. Others felt the exhibition should have been more modest, that it should have used less museum space. Still others believed that the extensive media attention was disproportionate to the importance of the exhibition. But any such reservations were clearly in the minority; and it was certainly not what the visitors who thronged to the museums thought: their comment cards were universally enthusiastic. Nor was it what the reviewers, who praised the exhibition so highly, wrote.

Although I do object to public relations being used in the art world in an effort to win undeserved recognition, no damage can possibly result from media attention to works of art that are of the highest order. Did museums compromise their judgments by showing an exhibition recommended and financed by an interested corporation? Did public relations do any damage by counseling the sponsor and helping to attract widespread public interest in the exhibition? I think not. The works in the Alexander exhibition spoke for themselves, and people flocked to see these extraordinary treasures that would otherwise have been accessible only to visitors to the museum in Salonica. Nobody forced the media to praise the exhibition. The involvement of public relations people in the project helped bring information about the exhibition to the attention of writers and commentators who were free, as always, to make up their own minds about what they saw.

The idea of hype in the art world is an illusion. Public-relations activity in support of major cultural events should be looked at as a natural part of the process by which outstanding works of art come to public attention. Without such efforts many works of art would be seen only by a privileged few.

Compare, for instance, the fifth-century-B.C. *Charioteer* in Delphi, which draws over 500,000 visitors a year, to Claus Sluter's fifteenth-century *Well of Moses* in Dijon, which probably does not draw 2,000 visitors a year. In the opinion of many art historians these works are equally important; yet many who enjoy the *Charioteer* are deprived of the *Well of Moses*. That too many people crowd in to see the former is the price we pay for whetting cultural appetites. Being unaware of the extraordinary qualities of Sluter's masterpiece is the price we pay for inadequate communication about one of the great art treasures of the world.

Overexposure is a problem in the arts, but I cannot think of a single instance in which this was caused by public relations. There are, for instance, over 80 casts of some major Rodin sculptures because of the permission given by the sculptor to the Rodin Museum in Paris for casts to be made after his death. *The Thinker* and *The Kiss* have therefore become so commonplace that one becomes numb to the forms. The same is true of popular multiples like those made of Robert Indiana's *Love*. Da Vinci's Mona Lisa and Michaelangelo's early *Pieta* have been so widely reproduced as to become cliches.

The villain in overexposure is not public relations but popularity, and it is a mistake to think that one causes the other. Popularity is the result of an infectious enthusiasm that spreads by itself. It cannot be manufactured. It has often been harmful in the world of art, stifling the inventiveness of artists who have become too popular too soon, or who would rather achieve public acclaim than satisfy inner compulsions. But a museum that wishes to make an impact on the cultural sensitivities of its visitors has no reason to be afraid of the popularity of its exhibitions. An exhibition is there for as many people as possible to enjoy during a limited period of time, and the more attention that is focused on it, the greater its contribution is likely to be.

PUBLIC RELATIONS VERSUS INTEGRITY

Can a museum offer public-relations benefits to a sponsor without compromising its integrity? To answer this question one must analyze why corporations sponsor art projects, and see whether their motivations justify anxiety on the part of a museum.

Probably there is no single motivation that affects all corporations that fund arts projects. At one end of the spectrum is a specific marketing objective. An example of this is a program recently developed by American Express for contributions to local cultural projects based on a formula tied to the number of credit cards issued in each community. The program is based on a working partnership among card members, merchants, and needy art groups. In a widely advertised local campaign conducted in a target market, American Express pledges a cash donation to the recipient arts organization. The amount of the donation is based on each card transaction during a given time, usually three months, as well as each purchase of American Express travelers cheques,

each new card issued, and each travel package purchased at one of the firm's travel service offices. Since the project was created in 1981, marketing programs have been launched in 20 major U.S. cities, Puerto Rico, Canada, and the United Kingdom.

In the words of American Express chairman James D. Robinson III,

Our cause-related marketing program is one viable solution. It opens an entirely new channel of monetary support for non-profit organizations. And, perhaps more importantly, it harnesses the creative marketing talent of a successful company like ours and puts that skill to work improving the quality of life in communities around the world where we do business.[1]

An equally direct sales promotion program was launched in the late 1970s by Spring's Mills, which contracted to pay the Metropolitan Museum of Art a royalty on sheets and pillow cases and other textile products featuring designs inspired by works of art in the museum's collection. The names of the artists and reproductions of their works were referred to in advertisements, displays, and printed materials, and the promotion was so successful that Spring's paid over $2 million in royalties in the first three years of the program.

At the opposite end of the spectrum is the example of the architectural program initiated by Cummins Engine in its headquarters city of Columbus, Indiana. In order to give the citizens of the community the benefit of great architecture in their hometown, the company agreed to pay the design fees for any building that would employ an architect approved by a committee of interna-

---

1. Kellee Reinhart, "American Express and the Arts," *Horizon,* 25(7):30 (Oct.-Nov. 1982).

tionally recognized authorities. The result has been dozens of buildings—churches, schools, libraries, post offices, fire stations, courthouses, and others—designed by the greatest architects of our time.

In talking about this program, J. Irwin Miller, the former chief executive officer of the company, has said repeatedly that it had no public-relations purpose at all—and that its goal was simply to stimulate the creation of outstanding works of architecture. For him good architecture was an end in itself. He believed it was consistent with his responsibility as a corporate manager to use company funds for something he felt was a contribution to civilization. I once told him, after hearing a speech he made on this subject, that I thought this was the best kind of public relations. Doing what one feels to be important is, I believe, the first principle of public relations. Calling attention to one's achievements—not in a self-congratulatory fashion, but for the benefit of others—is intellectually valid only when the first principle has been observed. Mr. Miller liked that definition of public relations and agreed that it could apply to his program.

The range of motivation in business support of the arts resembles levels of ethical behavior. It has been said that the highest moral act is when a person anonymously helps a total stranger and expects no thanks. The next level is when a person anonymously helps a friend and makes it difficult to be thanked. The third level is when a person openly helps a friend and is gratified by the friend's appreciation.

One of the generally accepted conditions of corporate public relations is that the recipient of any corporate gift will give credit to the company for its good deeds. Having the name of a corporate sponsor displayed at the entrance of a museum exhibition is a condition of virtually every corporate grant. Many publications have adopted the policy of mentioning the name of a corporate sponsor in reviews in order to give due credit. A few holdout publications still refuse to give corporate credit on the grounds that it is free advertising, not realizing that in doing so they may be jeopardizing the prospects of future corporate support.

A more commercial purpose—and at a lower ethical level—is sought by arts projects invented by a corporation for its own promotion. An example of this is the 1982 exhibition at London's National Portrait Gallery of entries to the annual Imperial Tobacco Portrait Award. It would be difficult to review this exhibition without mentioning the corporate sponsor. Even more commercial was "The Great Cover-Up Show" at London's Science Museum, an exhibition that included samples of protective clothing developed by the sponsor, British Petroleum.

At a time when the Business Committee on the Arts in the United States and the Association of Business Sponsorship of the Arts in the United Kingdom are encouraging corporations to make up the gap created by decreased government support, overt public-relations benefits are obviously being stressed. Although it is universally believed by sophisticated students of business that the gap-closing expectations are unrealistic, additional support will obviously be offered only if public-relations values are respected and accepted by the art community.

The question is where to draw the line between corporate public-relations values and curatorial integrity, if indeed there is a conflict between the two. My own judgment is that museum curators will not compromise their principles for a corporate public-relations purpose, nor will corporations press them to do so. I have yet to see a professional curator decide to mount an exhibition he or she did not honestly believe to be meritorious. Neither public relations nor money can call the tune in the art world. What is even more significant is that it would not serve the interests of a sponsor for a curator to plan an exhibition he or she does not believe in. The whole idea of corporate support is to provide funding for exhibitions when the curatorial staff believes it to be worthwhile.

Some have speculated that museums may be consciously or unconsciously attracted to blockbuster exhibitions because of their public-relations benefits to sponsors. It is true that public-relations advisers to corporations recommend exhibitions that are likely to be considered major events. It would be odd to recommend an exhibition that one knows in advance will be denigrated or ignored. But curators and corporations have the same objectives in this respect. Indeed curators of major museums in Europe, which do not depend on corporate support, feel the same way. Creating exciting exhibitions appears to be a trend of the times, whether or not business is involved through sponsoring. Museums all over the world are responding to the public interest in newsworthy events.

There is, incidentally, no reason museums cannot seek corporate support for their permanent collections. This idea was once suggested by Philippe de Montebello when he became director of the Metropolitan Museum of Art. Many artists and scholars would be delighted with such an idea since it would help draw the public's attention to the masterpieces on view. Thus, for instance, when the Tutankhamen exhibition opened in London, knowledgeable people in the art world pointed out that the British Museum has greater works that people didn't take the trouble to look at. It would be possible, I believe, to mount special exhibitions, as it were, of works of art on permanent view, accompanied by brochures, catalogues, lectures, conferences, and so on. This would be a useful counterbalance to the special exhibitions that have become such a dominant feature of contemporary museum schedules.

PUTTING PUBLIC RELATIONS IN PERSPECTIVE

It would not be an exaggeration to state that public relations often seems far more dangerous than it is. This is certainly the case insofar as museums are concerned. Museums may be criticized for becoming too large, for devoting too much space to stores and cafeterias, for providing architects with opportunities to create monuments; and all this may be attributed to an overdeveloped interest in public relations. But these trends would be under way with or without the professional practice of public relations on behalf of museums.

The pity is that some critics have publicly expressed concern about the more imaginative examples of corporate sponsorship of the arts. When Philip Morris announced that there would be a branch of the Whitney Museum at its new corporate headquarters in midtown Manhattan, there was speculation as to whether there might be a backlash against corporations adopting cultural institutions. Whenever there is a substantial source of funding from business sources or even from private fortunes created by large corporations, there are those who see cause for alarm. This happened when Norton Simon acquired —or would "rescued" be the more accurate term?—the Pasadena Museum and when it became clear that the Getty Trust would be spending over $50 million a year on acquisitions and other projects. The Annenberg-Metropolitan Museum explosion was another such example. The fear is that money that comes from business, even indirectly, can corrupt. The art world should, therefore, beware!

My own conviction is that business executives who recognize the importance of the arts in our society demonstrate a potential for leadership when they find common ground between their business interests and the cultural life of the community. I also believe that public relations can be a useful guide in exploring this common ground and in developing techniques to make joint efforts worthwhile for all concerned. Neither the arts nor corporations want to be exploited when they play a role in each others' affairs, and with mutual respect there is no reason they should be.

It is time to put to rest the specter of public relations as a potentially destructive influence in our cultural life. It is hoped that there are only a few who still feel a twinge of discomfort at the mere mention of the phrase "public relations" in connection with the arts. There will always be an abhorrence of the misuse of public relations, but there will be an increasing opportunity for this professional specialty to make a contribution to the vitality of American cultural institutions and to the enjoyment of the arts by an ever growing and appreciative audience.

ANNALS, *AAPSS*, **471**, January 1984

Managing Culture:
How Corporations Can Help

By DONALD C. PLATTEN

ABSTRACT: Between 1955 and 1979, arts organizations thrived as recipients of contributions, particularly when compared with churches, schools, and other recipient organizations. Three-quarters of donations to arts organizations came from individuals, and the rest from corporations, foundations, and bequests. In an era of economic malaise, growth in arts funding clearly cannot be sustained at former levels. Tighter budgets warrant more innovative giving programs as well as shrewder financial management among recipients. Chemical Bank, for example, has instituted two giving programs that feature unrestricted, longer-term grants. It expects that recipients will have the flexibility of applying funds where they are needed most, and also the ability to spend more time pursuing their main objectives instead of fund raising. The bank has also expanded such giving techniques as on-site management consulting, in-kind contributions, and diagnostic workshops, Much of the bank's thinking regarding the management of nonprofit organizations stems from its experience in providing them with cash management and other services. If tailored by other corporations to their own geography and style, such programs could benefit American culture significantly.

Donald C. Platten retired in October 1983 as chairman of Chemical Bank. He joined the bank upon graduating from Princeton University in 1940 and eventually became administrative head of its New York City branch network. He later took charge of its international division and supervised the bank's expansion overseas. An active participant in civic affairs at all levels, he served as a member of President Carter's Commission for a National Agenda for the Eighties, as chairman of the New York City Mayor's Management Advisory Committee, and as member of a number of corporate and nonprofit boards.

A few years ago, while reading about the budgetary difficulties of a cultural institution in New York City, I began to wonder how different the city would be without such institutions. After all, Lewis Mumford had once said that museums were institutions invented by people in sheer defense against the threatening suffocation of the city. Where would New York be without its museums? As I made a list of the most prominent institutions it became painfully clear how truly impoverished the city would be. That conclusion led to a study of how Chemical Bank could improve its giving programs.

As part of that project Chemical undertook to chart overall patterns in U.S. charitable contributions over the years. We found that the proportion of contributions received by cultural organizations from 1955 to 1979, relative to the total pool of contributions, more than doubled, as shown in Table 1, while contributions to other recipient groups—such as churches, schools, hospitals, and social welfare organizations—did not fare as well. That growth is attributable to several trends:

—an increased interest in the arts, which has spawned the establishment of arts organizations in communities across the country;

—more aggressive fund raising by arts institutions;

—the relatively new interest of the private sector in supporting cultural efforts.

Certain civic and public institutions also showed healthy growth during that period. In the meantime, by contrast, the share of contributions received by religious, health, educational, and welfare organizations all began declining.

About one-quarter of donations to the arts between 1955 and 1979 came from corporate contributions, which rely on profits, and from bequests and foundations, which rely on stock portfolios. The other three-quarters came from individuals. See Table 2.

Unlike bequests and foundations, which declined over the period, corporate support rose from $415 million in 1955 to $2.3 billion over the period. See Table 3. The growth pattern of contributions from corporate sources has been relatively erratic.

With the fall in overall corporate profits and with substantial retrenchments by government, it is obvious that

TABLE 1
CHARITABLE CONTRIBUTIONS TO ARTS AND HUMANITIES ORGANIZATIONS

Year	Total Contributions (billions of dollars)	Contributions to Arts and Humanities (billions of dollars)	Contributions to Arts and Humanities (percentage of total)
1955	6.66	.199	3.0
1960	9.39	.188	2.0
1965	13.29	.226	1.7
1970	20.75	.623	3.0
1975	29.68	1.72	5.8
1979	43.31	2.70	6.2

SOURCE: *Giving and Getting: A Chemical Bank Study of Charitable Contributions through 1984* (New York: Chemical Bank, 1980), p. 14.

such growth in arts contributions cannot be sustained. Deficits among some cultural institutions have become high, and more than a few institutions are worried about survival. It became clear to us at Chemical that the current setting, in which every dollar counts, warrants across-the-board increases in our giving to such institutions.

Artists, social workers, and others in the nonprofit sector have faced this problem for years: how can the practical matters of management be handled so that maximum time and effort may be spent toward creative or charitable objectives? Occasionally an organization has fallen short of its goals because of insurmountable financial difficulties. Indeed, the nonprofit nature of the endeavor, with the attendant need for seeking funds, can create conditions that frustrate the organization's efforts.

Besides single-year funding, the other significant financial difficulty that continues to bedevil nonprofit managers is that of grant restrictions. Even the most practical business people from donor organizations seem occasionally unmindful that contributions toward capital and operating expenses may be even more needed by a particular arts institu-

tion, especially one in a survival mode, than contributions toward what may be a marvelous exhibition or performance.

Restricted giving, moreover, tends to shift control over artistic objectives away from artists and into the hands of donors. Through the years the practical effect of that has been to reduce risk taking by the arts institutions and sometimes to limit performances and exhibitions to the recognized artistic giants. Corporate executives may occasionally forget that the established artist of today was once a struggling newcomer. Shifting the center of control over program content to outside organizations can also have the effect of favoring those nonprofit organizations with a talent for guessing the predilections of potential donors.

To help remedy those problems, the Chemical Bank corporate contributions program has been geared specifically toward making contributions in a way that assists organizations in achieving management objectives in addition to funding objectives. Two of our programs in particular—the Basic Grant Program and the Higher Education Grant Program—reflect the principles of unrestricted giving and longer-term commitment.

TABLE 2
TOTAL CONTRIBUTOR CATEGORIES (PERCENTAGE OF TOTAL)

Year	Individuals	Corporations	Bequests	Foundations
1955	85.7	6.2	3.6	4.5
1960	81.3	5.1	6.1	7.6
1965	78.0	5.9	7.7	8.5
1970	76.7	3.8	10.3	9.2
1975	81.7	4.0	7.5	6.8
1979	84.4	5.3	5.1	5.2

SOURCE: *Giving and Getting: A Chemical Bank Study of Charitable Contributions through 1984* (New York: Chemical Bank, 1980), p. 11.

TABLE 3
CHARITABLE CONTRIBUTIONS BY CORPORATIONS

Year	Total Contributions (billions of dollars)	Contributions by Corporations (billions of dollars)	(percentage of total)
1955	6.66	.415	6.2
1960	9.39	.482	5.1
1965	13.29	.785	5.9
1970	20.75	.797	3.8
1975	29.68	1.202	4.0
1979	43.31	2.300	5.3

SOURCE: *Giving and Getting: A Chemical Bank Study of Charitable Contributions through 1984* (New York: Chemical Bank, 1980), p. 10.

BASIC GRANT PROGRAM

Chemical has recently inaugurated an approach to cultural contributions that amounts to a two-pronged assault on the management problems besetting nonprofit organizations. With Chemical's Basic Grant Program we pledge to selected nonprofit organizations three annual grants with no restrictions on how the funds are applied.

Those grants, which increase in the second and third year, are frequently in support of such well-established institutions as the American Museum of Natural History and Lincoln Center. But far from being limited to the renowned, fully established cultural institutions, Basic Grants have also supported emerging grass-roots cultural organizations, such Playwrights Horizon, which, while struggling to become established, yearn for a chance to shift some of the expense and energy from fund raising to producing the cultural programs that constitute their reason for being.

In evaluating a potential Basic Grant recipient, we ask the following questions:

1. Impact. Is the institution making an important contribution in general, and is it absolutely vital to the New York scene or to a particular constituency in New York? Is the program ongoing, serving a large New York City population annually? Is the program flexible enough to respond annually to the interests of the New York City population? Would its effect on the city be significant without a basic grant?

2. Leadership and reputation. Does it provide a unique service, not duplicated by smiliar institutions in the city? Does it provide leadership and serve as a model for smaller institutions in the same discipline? Is its reputation for service and excellence unparalleled?

3. Finances. Does it have a sound financial plan: a realistically balanced budget, with a good funding mix and cost effectiveness? What are its future funding plans? Does it take decreased federal government funding into account, and what plans is it making for filling the gap? What plans does it have for earned income?

4. Management. Is the management effective and creative? Is there a five-year plan in place for program and budget? Is the board of directors active, representing broad interests and the constituencies the organization serves?

5. Benefit to bank. Is the program of direct benefit to our employees and customers?

As the last item suggests, we expect the benefits to flow to Chemical Bank as well as to the recipients. A commitment to our host city can only result in the long-range expansion of our own business.

During the course of the three-year grant commitment, recipients of Basic Grants can also approach Chemical Bank for programmatic grants. Extensive follow-up of each grant includes a written annual report on activities and frequent telephone contact. The bank will work closely with recipient staffs to determine to what extent a supplementary contribution will improve their effectiveness and expand their audience.

Only time will tell how effective the Basic Grant Program will be, but it should be remembered that a single donor organization cannot make the crucial difference in the management of a significant nonprofit institution. That effect can occur only after the more general adoption of the concept. Says Gigi Ledkovsky, an official of the National Dance Institute, which has received a Basic Grant from Chemical, "With the ability to make realistic projections comes the responsibility for implementing the long-term strategic planning and board [of directors] development we need."

HIGHER EDUCATION GRANTS

Complementing our Basic Grant Program is our Higher Education Grant Program, through which we have committed $1.98 million in unrestricted funds to be distributed in annual installments during a three-year period. While we will continue our present support of higher education through matching gifts and other programs, we feel it is particularly important now to make a strong commitment to our colleges and universities so that they can meet today's challenges. As the selected institutions confront declining enrollments and less federal funding, better planning and more accurate financial control may be critical to their survival.

Notwithstanding the unrestricted nature of the grants, we have expressed the hope that some of the spending decisions be tilted toward student aid. We recognize that other areas of need exist, and we leave the decision up to the school, but we are alarmed at the increasing number of qualified students who may have to forgo higher education. Many students are unable to cover their education costs lately due to lack of funds. Furthermore, for many other areas, such as subject-related research, corporate funding is normally easier to find. We have found that most schools intend to follow our suggestion, with many saying that student aid had already been identified as an area of critical need.

The genesis of the Higher Education Grant Program was like that of the Basic Grant Program. When it became clear that the Basic Grant concept would be welcomed by the recipients as a valuable means of bolstering the likelihood of their long-range prosperity, we began to look at educational institutions in a similar light. What would the future of New York and the nation look like if our educational institutions should decline or their diversity begin to narrow?

We decided that our funding of higher education should not be based on a relationship between a corporation and a college but rather on the college's own contribution to education and research. Therefore, rather than follow the usual practice of waiting for institutions to come to us for funding, we selected the recipients ourselves. These include three categories of recipients: major research universities across the United States, such as the Massachusetts Institute of Technology; private liberal arts college in the Northeast, such as Amherst College; and private colleges and universities in the New York metropolitan area, such as the Pratt Institute.

Since Chemical Bank feels a particular responsibility to institutions in its own back yard, the program includes a high percentage of New York City institutions. In fact, the rationale of the Higher Education Grants Program in general retains the same New York City focus of the Basic Grants Program. The problems of education are national in scope, and the problems of New York will be addressed by people studying and teaching in institutions throughout the country.

Of the schools receiving grants under the program, less than 10 percent had even approached us during the same calandar year. We have told all grant recipients that we will reexamine them in three years for possible continuing support.

SOURCES OF AWARENESS

Awareness of managerial needs has come to permeate Chemical's approach to corporate social responsibility. To a significant extent it emerged from a technique developed in the course of our banking activities with nonprofit organizations. Chemical has emerged as a pioneer in applying advanced technology to collecting, investing, and disbursing cash for nonprofits. We have succeeded in that business by clarifying to the managements of many nonprofits that while successful fund raising is important for delivering effective service, it is also important to get the maxium benefit out of every dollar of support raised. Nonprofits can do that by taking steps to

—collect incoming funds more quickly, so that checks that now languish in the mails or in processing are put to use sooner;

—invest idle funds more quickly, so that money does not sit in a checking account, not even overnight, when it could be earning interest;

—pay out funds more efficiently, so that paid staff time is not wasted on the mechanical details of controlling disbursements.

A banker from Chemical's Not for Profit Group will help those organizations analyze their financial operations to determine which combination of services can save time and money for the organizations. Our experience derived from advising hospitals, schools, and other nonprofit customers has furnished us with much of the insight needed to evaluate and assist grant recipients who manage the delivery of cultural services.

Also helpful as a source of insights has been Chemical's so-called streetbanker program. Streetbankers are bank representatives assigned to less affluent neighborhoods to make grants, offer bridge funding, which covers temporary cash-flow difficulties, and provide bridge funding if requested by small businessmen, community organizations, and others. This method of blending good business sense with good people-sense has produced a bumper crop of ideas for neighborhood organizations and for the bank in its attempts to assist those and similar organizations.

IN-KIND CONTRIBUTIONS

Even when Chemical decides not to contribute to a particular group financially, it can frequently furnish assistance of other kinds. For example, now in its fourth year is Chemical's Public Education Office, which offers seminars and workshops to many cultural, nonprofit, and small business organizations. The seminars help managements of those organizations to take advantage of the options and resources available for managing and developing the organization. Among the topics covered are board management, referral agencies, bank services, and fund raising.

Chemical employees can also enroll in our Volunteer Center, where workshops are offered to acquaint them with the needs of nonprofit organizations. Topics covered in those workshops include "What It Means to Be a Board Member" and "Internal Fiscal Control for Nonprofits."

Nonprofit managers, furthermore, can enroll in a diagnostic workshop aimed at identifying weaknesses in fund raising, board development, or other management areas. In some cases the deficiency can be remedied by one of our own workshops or by on-site consultation, which Chemical can also provide. In other cases we suggest a technical assistance organization.

Our confidence in the impact of our nonfinancial contributions remains buoyant, and our budgets for both the Basic Grant Program and the Higher Education Grant Program continued rising without regard to the recession. We have increased our budget for arts institutions for 1983 from 11 percent to 17 percent, well above the national average.

In addition to enlarging our reservoir of good will through those programs, Chemical has had the satisfaction of becoming a co-worker with managers of cultural institutions. That relationship helps them build a sturdier long-range financial base, thereby enabling them to spend less time pursuing dollars and more time pursuing their main objectives. If tailored by other corporations to their own geography and style, that kind of relationship could help endow American culture with an exciting future.

Supply, Demand, and the University

By SHELDON HACKNEY

ABSTRACT: One reason there never seems to be adequate funding for the arts is that supply can never keep up with demand. Because of their mission and the environment they provide for creative minds, universities contribute to the problem by fanning the sparks of artistic desire. At the same time, because of their role in educating the audiences of the future, they are equally a part of the solution. In good financial times no less than in bad, Americans have tended to regard support for the arts in a puritanical light. Universities therefore make their most solid contributions to the arts in kind, by encouraging artists and the arts as part of the primary educational mission and by exposing all students to both the old and the new in art, music, and drama. Even though direct subventions are bound to remain inadequate, institutions can effectively provide support for the arts by resuming some responsibility for instilling aesthetic judgment in the citizens and consumers of tomorrow. Universities have a historical obligation to develop the highest in human awareness. This includes helping to determine tomorrow's tune by taking responsibility for informing the tastes of those who will pay the pipers of the future.

Sheldon Hackney is president of the University of Pennsylvania. A historian, he attended Vanderbilt University and received his M.A. and Ph.D. from Yale. He was professor and provost at Princeton University and president of Tulane University before coming to Pennsylvania in 1981. The author of Populism to Progressivism in Alabama *and* Populism: the Critical Issues, *and coeditor of* Understanding the American Experiment: Recent Interpretations, *he has contributed articles on the history of the South to leading academic journals.*

WHY do the arts always seem to be in crisis? Whether we think of Mozart starving in a garret with feeble support from Emperor Joseph II, El Greco suing the powerful churchmen of Toledo for payment, the Arts Council of Great Britain, or the latest subventions of Congress to the National Endowment for the Arts, society has yet to find a satisfactory solution to adequate patronage of the arts. Yet it is also true that the aspiring novelists, poets, painters, and actors who decry the philistinism of America do so at the present time in greater numbers than in any other society throughout the history of mankind.

This apparent paradox should be no surprise in a society committed to democracy and pluralism. Art itself was removed from its pedestal in the course of the present century, opening up new avenues of creativity and elevating an array of humbler crafts to the status of art. At the same time, popular art has received increased attention as well as support. The emphasis on individualism and the recognition of the role of self-expression in a child's intellectual development have each tended to encourage people to indulge what is a powerful human drive for creative activity. In addition our standard of living gives more people time to stand and stare, to pause and smell the flowers, to set about seeking new perceptions of reality and fresh expressions of themselves. Affluence and freedom amplify our artistic instincts, but the existence of a vigorous underground community of the arts in China and the Soviet Union underlines the fundamental nature of the artistic urge. Consequently, rising standards of living and the availability of money for the arts only help to ensure that there will never be enough support to go round. Supply will always exceed demand. It is a clear example of the freeway principle: instead of reducing pressure on the roads, improved highways merely tend to increase the volume of traffic. In artistic pursuits, as in all else, nature abhors a vacuum.

In this situation universities contribute to the problem as well as to the solution. Despite the supposed animosity betwen academia and the arts, our educational institutions help to fan the spark of artistic desire by exposing students to the best works of the past and by allowing them to come in contact with creative minds working at the forefront of knowledge and art. If the vast numbers of potential artists attending college never actually materialize, a fire is nonetheless stoked which may break forth at a later stage. At the same time, the university contributes to the solution, as it can certainly claim responsibility for producing informed consumers and patrons of the arts. In this capacity it plays an important role in the drama of the arts in a changing world.

During the boom of American higher education in the fifties and sixties, there was more than a passing notion that universities would become the new Medici, the Maecenas of art in modern America. At a meeting entitled "The Arts and the University" held in Lima in February 1964, a member of the Ford Foundation predicted the day when "the university may finally become the patron of three-quarters of all that goes on in the arts in the United States."[1] Indeed the innovative directions that resulted from student demands for a refreshed look at curriculum and the form and content of teaching did produce a flow-

1. Quoted by Jack Morrison, *The Rise of the Arts on the American Campus* (New York: McGraw-Hill, 1973), p. 4.

ering of new programs and facilities in the following decade.

SOME PROBLEMS

Even if university patronage of the arts did not materialize to the extent predicted, many institutions became involved in ambitious artistic ventures. As a result, by the eighties they find themselves faced with problems similar to those of exclusively cultural institutions at a time of government cutbacks and increased competition for private or corporate moneys in a depressed economy. Since a major source of unrestricted revenue in a university is student fees, and a current priority at institutions of higher learning is to find the wherewithal to replace government moneys that make it possible for many students to attend university at all, one becomes acutely aware of the reverse slope of a sort of Laffer curve that warns that it may no longer be practical to increase tuitions as a means of funding operations. Colleges and universities that subsidize well-established programs in the arts receive a range of other urgent demands on their resources.

In straitened times the campus is thus particularly badly placed to salvage threatened cultural enterprises; its own dilemmas are too similar in kind, too subject to the same economic realities. The labor-intensive nature of the cultural institution is illustrated by the fact that an octet still requires the same number of performers now as in Mendelssohn's time. Cutting it by 50 percent may increase productivity but does not ensure that it will be equally functional in the guise of a quartet.[2] In the world of art, progress is our most important

enemy. As economic productivity increases, the labor-intensive activities of the service sector and cultural world get more expensive relative to the price of goods being produced by ever more efficient means.

The same is true of universities. Without subsidies from other sources, tuition would have to rise by more than the inflationary rate in the general economy. At a time when even the Metropolitan Museum of Art is encountering financial difficulties, those responsible for the health of institutions of higher learning may be excused some nervousness, particularly since almost three-quarters of university museums have an expenditure of less than $500,000 per annum while 81 percent of non-university museums expend in excess of that amount.[3] Even the Fogg Museum, with $21 million already in hand, recently ran into controversy concerning the appropriateness of going ahead with a long-planned addition. The question was positively resolved; yet the fact that there was insufficient space to display major works by Degas, Gauguin, and Picasso or the finest collection of paintings and drawings by Ingres outside of New York, was not at first persuasive enough to convince the governing board to approve the project.[4]

---

2. "To dramatize this point—it is estimated that the average manufactured product takes one-twentieth as many person hours today as it did during Mozart's lifetime, but a Mozart quintet takes exactly as many person hours to perform now as it did then." William J. Baumol, "Financial Prospects for the Performing Arts" (1979 speech), quoted by Patricia McFate, "The Effects of Inflation on the Arts," *The Annals* of the American Academy of Political and Social Science, 456: 84 (July 1981).

3. Jay D. Starling and John P. Plumlee, "The Association of Art Museum Directors Survey Report," photocopied (Dallas, TX: Southern Methodist University, n.d.), tables 4 and 5.

4. John Russell, "To the Rescue of the Fogg Museum," *New York Times,* 28 March 1982.

In a democracy the arts run into pressures against public moneys being used to subsidize what is viewed as an elite activity. This is particularly true in the United States. Here, unlike Europe, much of the enterprise of universities also has been traditionally suspect of elitism. A Rockefeller Panel report (1965) describes a recurrent attitude toward the arts both on and off campus:

Influential voices among us . . . question the expenditure of so much of our treasure upon the arts, the values of which cannot be charted like the movements of the solar system, or demonstrated by a litmus test, or worked out mathematically to the nth decimal place. Others are convinced that political freedom coupled with the maintenance of the free enterprise systems is enough for the artist, and for society to undertake, given its many other burdens. They require information on the practical, immediate, social benefits of the arts. It is very much in the American character to demand such proofs.[5]

At universities, even in more prosperous times, the accusation of "frills" was heard. And the world has changed since the good old days when students were clamoring for a more arts-oriented program. Today students are far from convinced that what they want is more cultural enrichment rather than more courses in business. It is not surprising that arts programs feel themselves embattled, if not in retreat.

One of the reasons our pluralistic democracy has survived so well is that we have been able to let the market decide so many things. The traditional politician's response to conflict has been

5. *The Performing Arts, Problems and Prospects,* A Rockefeller Panel Report on the Future of Theater, Dance, and Music in America (New York: McGraw-Hill, 1965), p. 6.

to give a little bit to every group—to get money into the hands of everyone and leave it to the recipients to decide how to spend it. Private philanthropy has saved those many segments of so-called high culture that would otherwise have failed under this formula. The government has also recognized the general interest in art by allowing nonprofit cultural institutions to be tax exempt.

In this market-driven system a university's most important role remains that of attempting to even the odds by educating the audiences for the arts and by nurturing forms, both experimental and archaic, that might otherwise not survive.

THE SOLUTION: IN-KIND CONTRIBUTIONS

Universities support aspects of their fine arts programs—theater, musical performance, dance, film, art galleries—by direct subventions from their budgets. The University of Pennsylvania, for example, supports the Institute of Contemporary Art, the Annenberg Center for the Performing Arts, and music and the fine arts on a departmental level under the College of Arts and Sciences and the Graduate School of Fine Arts. In 1983 the Arthur Ross Gallery was opened for the display of the university's collection as well as special exhibitions. Outside performers and student productions are also supported by the allocation of special university funds.

There are a number of other functions that are historically within the purview of institutions of higher learning and through which they make an in-kind contribution. Because their mission is to teach both what is old and what is new, academic institutions are well suited to protect the values of the past even while encouraging creativity and renewal of the inherited store of human experience through encouraging established artists and their students to produce the aesthetic artifacts that give expression to the contemporary world.

In the opinion of Janet Kardon, director of the Institute of Contemporary Art, universities are the only place where such experimentation survives. Her words are echoed by the chairman of the University of Pennsylvania's music department when he states that for the last 20 years university departments have been the sole promulgators of contemporary music. Orchestras and operas increasingly appear to see their mission as a musical museum, and conservatories direct their attention to the repertoire of the past, which their students, if they are lucky, will find employment playing. But universities appoint composers to their faculty, giving them time and support for their work and the irreplaceable opportunity of having their works performed in a laboratory-like environment.[6]

A second distinction should be made with regard to the teaching function of the university, this time as it applies to students. One possible object of a program for the arts is to train professionals for a sphere of operation outside the university. Yet, as Robert Brustein— former dean of the Yale Drama School and currently director of the American Repertory Theater at Harvard—has pointed out, rather than setting up to compete with conservatories to train

talent, the university still performs its most important function through its traditional role of liberal educator.

The undergraduate school [should] provide the soil and climate for the seed that the professional school will later transplant and cultivate. Colleges are equipped neither by inclination nor charter to be professional conservatories or vocational schools, nor should they attempt to half-hearted training in order to please their artistically inclined students. But they can provide a valuable pre-professional service by arousing curiosity in a student's mind, an appetite for the arts, and—most difficult and necessary of all—a respect for excellence and a sense of humility. In this manner colleges can function —as they are now forced to function in America—as a substitute for the culture that Europeans absorb quite naturally from their homes and their society.

Any professionally oriented training on campus, thinks Brustein, should be confined to the graduate school. This does not mean, however, that where such programs do not exist, amateur standards—associated with the artistic dabbling recognized as a valued function of liberal education—should be allowed to compromise the "distance between attempt and accomplishment, between neophyte effort and artistic achievement." The university should concentrate on what it has traditionally done best.

Colleges have a potential for service beyond the declarations in their catalogues. Without changing their function, they are capable of instilling a sense of literature, a love of music, a feeling for art and a response to theater in their students—often for the very first time.[7]

---

6. Composers George Rochberg, Richard Wernick, and George Crumb are members of the University of Pennsylvania faculty. The Penn Contemporary Players perform their works as well as other new pieces.

7. "The Spirit of Excellence: Theater and the University," *The New Republic,* 171: 15 (16 Nov. 1974).

Quality, moreover, should never be compromised, whatever the shifts in philosophy or fashion.

A liberal education in the arts is even more important for those who aspire to be artists of some kind than for the consumers of art. American students do not arrive at college having already read all the great dramatic works that all actors aspire to perform. The University of Pennsylvania's poet in residence, Daniel Hoffman, reports turning away a considerable proportion of hopeful young poets from his seminars in creative writing with the admonition that, if they hope to express themselves, they should consider reading some of what similarly inclined contributors to their language have already set down in that medium. If the university has a special obligation in this regard and at this particular juncture, it is probably to dispel the illusion that there can be some sort of aesthetic noble savage—an untutored genius who is capable of profound insights precisely because he or she has not consciously studied or learned from the vast storehouses of riches already produced by the human mind.

The third and most important aspect of in-kind contributions of the university to the arts is even less distinguishable from what many would consider the university's traditional role. We have suggested that even if the future professional manages to pick up some experience and polish as a practitioner, the major contribution of the university is preparation in the liberal arts, the underpinning of all the arts and professions. Surely the reason that in England Shakespeare belongs to the people rather than on a pedestal is that it can be assumed by the actors that what they are saying makes perfectly good sense. They do not find themselves gabbling off lines that are viewed as too anachronistic ever to be comprehensible.

It is no longer true, if it ever was, that if you wanted to be an artist you went to art school, and that if you did not know what you wanted you went to college. This formulation is only slightly less preposterous than the old saw about education in the arts, "Those who can, do; those who can't, teach." A sign of the times is the number of successful artists in various areas who have at least a bachelor's degree, possibly a master's degree, as a result of protracted studies at regular colleges and universities—Meryl Streep would be a celebrated example—not to mention business graduates with degrees in arts management or the increasing number of doctoral degrees among museum directors.[8] But the rest of the student body will also have a role to play in the future of the arts that may prove equally important to their survival, for all artistic endeavor depends on both the creator and the receiver. Even works from the past will not be preserved unless there is a receptive audience in addition to those trained in production or performance. Experimentation will wither on the vine if there is no encouragement or support beyond the immediate initiates.

Those who are responsible for the fine-arts component in the university curriculum make much of the need for such programs, not only as a necessary and enriching ingredient in general education, but also as they affect the survival of the arts. The continued health of

8. "Nearly 90% of the directors hold a masters degree and nearly a third have a Ph.D." Starling and Plumlee, "The Association of Art Museum Directors Survey Report," p. 9.

the arts depends on an audience and, beyond that actively engaged group, a general public equipped to make judgments on the place of the arts in society and on the funds that will be allocated by the government and by private or corporate sources of support. It is not enough to proclaim, as did the Rockefeller Panel report, that "the place of the arts is at the center of society" unless society acts as if this were indeed the case.

As they pass through our American universities, members of the public of the future have the chance to develop their artistic yearnings, or at the least to refine their aesthetic judgment, as part of a rounded education. Even Benjamin Franklin, the pragmatist, renowned for his hard-nosed attitude when it came to describing the educational program most useful in the American colonies, gracefully acknowledged the place of less practical forms of learning as "a distinguishing Ornament."[9] College graduates are very likely to sit on boards of cultural institutions, or to make contributions to what they adjudge to be the most worthy causes. It is unlikely that there will be any diminution of competition for such support. On the broader scene, graduates will be among the lawmakers, and at the very least they are the electorate, enlightened or otherwise, who determine how the nation's treasure shall be spent.

Patricia McFate notes a 1980 editorial in the *New York Times* to the effect that "cutting welfare benefits 10 percent is not the same as cutting land reclamation 10 percent. Nor is a lid on spending for food stamps the same as a lid on the

Endowment for the Humanities."[10] In response, others hastened to bring in comparable parallel expenditures involving funding for welfare and the arts compared with missile cost overruns, and even the fact that military bands, as a line item in national-defense spending, exceeded the highest total budget of National Endowment for the Humanities and National Endowment for the Arts combined. Even now, large amounts of money are available for entertainment, most of which is not expended in the cause of the arts. McFate quotes Robert Samuelson to the effect that people must decide for themselves whether to spend their money for entertainment by the Pittsburgh Steelers or the Pittsburgh Symphony.

Clearly the present financial crunch is not merely a question of the amount of funds, but also the ways in which the funds are allocated. Thus, at the very least, today's student body is arguably a captive audience, one that is not only amenable to receiving some ideas on subjects on which they may have few preconceived notions—other than that it is possibly too high-brow for them—but who, according to Brustein, may remain aesthetically underdeveloped if the opportunity is missed. For this reason the university art museum has a special role, indicated in a recent article by John Russell.

University museums have a constituency of a special kind. Great works of art that we see first in youth are never forgotten. We remember when, and in what company, we first saw them. They are a part of our youth, and of ourselves, in a way that other works of art are not.[11]

9. Benjamin Franklin, *Papers of Benjamin Franklin,* ed. Leonard W. Labaree (New Haven, CT: Yale University Press, 1959-76), 3:415.

10. McFate, "The Effects of Inflation on the Arts," p. 75.
11. Russell, "Rescue of the Fogg Museum."

In some ways this is but an analysis of what lies behind "knowing what one likes"—a thoughtless statement most often to be interpreted as "liking what one knows."

For universities not to take the opportunity of helping form taste by ensuring that students receive the widest possible exposure to the arts in all their manifestations; not to encourage the minor effort that will harvest a major reward, both personally and for the public good; not to take full advantage of writing something worthwhile on the aesthetic tabula rasa many students present is surely an abdication of responsibilty for an important function that they are in a position to exercise. In the long run, indifference to this responsibility can only be detrimental both to universities and to primary cultural institutions whose rewards are nonetheless generally recognized as worth the minor expenditure of effort and intellect: *per aspera ad astra!*

REDISTRIBUTING RESOURCES

What does this all have to do with paying for culture right now, when so many causes are crying out for sources of funds to sustain programs in jeopardy? The fact is the university's educational function has particular bearing on the subject. It is not as if there were no money available in the culture/entertainment sector, or even a dearth of young people able to dispose of it. In fact the question is not simply, either the the Pittsburgh Steelers or the Pittsburgh Symphony. It is a matter of the mix. At the university we have the opportunity, as well as a responsibility, to help cultivate taste for the good not only of the arts but for the development of the whole person through exposure to the range and diversity of the world undreamed of in many an undergraduate's philosophy.

Because of the growing separatism of the youth culture and the natural responsiveness of institutions of learning to changing values, there has been a tendency in recent years to overlook the fact that certain values, despite changing times and tastes, must nonetheless remain the preserve of the university. Ambivalence, provoked by the fear of labels of elitism, does a disservice to the traditional standards that are basic to the academy. In addition a timorous attitude tends to sell short the most energetic, gifted, and intellectually curious members of young society. A hesitancy to introduce subject matter for fear of being thought high-brow and undemocratic may actually prevent students from receiving an introduction to those unforeseen elements in education that often prove to be the most influential. In a volume dedicating a new art gallery at the Univerity of Pennsylvania, Provost Thomas Ehrlich commented,

The visual arts provide a vital dimension in education that is so obvious it is sometimes ignored. In considering that most elusive of all human activities—creativity—the visual arts reveal unique links between rational analysis and intuitive insight. With experience and knowledge our perceptions and abilities to make critical judgments become sharpened and educated and our lives enriched. . . . It is the education of the mind that disciplines the eye to recognize the beauty that artistic greatness can convey, the appreciation of the transformation of images from the artist's vision into something tangible. Some students come with natural talent, others only with interest, but all can be educated if they have the will to learn and the courage to inquire.[12]

12. "Education and Art," *"La Tauromaquia"*

Perhaps because of the influence of Benjamin Franklin and the Morrill Act, universities in the United States have always had to contend with accusations of elitism in the values they espouse. At the present time, in a highly educated nation the term often implies little beyond the maintenance of standards and the habit of distinguishing quality from its opposite. At an earlier moment in history intellectual snobbery may have invited a creative reaction. But the pendulum has swung much too far to the opposite side; and notions such as idealism, freedom, and a whole slew of what Abbie Hoffman recalls as "isums" and "wasums" of the sixties have been co-opted in the interest of commercialism, not of reinvigorating popular culture. Because of their toleration and openness, universities were particularly vulnerable in the sixties.

The university itself, traditionally the home for the best that had been thought and created, had begun to lose its nerve about its own purpose, and to question the importance of literature, theater, art and music. Only later would people begin to realize that the revolutionary values of radical students regarding art and the humanities were very similar to the philistine values of commercial society; and that the levelers on the left had joined hands together against the university and the creative arts in a common effort to obliterate all undemocratic (unprofitable?) standards and distinction.[13]

Long after the revolutionary idealism has been replaced, the universities and the arts have yet to recover fully from the incidental vandalizing of their operations—always a side-effect, and often the most lasting, of popular revolt.

It is time for universities to resume the responsibility, given up almost 20 years ago, to point out the exploitation to which the young unknowingly submit, to help guide students in their choices, including the ways they spend their considerable budgets for extracurricular entertainment. Let there be cultural pluralism but also awareness that the university must resist a takeover by commercial values in the guise of democracy, bad art masquerading as popular culture. Throughout history the gullible have been bilked for their innocence by charlatans, whether they adopted Italian names to deceive the pseudo-illuminati or employed some extravagant device to deter the crowd from pronouncing that the emperor has no clothes. Where, if not at universities, can judgment be nurtured so that a neo-discriminating audience will be able to distinguish the phony from the true, to learn that the value of art is not that it belongs to the elite or to the inhabitants of history, but that it is for now and for all people?

Providing standards for the way students spend their money as well as their time is only a continuation of a proper function of a university as a watchdog of quality and excellence, not as elite values, but as standards to be aimed at in a pluralistic society no less than in an aristocratic one. Coupled with continuing support for the fine arts on campus, with attention to maintaining the highest possible standards, this also holds out the hope for their future sustenance. Precisely because so little art is seen or heard live, as entertainment becomes increasingly individualistic and home-oriented, the theaters, galleries, and the many opportunities for participating in live music and entertainment on campus become even more important elements in a truly educational experience. The

---

and Other Prints, exhibition catalogue, University of Pennsylvania, Arthur Ross Gallery (1983), pp. 7-8.

13. Brustein, "Spirit of Excellence," p. 14.

discovery of the unanticipated pleasures of live art as an active communal experience rather than a canned passive spectator sport may further help provide acceptable alternatives to violence or cults, two manifestations of the dissatisfaction of the young with the status quo. It is already recognized that contact sports provide an acceptable outlet for aggressive tendencies. Perhaps, after all, there is a real link between the Pittsburgh Steelers and the Pittsburgh Symphony—with emphasis on the conjunction.

It is appropriate that universities, though not wealthy patrons in their own right, should at least exercise their historical obligation to develop the highest in human awareness, to help determine tomorrow's tune and indeed whether there will be a tune at all, by taking more responsibility for informing the tastes of those who will be helping to pay the pipers of the future.

Supporting the Arts in the Eighties:
The View from the
National Endowment for the Arts

By FRANCIS S.M. HODSOLL

ABSTRACT: The federal government's direct involvement in funding the arts has come relatively recently in our nation's history. The National Endowment for the Arts was established to this end in 1965. Local private giving to support the arts preceded the Endowment and continues as the principal factor. The federal government's role, intended to complement the highly active role of private citizens, provides national recognition that the arts are vital to the nation. Within the context of America's private giving, the National Endowment for the Arts has a number of specific tasks in support of the arts, which will be particularly important in this decade— a time of major economic and demographic change. The Endowment's six-part strategy for the 1980s encourages (1) longer-term institutional support for arts organizations; (2) projects that advance the art forms or bring a diversity of arts to broader audiences; (3) better management and planning by arts institutions; (4) development of partnership among public arts agencies; (5) greater private support; and (6) linkages among systems of arts information.

Francis S.M. Hodsoll is the fourth chairman of the National Endowment for the Arts, appointed by President Reagan in 1981. The first lawyer and career government official to head the agency, he brings extensive administrative and policy-making experience through two decades of government service in several agencies and departments, including State and Commerce. Prior to his present appointment, he served as deputy assistant to the President and deputy to the chief of staff, and was senior White House liaison for the Presidential Task Force on the Arts and the Humanities.

NOTE: This article was originally written by the author in his capacity as chairman of the National Endowment for the Arts and as a federal employee; it is therefore in the public domain.

THE federal government's involvement in the formal funding of the
arts in this country has come relatively
recently in our nation's history. The
National Endowment for the Arts was
established less than 20 years ago, in
1965. While the Works Progress Administration of 1935 supported artists as
part of a jobs program, the Endowment
was the first national funding agency
created on behalf of the arts themselves.

The federal government's involvement
in supporting the arts was designed to
complement the highly active role of
private citizens. As the Endowment's
enabling legislation noted,

the encouragement and support of national
progress and scholarship in the humanities
and the arts, while primarily a matter for
private and local initiative, is also an appropriate matter of concern to the federal
government.[1]

The Endowment's initial budget of
$2.5 million was only a 1 percent addition
to the base of private support for the arts
and humanities, estimated at $200 million
in 1965. Yet something more profound
than dollars was added to our system:
the Endowment added national recognition that the arts in and of themselves
were vital to our civilization.

This recognition coincided with a 20-
fold growth in private support and helped
stimulate a network of public support
agencies at state and local levels. Private
support of culture in 1982 was $3.56
billion; state arts agency support was
$121 million; local government support
has been estimated at over $250 million;
the Endowment's budget was $143
million.

HISTORICAL PERSPECTIVE

Private giving to assist the arts is an
American tradition. As President
Reagan's Task Force on the Arts and
the Humanities noted, "There is no
other nation in the world in which the
principle of private giving to sustain cultural institutions is so deeply ingrained."[2] Our system of arts support is
different from that of other nations,
most of whom rely on government as the
primary patron. Our pluralistic system
of arts support—involving individual
citizens, local governments, foundations,
corporations, and government—has
contributed to an unparalleled diversity
of artistic excellence in this country.

This system of private support grew
with the nation—from the fertile but different soils of our towns and cities. In
Boston, for example, where the arts
were first viewed with suspicion, limited
support was justified as part of education.
However, in nineteenth-century Charleston, South Carolina—the site of our
first symphony, opera performances,
and our first museum—the arts were
seen as part of the celebration of civic
advancement.

As the nation developed economically
during the nineteenth century, individual
benefactors took the lead in the founding
and development of what today are
many of our major museums and orchestras. Outside the major urban centers, individual subscribers of more
modest means made possible the numerous chautauquas, which brought
lecturers and performers of the day to a
broad audience.

This pattern of individual patronage
was broadened and enhanced by the

1. U.S., National Foundation on the Arts and
the Humanities Act of 1965, as amended, *United
States Code,* title 20, sec. 951 et seq.

2. Presidential Task Force on the Arts and the
Humanities, *Report to the President* (Washington,
DC: Government Printing Office, 1981), p. 3.

passage in 1913 and 1917 of our income and inheritance tax laws, which provided tax-exempt status for many cultural institutions and tax deductibility for gifts. With these laws the federal government has indirectly supported culture. In 1974 the forbearance of the government on tax income going to the arts and humanities was an estimated $400 million, perhaps larger; and in 1980 this estimate was over $1 billion.

FEDERAL ROLE

Within the context of America's tradition of private giving, the federal government has specific tasks:

—recognition: to demonstrate and advocate the importance of the arts by recognizing, at the national level, that which is artistically excellent;

—support for experimentation: to ensure support—as in the sciences—for new and experimental ventures that might be too risky to elicit sufficient private investment and to foster a climate for the unpredictable;

—preservation: to preserve art in danger of loss or deterioration;

—institutional stability: to enhance the financial base of the nation's most excellent artistic institutions so their artistry may advance, notwithstanding difficult economic times;

—cultural diversity: to encourage the kaleidoscope of American culture;

—availability and appreciation: to increase access to, and appreciation of, the arts for American citizens everywhere.

IMPACT OF THE EIGHTIES

These efforts are particularly crucial in the 1980s, as the overall economic growth rate that paralleled the arts boom of the sixties and seventies lessens. The task is not easy. The 1980s began with tremendous inflation, high interest rates, and growing federal budget deficits. A nagging recession has resulted in economic dislocation. These circumstances have affected all public and private institutions. Inflation and interest rates are down; but the federal budget deficit persists, threatening progress on the former.

Further, the 1980s are more than a time of changing economics. We also face changes in national demographics. Our population is aging. The median age in 1970 was 28.1 years; in 1980 it was 30 years. This figure is predicted to grow to 35.2 years in 2000. The population over 65 will increase from 26.2 million today to 31.8 million in 2000. According to the Bureau of the Census the country's population center—for the first time in history—has moved west of the Mississippi. In 1790 the first census showed the population center to be near Chestertown, Maryland. Today it is in a wooded area just outside the city of DeSoto in Jefferson County, Missouri. Our population is becoming better educated. According to the 1980 census, for the first time more than half the residents 25 years and older of every state have completed at least four years of high school. Seventeen percent of our population has now completed four years of college. Nonfamily households increased nearly 72 percent in the 10-year period 1970-1980, whereas family households grew only 16 percent in the same time frame. The number of single-parent families rose from one out of eight in 1970 to nearly one out of five in 1980.

Our technology is also undergoing a rapid transformation. The manufacturing sector is giving way—at an even faster rate than earlier predicted—to the service, information, and high technology sectors. A recent National Science Foundation study speculates that by the end of this century, one- and two-way home information systems, called teletext and videotext, will penetrate deeply into our daily lives with an effect as profound as the earlier impact of automobiles and television. An encyclopedia of the entire nineteenth-century repertoire of music can be recorded on a single video disc. The technology exists for multiple, interactive communications networks for any group with similar interests. Where will the money come from to program these new technologies, and who will determine that programming?

Avoiding artistic consolidation is a greater challenge than it once was. In the 1950s over 500 feature films were produced each year; today the number is closer to 60, at an average budget cost of $10 million. Publishing houses have, in many cases, become adjuncts of conglomerates. Thus, except for the small publishers and university presses, young poets and novelists find it much more difficult to get published. Performing arts repertoires are in many cases becoming less adventurous.

ENDOWMENT STRATEGIES FOR THE EIGHTIES

With these trends in mind, we have devised a six-part strategy for the Endowment:

1. Emphasizing longer-term institutional support. Through the Endowment's Challenge and Advancement Programs, which provide institutional support on a matching basis, we are assisting the best of our arts organizations, big and small, to achieve a financial basis on which they can face the future with confidence.

2. Encouraging projects that advance the art forms or bring a diversity of art to a broader audience. We are placing special emphasis on support of innovative projects that could affect the development of the art form. In addition, we support artists and arts organizations of national or regional significance and the touring, presenting, and media dissemination of their work.

3. Encouraging better management and planning by arts institutions. The Endowment is encouraging arts institutions to develop better management, including rolling three- and five-year planning, artistic and financial.

4. Developing partnership among public sector supporters of the arts. In the past year we have developed a $2 million test initiative to assist local arts agencies. Together with state arts agencies we are reviewing public support for arts education and for touring and presenting of the arts. We are encouraging to a greater degree state arts agencies and regional organizations to seek funding from Endowment programs for specific projects in the various art forms; and we are working with both state and local arts agencies on joint planning for the future.

5. Encouraging greater private support. The Endowment is working with the President's Committee on the Arts and the Humanities to encourage greater attention to and support for the arts. We are also supporting a variety of specific

projects designed to recognize, inform, assist, and advocate new private support for the arts.

6. Initiating the development of a system of arts information systems that anyone concerned with the arts can use. The Endowment is encouraging linkages among the information systems of state arts agencies, arts service organizations, and the Endowment.

These strategies, in my view, will help broaden the base of support for the best of our arts and will encourage greater financial stability. Our arts are the envy of the world. We must as a people continue to assure, in many and diverse ways, that they do not lack a variety of sources of support to keep them vital and flourishing.

ANNALS, *AAPSS,* **471,** January 1984

Our Government's Support for the Arts: Nourishment or Drought

By LIVINGSTON BIDDLE, Jr.

ABSTRACT: The National Endowment for the Arts, coming into existence in a period when federal support of the arts was not a popular cause in Congress, has survived and prospered with bipartisan support. From its beginnings the Endowment has operated under the principle that private support of the arts is of primary importance, and that the agency should be guided by the advice of private citizens. Endowment grants have supported artists and cultural institutions and companies, increased education in the arts, improved the aesthetics of city living, and encouraged development of ethnic projects. Challenge Grants, which bolster arts organizations, have been an immense success. The article presents the author's views regarding the essential and precedent-setting nature of the Arts Endowment, its meaning to Americans and the arts at the very core of life. The author discusses the catalytic impact of the Endowment since 1965, and expresses deep concern that a time of exceptional nourishment may give way to a time of drought.

Livingston Biddle, Jr., prepared the enabling legislation in the U.S. Senate for the National Endowment for the Arts and held positions in the Endowment, including that of chairman (1977-81). A practicing artist, he is the author of four novels, two of which were best sellers. He has served as chairman of the Division of Arts at Fordham University at Lincoln Center, New York, and once headed the Pennsylvania Ballet Company. He received an A.B. degree from Princeton University. He is married to the artist Catharina Van Beek Baart.

THE arts are at the very core of life. They have always been so. All great civilizations throughout history have placed abiding emphasis on their values, on the special enrichment of the human spirit they provide, on the legacies of talent and its expression they pass on to us.

It often seems to me that the basic importance of the arts is overlooked by those who criticize or question a governmental role of support. Of course our government should support the arts! It should be proud to make a strong and unequivocal commitment to their development.

In budgetary terms the commitment is presently minuscule. Even if it were to be doubled some day, the sum would remain relatively minuscule—a blip of shortest duration on the screen of manifold, far larger governmental expenditures. To suggest reducing the financial commitment by a demolishing 50 per cent in 1981, by an inordinate 30 per cent the year following, and by a distressing $20 million in 1983, simply cannot be linked in any compelling way with the principles of equitable fiscal restraint. Serious doubts linger. What value is actually being placed on the arts by the present administration? Do they continue as a special target? And if a commitment, carefully nurtured and fostered for 18 years, is to be so drastically altered and reversed, is it a commitment at all? Or is it indeed abnegation of commitment wearing a palatable disguise?

The doubts were there in the beginning when Congress first, in the early 1960s, began serious consideration of governmental support.

In those days to espouse the arts in Congress was to expose the protagonist to unseemly jibes, to suggestions of eccentricity, of unworldliness, of impracticality and visionary dreams detached from political reality. The arts were considered by a majority in Congress as frivolous, of appeal only to a limited audience, practiced by irresponsible bohemians, very possibly embarrassing —and hence political liabilities. One has only to recall debates of the period, notably one in the fall of 1965, when an amendment was offered in the House of Representatives proposing inclusion of the "rotatory undulations" of the belly dancer within the lexicon of the arts. Ridicule had been used successfully to expunge previous attempts at culturally directed legislation. Ridicule almost succeeded late in 1965. The House floor rocked with raucous mirth. The legislation—precedent-setting in its concepts and intent—almost was banished, for some other try, some other year.

A LASTING TRIBUTE

That it survived is a tribute—a lasting monument, in the view of this then House gallery spectator—to a small number of intrepid pioneers, adept in debate, eloquent in language, able to turn the weapon of ridicule against its users. But it was a very near thing.

Never since that afternoon has the concept of government support for the arts been that close to the precipice in Congress. The climate changed. As time advanced, the precipice of refusal and rejection was left far behind. The pioneers set out across the plains, with ranges of blue mountains ahead in the distance.

They should be called to mind. To me they will always be heroes: Claude Pepper, perhaps the first among them whose advocacy dates back more than forty years; Jack Javits, Hubert Humphrey; Claiborne Pell, my boss then and long thereafter, the initial and for many years chairman of the first Senate Subcommittee on the Arts; and in the House, Frank Thompson, who found the felicitous phrases to combat ridicule on that memorable day; Ogden Reid and Joe McDade; John Brademas, for so long a champion of the authorizing process for the arts; Paul Simon, his successor; and especially Sidney Yates, uniquely gifted in appropriations, who has so well guided the funding year after year, and who so skillfully developed such strong bipartisan support that it withstood the drastic reductions in funding recently proposed.

From earliest times Democrats and Republicans were linked in this endeavor. The budget grew from the tiny, modest $2.5 million at the outset, upward. It grew under Roger Stevens, the first chairman of the National Endowment for the Arts, a pioneer taking the message of the arts' importance across the country. It grew mightily under Nancy Hanks, chairman for eight years, wise and greatly competent, who passed on to me a budget close to $100 million. In my tenure the funds increased almost to $160 million annually, then ended after a final frenetic year, not at the initial $88 million recommended, not at $77 million later proposed, but at $143 million—to me a congressional miracle, which I attribute chiefly to the wondrous work of Sidney Yates, work that perseveres with yet other miracles very possibly in store.

It is difficult to describe this still youthful program, with its relatively small number of employees and its new approaches, without mentioning personalities. Small programs depend on them. The size precludes anonymity.

BASIC PRINCIPLES

But there are principles to discuss. What has made the agency flourish? And why have the arts so flourished in our nation since its inception?

Let us start with the law itself, passed by Congress and signed by President Johnson in a memorable ceremony in the Rose Garden at the White House on 29 September 1965. The president included this new departure for government within the framework of his Great Society program and had given it particular support.

Essentially, however, the law stemmed from congressional initiatives. In creating the National Endowment for the Arts, the legislation

—emphasized the fundamental values of the arts to our nation;

—found there was a growing desire among our people for the special benefits cultural well-being provides; and

—recognized that the private sector, by itself, was inadequate to meet these important needs, hopes, and aspirations.

A special kind of catalyst was required Congress determined, a special kind of seed money to provide new incentives for cultural growth. We grappled to find a uniquely American response. We studied the approaches other nations had taken and were taking to develop their own cultural assets. We looked back over the centuries and at the present situations. We realized that in almost all cases, in other countries of the world where strong cultural growth has been fostered, a nearly total subsidy was involved—from ancient times to the present, from the early years of patronage by pharaohs and popes and emperors to the transition to modern times and activities almost entirely supported by government.

But that approach of total subsidy was neither in keeping with our own traditions, nor with the adaptation of those traditions to this new endeavor. A uniquely American approach was sought and found. Its basic philosophy and guiding principles were based on the theme of partnership—between government and the private community.

In its Declaration of Purpose, at the very beginning, the law creating the Endowment expressly emphasized that while government has a clear, responsible, and positive role to play, private support for the arts is of primary importance. That principle remains steadfast, just as it should.

Further, the legislation emphasized that this new undertaking, first of its kind in our history, was to be guided by private citizens—by members of the National Council on the Arts and, significantly, by panels of private citizens, all experts in the arts and recognized for their experience and special knowledge. Thus the Endowment was envisioned not as a federal bureaucracy, but as a program guided by the knowledge and expertise of the private community.

To me the success of the Endowment rests on these basic principles. A catalyst was created in an American tradition, and it has produced unique results.

During my service as chairman I gave much attention to enhancing further the guiding role and responsibilities of the National Council on the Arts, and to strengthening the panel structure, so that the private-citizen experts in each of the major arts disciplines would be better able to review, most carefully, the

30,000 applications for help being received, and to recommend for additional council examination the most qualified. This is an awesome task. It needs, above all, the wisdom of private experts fully respected by their peers; for the process is fundamental to the assurance of quality, and to the assurance that no individual bias is placed on the program itself. It would be vastly unwise in my view to tamper with this basic procedure.

In my time, available funds permitted only 20 percent of the applicants, on average, to be successful. A far higher ratio was considered deserving. Reductions in funding were not then relevant. The agonies of panelists—with long lists of those whose work was adjudged meritorious, but whose needs could not be presently met—were very real. In no foreseeable future would quality be a valid issue to the Endowment's tasks.

It is interesting to note that this process was examined by a special presidential task force assembled in the spring of 1981, while I was still incumbent, and the process was endorsed after weeks of close scrutiny. Rumors—and Washington can grow a particularly virulent variety—circulated that the Arts Endowment would be reshaped in its entirety and some said abandoned. But the end result was a vote of confidence in its structure, its fundamental purpose, and philosophy. The legislation has stood the test of time.

MISUNDERSTANDINGS

Let us look briefly at other voices raised over the years in opposition. Those who have criticized the Endowment with attributes of articulate phraseology—for example, the so-called Heritage Foundation report published in 1981 as a guide to the incoming administration—have pronounced judgments and presented assumptions impaired, in charitable terms, by a startling degree of ignorance, as if emanating from some ivory tower aloof from the needs of factual examination. I prefer this explanation to suggesting a limited intellectual ability. After all, educated minds have been at work and, given the opportunity of intelligent inquiry and scrutiny, should really know better.

We have long heard rumblings of a politicization or "politicalization" of the arts, and of resultant spending by the Endowment of precious dollars on arts undertakings that have no abiding value.

I have asked others—and myself, over the years—what these terms really mean. They certainly imply that something detrimental to the arts is going on. They also can imply that our political process and the arts are antithetical, that American democracy, governed by the political process we have developed, and support of the arts are inevitably at odds. Taken a logical step further, we could conclude that in the United States democracy and the arts are by their definitions incompatible.

Since I do not believe that this is quite the intended thrust of the criticism, I am persuaded that politicalization, in the phrasing used even earlier than 1981, conveys a derogatory partisanship, placing one political view or party into unseemly conflict with another. The facts, until very recently, simply do not support such a contention.

The Arts Endowment, as noted, was created with a special demonstration of bipartisanship. Regard the original sponsorship in both Senate and House of Representatives in the beginning 1960s. Regard the increasing support provided by a succession of presidents from both our major political parties. It seems ironic that the first administration to break with the foundation of bipartisan encouragement is the very administration that now decries as worthy of attack a politicizing of the arts.

Ignorance of the beginnings of the Endowment and of its development must be involved. Otherwise the tones are far darker and would lead to implications that somehow the founding fathers set in motion a governmental process unfriendly to the achievement of cultural goals.

Moreover, what are the arts of alleged unabiding worth, spawned by alleged political bickering and confusion? Please, again regard the Endowment's history and its basic premise. Critics so often disregard these aspects, and they place an unavoidable trip-wire across their paths. What has the catalyst, working with the private community since its inception, fostered which we would discard? Is a symphony orchestra of no lasting value? Is a theater company? Or a dance company? A museum? A writer? A painter? A sculptor? Let us face it— the Endowment helps all the arts. It does not invent them. Where is the value that lasts, or that fades? Who is omniscient enough to predict an unalterable future?

I remember, when a new administration recommended slicing the Endowment's budget in half, seeking out one who reportedly was proferring the knife with highly influential advice to his superior, the Lord High Wielder of the weapon itself. We had lunch together. Why cut the arts? I asked. What was the rationale? It was very simple, said my companion; the Endowment was supporting art that the people did not want, art of no value. How so, I inquired? Could I be given an example?

Well, he said, he did not really know too much about the arts, but he did know what an audience liked. And that was to be assisted? I inquired. Of course, he said; the rest was of no real consequence. A symphony perhaps, I suggested. A symphony—yes, he agreed; but not just any symphony. A classic one. What was his own favorite? I asked. He was silent for several seconds. Beethoven, I suggested, perhaps Beethoven's Fifth Symphony. He brightened instantly. Exactly, he said; that's it precisely. I asked what made it a classic. It has stood the test of time, he said at once.

I asked him if in his view it had stood the test of the early nineteenth-century audiences. When there was no immediate reply, but rather a look of entering somewhat unfamiliar waters, I reminded him that Beethoven's work was considered to possess pioneering elements, an avant garde quality for his own time. Critics found some of his harmonies bizarre. Many great artists, I suggested, are discovered and uplifted in lasting reputation, not in their lifetimes but by future generations. The arts are never static. They constantly evolve.

These appeared to be new thoughts, but the recommended cuts remained unaltered and, as the months passed, grew even more severe.

If one examined a map of the United States that pinpointed arts activity in the 1950s, one would find the arts concentrated primarily along the eastern seaboard from Philadelphia to Boston, in and around Chicago, in a few areas of Texas, and in California, with a focus on Los Angeles and San Francisco. Today there is a vast difference. The arts have come alive all across the country. People do not just like the arts. They are giving to them a deeper affection.

Let us examine some particular statistics. Since the Endowment's creation, the number of professional theater companies has grown from 40 to 500; symphony orchestras, from 58 to 145; opera companies of substance, from 31 to 109; professional dance companies, from no more than 35 to 250. Audiences have grown at similar ratios, with the audience for dance increasing almost 15 times. What was once static became full of dynamic growth. The central importance of the arts, wherever their roots are deepening, is manifest.

As one who has studied and has had a share in these developments in all their aspects, I am convinced that the National Endowment for the Arts has been the single most significant catalyst for this growth. Let us now look briefly at some particular National Endowment programs.

Through Artists in Education, the Endowment has assisted artists with new opportunities to develop their work in educational settings, and students to increase their understanding with firsthand knowledge in a broad spectrum of the arts. The artist does not replace the teacher. The artist supplements instruction with the enrichment of a demonstrated excellence. Since its beginnings the program has enabled over 21,000 artists to reach more than 10 million students in close to 45,000 schools, with each federal dollar generating additional support of up to six dollars in a combination of state and private funding.

In dance, the Dance Touring Program originated by the Endowment has entirely altered presentation of this art form, giving it nationwide appeal. The Dance Theater of Harlem has grown from a school aided by the Endowment into a company of international renown. The

American Ballet Theater and the Robert Joffrey Company have been rescued through special emergency grants. Dance went out from its New York City base of the mid-1960s and has become the fastest growing American art form.

The Design Arts Program concentrates on architecture, landscape architecture, and design concepts concerned intrinsically with the best kind of environment for our daily life, aesthetically and in practical terms. This program, essentially through small planning grants averaging $25,000 each, has triggered vitality and rebirth for growing numbers of cities, from Albany (New York), to Winston-Salem (North Carolina), to Savannah (Georgia), to San Antonio (Texas). Such cities have become focal centers for imaginative new ways of rescuing historic areas from decay, saving the best of the old and renewing it for the future.

Expansion Arts provides relatively small grants for developing organizations. One of my most vivid memories comes from a trip to Houston, Texas, to a new grantee in a then-deteriorated section of the city. Going there was like traveling through a desert and suddenly coming to an oasis. The small houses were well kept, windows unbroken, plots of grass tended in small front yards. There was a feeling of hope. The focus was on an old theater being rebuilt literally by hand. Inside the director said that he had envisioned, at first, a small health center in the building. Then he continued in what I have found most memorable phrases. "We found that physical well-being was not enough of a goal, so we turned to the arts," he said to me, "because, above all, we felt something special was needed here for the human spirit." The old theater was alive

with music, with work in the visual arts, with work in theater itself. Experts provided training and guidance.

Down the street was a school. The rooms were bright with particularly brilliant colors. The principal told me that the art classes, started because of the adult interest in the theater, had caused truancy to drop from over 80 percent to less than 15 percent in a few months' time. "And the pupils are learning to read, write, do arithmetic," he said, "because the arts have showed them that learning can bring pleasure."

That memory has lingered with me ever since because it speaks so well to what perceptions of quality in the arts can accomplish even in places where other benefits in life are so sparse. Talent is not restricted by economic boundaries. Talent grows where it is nourished.

Through the Folk Arts Program our country—for the first time, I believe— has become aware of the artistic and historic importance of our indigenous arts, those authentic to our own heritages. These arts include Alaskan soapstone carvings, the ancient art of the hula in Hawaii—so different from commercial adaptations and full of such dignity and legend and mystery, Creole traditions in Louisiana, Appalachian music, and the individual beauty of a work by a New England craftsman.

Inter-Arts deals with cross-discipline approaches, with a variety of art forms, with organizations that present a varied menu. A recent study revealed a network of such organizations responsible for almost 50,000 performances a year, with ticket sales totaling $188 million. But there were $120 million in unsold seats! An increase of 10 percent would mean $19 million more for the artists involved, giving them expanded opportunities. Inter-Arts helps analyze and remedy such situations. It is the kind of help not immediately visible, but of growing significance, as the complex nature of arts support is examined and understood.

The Literature Program gives assistance to the nation's small presses, so often today the only source of assistance for talented writers needing the opportunity of publication for the first time. In my own experience as a writer, as one who produced in earlier years four published novels, it was not too difficult then to find a commercial publisher who would take a risk with a beginning author. Today such opportunities are increasingly rare. The small not-for-profit press has become an indispensable literary asset and strength for future writing. Small grants in this field make a world of difference, as does individual help for qualified writers, also an important part of this program.

The Media Program has helped to initiate and support such television series as *Dance in America, Live from Lincoln Center,* and *Live from the Met.* Excellence in the arts, through television, has entered the family living room in this way. The Endowment originated the American Film Institute, significant both archivally, in the preservation of films from our past, and creatively, through the training of film makers. The Institute is winning recognition, a consistent level of praise, and assisting careers in what many consider the most American of all art forms.

The Music Program aids the nation's symphonies in their remarkable recent growth; but it has also pioneered in the development of chamber music groups, and in the increase of choral groups. It has given new importance to jazz, its

special harmonies and rhythms often called America's classical music; and it has provided particular assistance to American composers.

In its program for museums the Endowment has stimulated large numbers of museums to enhance their collections with the works of the best American artists; it has also provided initiative and help for special exhibitions—some of major national and international importance, others with a more localized interest and quieter appeal, and each of a basic value to the size and type of the museum served. In addition, the program has helped museums renovate their facilities and install the essential protection of climate control, without which the delicate objects in so many collections simply will not last.

In the field of opera and musical theater, before the Endowment a majority of talented American singers had to receive their training in Europe, and they pursued careers abroad. Now the careers are developing at home. Luciano Pavarotti recognized this change when he created an international competition for opera in Philadelphia rather than in his native Italy. The center of opera is shifting to the United States, and the Endowment has played a key role in the change. "Musical Theater" was added to the title of this program in 1979, to allow the whole field a fuller and freer development, without the constant eye on the limits of commercial considerations. Hence new American operas are coming into being. There is a feeling of yeast, of the mixtures of past and present rising, of new talents emerging. American singers, conductors, directors, designers, composers, and librettists have all benefited from this new experience in the arts, as have new audiences in all parts of the country.

In theater another metamorphosis has occurred through Endowment assistance. Just as in dance, this major art form is now well represented nationwide, not just in a handful of isolated areas as it was in the middle 1960s. Again, a sense of vitality is present, and the audience responds in the far reaches of the country, where a few years ago "going to the theater" was a foreign phrase.

In the Visual Arts Program the emphasis is on individual grants, particularly needed because such support from other sources is so relatively lacking. Individual support is basic to this program's work and to the development of talent, but there are other aspects. Through Art in Public Places, the Endowment's efforts have invigorated scores of cities, large and small. Public places take on new dimensions as works of art are introduced. City fathers are finding that art and building have integral relationships. Sculpture on a city street is no longer a rarity; and we can begin to think of the great squares of other countries where the artist, the architect, and the builder were in the closest kind of partnership through many centuries. As a country we are beginning —just beginning—to see with those eyes.

These are a few highlights of the Endowment's work, an outline minus many details. This work is growing in service as the funding has grown to furnish strength for the catalyst.

INTERNATIONAL PROGRAMS AND CHALLENGE GRANTS

Periodically the legislation has been reauthorized by Congress. Few changes have been made; but in 1976 the law was modified to allow the agency to assist international arts projects that could enhance cultural understandings and increase opportunities for American artists. Programs were initiated with Belgium, Japan, and Mexico, and most recently with the Scandinavian countries.

The widest possible variety of the arts was celebrated—dance, music, literature, theater, and the visual arts among them. American artists and cultural institutions shared in these events. New avenues were opened for cultural exchange and reciprocal programs abroad. The National Endowment for the Arts and the National Endowment for the Humanities combined forces in these undertakings and worked with the United States International Communication Agency (now the United States Information Agency) to establish new bridges of cooperative effort.

Just as potentials for future Endowment emphasis were expanded philosophically in 1976, so was there also enacted a refinement on matching formulas. The Challenge Grant Program was created by those of us who felt that private assistance to the arts could be stimulated and encouraged beyond the ratio required by law: one federal dollar to one nonfederal dollar. Minimum ratios of three to one and four to one, in special circumstances, were prescribed. Challenge grants, at first thought to bolster chiefly major arts organizations, were developed and gradually expanded in their application. They require an emphasis on planning, an exercise and a skill beneficial to arts organizations large and small, too often harassed in the past by the vexing problems of the moment. Challenge grants sometimes can help develop endowments, a major need for all organizations in the arts, and a luxury only a relative very few can yet afford.

Challenge grants have proved successful beyond fondest Congressional hopes. The overall ratio of match to the federal investment now is seven to one, and it is climbing as the program has grown. One example: the Boston Museum of Fine Arts needed an extensive new wing to help house and display its magnificent and expanding collection. A large challenge grant of $1 million was awarded, for the cause was especially worthwhile. The resulting $4 million formed the nucleus for added giving; a halfway point was reached, and the momentum continued to a final most happy conclusion. Today a visitor to this great Boston museum can enjoy the unique elegance of I. M. Pei's architecture with its vaulted glass ceiling illuminating the masterpieces. The Endowment's challenge grant was praised at dedication ceremonies as key to the entire project. It is not surprising that these special grants are subject to such intense competition, with requests far exceeding funding available at any given time.

MOMENTUM, COMMITMENT, AND VALUES

Fundamental to the Endowment's success has been the principle of momentum. Each year we argued and pleaded with Congress and friendly but economically minded administrations—under Presidents Johnson, Nixon, Ford and Carter—not just for added funds but for momentum, not just to help the nation's 145 symphony orchestras with $10 million annually instead of $8.6 million, for example; for the numbers by themselves lack consequence. It is what the numbers imply that matters in terms of momentum; in terms of how this momentum is the multiplier, the snowball gathering

size with added private philanthropy; and in terms of unfaltering commitment. The gains since 1965 have been gains in momentum much more than in federal dollars. The gains have been in the strength of the catalyst.

Now in many quarters gains are perceived to falter, to weaken. There is skepticism regarding the proposed substitute strength of the private dollar "taking up the slack," "filling the gap" in recommended federal reductions, and otherwise doing what seems expected by such phrases. Intentions may be admirable, but there seems to be a considerable gap between good intentions and a full, complete understanding. Reports indicate that corporate support can at critical times diminish rather than steadily increase.

Be that as it may, momentum and commitment cannot rest alone with the National Endowment for the Arts. It should serve as a catalyst in related areas of government, at the state and federal levels. The federal-state partnership for the arts has been immensely effective, and great numbers of community groups have joined in efforts at the local level, but the federal commitment should be more broadly based. That was a primary reason for creating in 1965 the Federal Council on the Arts and the Humanities, consisting of agency heads whose work was associated with cultural progress. The Smithsonian Institution and the Library of Congress with its cultural emphasis—renowned chamber music concerts are one example—have enlightened the nation's capital for years; but there are newer areas of cooperation.

Under the leadership of Joan Mondale, during President Carter's term, the federal council was rejuvenated. Programs were initiated with the Transportation Department, to enliven and beautify transportation facilities—airports, railway stations—with the arts. Through the Veterans Administration works of art were introduced into veterans' hospitals. Cultural impetus was given to the international arena, through the International Communication Agency mentioned earlier. The Education Department placed growing stress on the educational values of the arts. Special arts programs and projects were begun in our country's parks through the Department of the Interior. Programs in economically deprived areas showed how inner cities can benefit from the arts, both in spirit and in physical terms: create a center, however small, with a focus on the arts, and the neighborhood undergoes a change. Even the Small Business Administration joined these efforts to demonstrate, through seminars and and regional meetings drawing capacity audiences, how the artist can learn the practicalities and benefits of business experience.

There was a growing feeling that the arts should be a pervasive force, not limited, not isolated. The tangible values of the arts were examined and reviewed.

They are manifold. Tangibly the arts can become focal centers for giving new vitality to life. Study the recent history of Winston-Salem, North Carolina, where major importance was given to the arts, and you will discover a whole city transformed: artists' studios in the center of town, a fine new theater, a new adjacent park, ballet, orchestral music, one of the nation's most excellent schools for artistic training—and several hundred millions of dollars of new and expanding business enterprise, and new residents coming not just from North Carolina but from many other parts of the

country. Winston-Salem received one of the first community planning grants from the National Endowment for the Arts. There was an inspirational reaction.

The arts are also labor intensive, providing employment for growing numbers of their practitioners. Remember that an important symphony orchestra employs 100 musicians, who pay income taxes and who are just as unemployed as anyone else when they are out of work, as are dancers, for that matter.

Ten years into the Endowment's life I conducted research on the economic impact of the arts on Rhode Island. I found that Endowment assistance had helped create and develop 200 arts groups, with 2000 employees, salaried at $20 million annually. Such size, said Senator Claiborne Pell, "equates with an important business in Rhode Island."[1] And it is the same all across the United States. The arts have a significance to business life, all the way from such a small object as a photographer's light bulb to the bricks and mortar of a large cultural center.

We can think of the arts as major forces for tourism. Witness a festival like Spoleto, in South Carolina, where Endowment seed money has helped to rejuvenate old Charleston. Witness New York City, where the arts constitute one of the largest factors in the city's economic life and, incidentally, in the increase of real estate values taxable to the city. Witness Lincoln Center rising from a then slum area to house in a brilliant setting the preeminence of the Metropolitan Opera.

We can even think of the arts as increasing income tax revenues in important ways. Not long ago a study of the

1. My conversation with Senator Pell, circa 1975. I worked with him over a number of years.

New England states showed that the federal income tax returns from the arts organizations surveyed totaled $10 million a year. That is just $2 million less than the Endowment's total investment in the arts in those states during the year involved. In other words, in terms of taxes, the federal investment was returned virtually intact. Some business leaders have pointed out that on this basis alone the arts are extraordinary investments.

But these assets which the arts furnish, appealing as they may be, are not at the core of their value. Of profoundest significance are the great intangible benefits of the arts, which have existed from the start—in terms of talent and its development, in terms of imagination, new insights, new perceptions, and new dimensions of understanding, and in terms of unique enrichment for the human spirit.

DANGERS OF DROUGHT

Let us make no mistake, however: the endeavor to build truly lasting support remains fragile. The arts exist within narrow boundaries dividing financial solvency from failure. I have spent so much of my life in these areas that I can testify from personal experience as well as from the innumerable case histories I have studied and reviewed. The margin between success and failure is exceeding thin for the major organizations as well as for those of smaller size. It is because of the uncertainties, the dangers inherent in this slender margin—this ever present sword of Damocles on its slender cord—that the Endowment's catalytic strength is so significant. This is also the reason that Endowment help is so sought after, and why it is so crucial to the survival and nourishment of the arts. The roots of so many growing arts organizations are still reaching for fully hospitable soil. The quest is far from complete. Weaken the catalyst, and the multiplier effect can work in reverse.

I have been enormously fortunate in my own experiences, shared with an artist wife who loves the arts as much as I do and whose special insights are especially cherished. We have heard grand opera performed by Beverly Sills. We have witnessed a spring ritual dance of Hopi Indians performed on a lonely rain-swept Arizona mesa. The arts have such immense variety. They spring from our ethnic backgrounds and from our heritages. There are the arts that have a special impact enhanced by tradition, and there are the arts on the frontiers of new expression.

Above all, government support has recognized the variety of the arts. Perhaps that recognition and the response to it has brought about the greatest single change from past decades when support was limited, static, concentrated on the relative few. The glory of our country lies in its diversity, in its almost infinite variety. The glory of our country's arts is similarly lodged.

I have talked to those who equate the arts with the marketplace, who point to commerical success as the criterion for excellence. Government support deals not with this area, for help is not needed. Government assistance deals with the not-for-profit, and often with those areas where the private dollar by itself might not venture at all, with the frontiers where art is constantly evolving, where controversy is not an enemy but a necessary companion.

Ever since Roger Stevens was wise enough to urge the first National Council on the Arts to consider help to the off-off Broadway theater, the Endowment has aided the artist in exploration. I have a nightmare on occasion of all the symphony orchestras in the United States playing only Beethoven's Fifth Symphony, all the theaters extant presenting only *Uncle Vanya,* all the opera companies performing only *La Boheme,* because they are marketplace, box-office winners. How dull the arts would become!

We welcome the old favorite masterpieces, but they are best in a setting as varied as the colors on an artist's palette, whose prime colors have that infinite variety when skillfully mixed and blended. And those who espouse the marketplace as the determinant of a popularity beyond which no government support should wander should be asked and asked again and again, What about Beethoven, who dared new harmonies in his own time? What about Wagner? What about Mozart? Or Rodin? Or Van Gogh? Artists have always questioned contemporary conventions; and so many of them, who later centuries have come to revere, were in their own day criticized, abused, even reviled. Controversy becomes a special attribute, for it opens our eyes and minds; at last resolved, it can open our hearts.

So we need wisdom, a fullness of appreciation, and most of all, I suspect, a deep understanding and love of the arts as being indeed at the core of life—not tangential to it, not on the fringes, but at the center. The rhetoric, the financial support will follow.

But the undergirding commitment must be there. Currently it is perceived to waver, its voice lacking in resolve, its eyes lacking in boldness of vision. At the highest levels a time of drought for the arts appears. We look to the hills, but the rain clouds have not yet formed, or they travel in different directions. Pallid substitutes take the place of the old ringing endorsements of commitment and dedication.

Much of our country was once a desert to the arts. Then came the greening. Some will say that the seeds can remain dormant, that after a while they will grow again. But have you ever looked at an untended garden after a drought? Have you ever returned to your own garden after a parched period when watering was neglected? Some life is left in the big, hardy plants, if not their bloom. But the fragile flowers, the newly planted—they have withered; and it is too late in the season to find replacements.

Federal Support for the Arts Has a Future

By CLAIBORNE deB. PELL

ABSTRACT: As one who has been intimately involved for 23 years with the federal programs that support the arts in this country, I have been particularly concerned about recent Reagan administration efforts to reduce the budgets of the National Endowments for the Arts and for the Humanities and to lessen their impact on our cultural scene. The administration's approach to federal arts policy began with some basic misconceptions about the sources of the impressive growth that took place in the sixties and seventies in both the number and quality of American cultural institutions. Moreover the administration contended that as government support for the arts increased, there was a decrease in moneys from the private sector. Statistics seem to indicate that the opposite is true. The federal government through the National Endowment for the Arts has had a major impact in aiding and expanding our nation's cultural institutions. Much of this effect has been achieved in partnership with private resources. This critical government role as catalyst and facilitator must continue to spark increased nonfederal support for the arts.

Claiborne deB. Pell has served as the United States senator from Rhode Island since 1961. He holds influential senatorial posts in a number of fields, including human resources, education, arms control, health, employment, human rights, foreign relations, arts and humanities, and oceans and environment. Pell earned his A.B. degree from Princeton and his M.A. degree from Columbia University. He is the author of two books: Power and Policy *and* Megalopolis Unbound; *he coauthored* Challenge of the Seven Seas. *Pell was the principal Senate sponsor of the 1965 law establishing the National Endowments for the Arts and the Humanities.*

THE direction of federal support for the arts became alarmingly uncertain only a few weeks into the Reagan administration. The drastic reductions proposed for the 1982 fiscal year came as a surprise to those of us in the Congress who had nurtured the steady growth of our twin Arts and Humanities Endowments over the preceding fifteen years, growth that had enjoyed the unique bipartisan support and encouragement of presidents and congressmen alike.

THE THREAT TO
FEDERAL SUPPORT

The administration proposal was to reduce the budget authority of the National Endowments for the Arts and for the Humanities by half. A "savings" of 50 percent was foreseen in the programs beginning in the fiscal year 1982. Furthermore, it was recommended at the same time that budgets for the fiscal years 1984 and 1985 be held at the $100 million level.

The Office of Management and Budget (OMB) under the guidance of its director, David Stockman, stated its rationale for these cuts as follows:

Reductions of this magnitude are premised on the notion that the Administration should completely revamp federal policy for arts and humanities support. For too long, the Endowments have spread federal financing into an ever-wider range of artistic and literary endeavor, promoting the notion that the federal government should be the financial patron of first resort for both individuals and institutions engaged in artistic and literary pursuits. This policy has resulted in a reduction in the historic role of private, individual, and corporate support in these key areas. These reductions in federal support are a first step toward reversing this trend.[1]

The most extreme interpretation of these words would be that government does not really have an obligation to support the arts financially or philosophically and should therefore stop or drastically curtail its activity in this area. Others, of a more moderate bent, would hold that government support should extend only to our so-called national treasures, leaving the rest of our artists and cultural institutions to fend for themselves. However one interpreted the OMB rationale, it was a startlingly new concept, which posed serious social and economic consequences for a multitude of communities and institutions.

Mr. Stockman advised the president that such cuts "could generate strong opposition" from the Endowment's "broad and articulate public constituencies."[2] Despite this warning, however, he proceeded to recommend the 50 percent reductions. Some members of the administration tried to put the best face possible on the proposed halving of the Arts Endowment's budget by spreading the word that Stockman had originally asked for the complete elimination of the agency. This generous gesture, if true, was hardly reassuring to the arts community and to their supporters in Congress. With the formal submission of the proposed budget revisions, the battle of the budget was officially under way.

I particularly objected at the time to two of OMB's justifications for the reductions. First, I strongly disagreed with the point that the arts were a "low prior-

---

1. U.S., Executive Office of the President, *President's Budget Reform Plan,* pt. 3, *America's New Beginning: A Program for Economic Recovery* (Washington, DC: Government Printing Office, 1981), p. 6-39.

2. U.S., House of Representatives, Democratic Study Group, "Special Report: The Stockman Hit List," 7 Feb. 1981, p. 37.

ity item,"[3] and second, I took issue with the contention that federal support for the arts over the previous 15 years had discouraged or driven out private and corporate support. In fact, in the 10 years prior to the Arts Endowment's establishment, contributions to the arts from the private sector had risen less than 3 percent from an estimated $199 million in 1955, to $205 million in 1964. In the succeeding years, however, when the Endowment has been performing its crucial role as a catalyst, total philanthropic support for the arts and culture had grown to $2.7 billion and corporate support alone had increased from $22 million in 1966 to $435 million currently.

Since its beginning in 1965, the Endowment has also been largely responsible for encouraging growth in support for the arts from state governments, in local arts agency support, in the overall increase in the number of arts institutions, and especially in the size of audiences.

Perhaps the most fundamental concept of my original enabling legislation was that private initiative should always be the principal and primary source for the support and encouragement of the arts in the United States. I envisioned the Endowment as a catalyst that would help spark nonfederal support for the arts in a new and unique role for public moneys. The fact that Endowment grants were to be matched on a one-to-one basis was the key to the entire proposal.

After seeing the success of this plan, the legislation was later amended to provide for the Challenge and Treasury Department grants, which required a match of three nonfederal dollars for each federal dollar granted by the

3. U.S., Executive Office of the President, *America's New Beginning,* p. 6-39.

Endowment. I could not have been more pleased when the incoming private dollars began far exceeding those required by the federal guidelines. The concept of "Endowment as catalyst" was clearly working, and it was proving to be of tremendously important assistance to cultural institutions.

IN DEFENSE OF FEDERAL SUPPORT

When the appropriations hearings got under way to address the cuts in the first Reagan budget, the arts community turned out in impressive numbers and with eloquent pleadings and telling statistics with which to make their case. These articulate arts witnesses were supported by representatives from the corporate sector, who were justifiably worried that massive reductions by the government would send a signal that the arts were in fact dispensable. If this belief took hold it would certainly not encourage the private sector to contribute additional sums at a time when they were actually of critical importance.

After lengthy hearings and complicated negotiations between the House of Representatives and the Senate, a final budget of $143 million was approved for the Arts Endowment in fiscal year 1982—approximately a 10 percent reduction from the year before but in reality a more serious blow, owing to the toll taken by inflation. The important element, however, was that the arts constituency in this country had proven to be a powerful force with which Congress and the president could not avoid dealing. Indeed the strength and effectiveness of the outcry may have surprised the administration and convinced it that further major alterations in federal arts policy should be undertaken more cautiously and with an eye to the freshly mobilized and confident arts constituency.

The administration soon responded by appointing the Presidential Task Force on the Arts and Humanities and directed it to conduct a thorough reassessment of federal arts policy. Many who feared that there would be fundamental alterations in the Endowment's structure and purpose were reassured when President Reagan called our cultural institutions "an essential national resource" that "must be kept strong"[4] despite the need to reduce government spending. Others were suspicious that the task force findings were already a foregone conclusion and that the Arts and Humanities Endowments, as we know them, were to be drastically transformed into a government corporation along the lines of the Corporation for Public Broadcasting.

Nevertheless a distinguished group of citizens from the artistic, corporate, and university worlds was appointed by the president to conduct an extensive review of both Endowments. An indication of the future of federal support for the arts can be found in the report that the task force presented at its final meeting. First, it concluded to everyone's great relief that there is indeed a valuable federal role in the arts and humanities. The low priority assigned to the arts by OMB had clearly undergone an important alteration. In addition the task force found the basic structure of the two Endowments to be sound. I particularly welcomed this finding, as my confidence in the two agencies and the way

4. U.S., Executive Office of the President, Statement on the Establishment of the Presidential Task Force on the Arts and Humanities, 6 May 1981.

they operate has remained steadfast over their entire life span.

Those of us on the Senate authorizing subcommittee exercise our oversight authority by setting the direction of the Endowments' programs. Reauthorization of the Endowments, which now occurs every four or five years, gives us the chance to address specific problems in a program and to hear proposals for change. Some fine tuning has been carried out over the years, but, in general, the original legislation has remained largely unchanged as a testament to its effectiveness as well as to the success of the Endowments.

A further finding of the task force was that support for the arts from the private sector should be increased. The success of the Challenge Grant Program was undoubtedly a guidepost here. But the task force recommendation went further to ask that corporate, foundation, and individual giving be increased so as to make up the shortfall in federal spending. It was speculated at the time that if any one of the top 500 corporations gave the legally allowable 5 percent contribution to the arts, the funding problem would be solved. Furthermore only 30 percent of the nation's corporations were said to be making charitable donations, and that a great deal more could be accomplished if these vast untapped resources were mobilized.

Though business will undoubtedly find it difficult to increase its gifts in the present economic climate, I wish to encourage all efforts in this direction. The Arts Endowment has a superb track record of being able to attract private money. Through the existing mechanism of Treasury Funds and Challenge Grants, the agency is set up to receive gifts that have the wonderful effect of doubling or tripling the funds that it can actually award to a particular applicant institution. This ability to attract private money has been incorporated into the Endowment's structure and has already proved to be a huge success. With skillful direction and encouragement, the much needed increase in private support can be achieved by expanding this partnership.

THE NEED FOR FEDERAL INVOLVEMENT

Of course a period of dramatic economic growth would help everyone, but I am skeptical that a major recovery is coming soon. Private philanthropy alone is simply not going to fill the gaps that are now occurring with alarming frequency among our arts institutions. Foundations, also pressed by economic conditions, are finding it virtually impossible to increase their giving commitments. It is regrettable but true that corporate and foundation philanthropy can only in rare instances address base budget problems no matter how sincere the interest. Some redirection of foundation funds can be expected to assist in some of the most desperate situations, but this sector cannot possibly be expected to come to the rescue without an assist from the federal government.

Large capital endowments can provide a welcome cushion in hard times, but even our major cultural institutions are just beginning to seek funds for stockpiling in such a reserve. Wisely, the Endowment's Challenge Grant Program permits both the federal and private

matching moneys to be used for building such cash reserve funds. Again, it would seem prudent to explore ways of developing and improving this now well-tested method of raising capital funds. It should also be structured so that institutions of all sizes can participate.

Though each segment of the private sector must be approached and encouraged to assist in ever more creative ways, I want to stress that I believe that the American government should very definitely continue to be actively involved in the business of the arts. I do not agree with some who see the foundations and corporations being forced into taking over programs that the government is abandoning. They have neither the resources nor the desire to do this. The government must continue to play its crucial role as catalyst and ensure that the symbiotic relationship between public funding and private initiatives remains a vital one.

The arts in this country are flourishing as never before, and their audience is expanding. It is, in fact, not the arts that are financially threatened, but only specific arts institutions and activities. Now that the structure and methods of the Arts Endowment have been endorsed by this administration, the only real gap is the gap caused by high inflation and reductions in government support. New ways can be found to increase the participation of the private sector by expanding its partnership with the established government arts programs.

ANNALS, *AAPSS,* **471,** January 1984

Notes on the Presidential Task Force
on the Arts and Humanities and
President's Committee on the Arts and Humanities

By BARNABAS McHENRY

ABSTRACT: Created in 1981 by President Ronald Reagan, the Presidential Task Force on the Arts and Humanities produced a series of resolutions including a recommendation leading to the formation of the President's Committee. The Task Force did not question federal funding of the arts or the humanities, but it did suggest encouragement of federal matching grants and increases in private support. The President's Committee began its deliberations where the Task Force ended: the investigation of ways to further private support of the arts and humanities. Among the items on its agenda are the encouragement of community foundations to enter the area of cultural funding; presidential fellowships in the arts and humanities; development of an information system for the collection of data on funding; recognition awards; city pairing and sharing for cultural institutions; and various tax proposals.

Barnabas Mc Henry is a graduate of Princeton University and Columbia Law School and is the general counsel and a director of The Reader's Digest Association, Inc. He was the vice-chairman of the Presidential Task Force on the Arts and Humanities and is co-vice-chairman of the President's Committee on the Arts and Humanities. He is a trustee of many organizations, including the Metropolitan Museum of Art, Metropolitan Opera Association, Inc., New York Zoological Society, the School of American Ballet, Inc., Central Park Conservancy, Boscobel Restoration, Inc., and Scenic Hudson, Inc.

T HE Presidential Task Force on the Arts and Humanities—hereinafter referred to as the "Task Force"—was created by executive order on 5 June 1981,[1] and was granted 117 days of existence in which to prepare a report to the president on the federal arts and humanities establishment. The Task Force report was delivered on 14 October 1981,[2] 14 days late, and it contained absolutely no surprises. There were, however, some interesting discussions, disputes, and results of the Task Force that are not widely known. It is the purpose of this article to chronicle the Task Force's major activities and to explain how and why the President's Committee on the Arts and Humanities—hereinafter referred to as the "President's Committee"—came into existence and what the President's Committee may be expected to achieve.

The Task Force was made up of 35 members,[3] most of whom could be characterized as personalities. At the

1. Executive Order 12308, 5 June 1981, *Federal Register,* 46 (110): 30485-86 (9 June 1981).

2. Presidential Task Force on the Arts and Humanities, *Report to the President* (Washington, DC: Government Printing Office, 1981).

3. Members of the Presidential Task Force on the Arts and Humanities: Dr. Hanna H. Gray, cochair for the humanities; Charlton Heston, cochair for the arts; Daniel J. Terra, cochair for government; Barnabas McHenry, vice-chair; Margo Albert; Dr. Edward Banfield; Anne H. Bass; Dr. Daniel J. Boorstin; Dr. William G. Bowen; Joseph Coors; Armand Deutsch; Virginia Duncan; Robert F. Fryer; Henry Geldzahler; Gordon Hanes; Nancy Hanks; Dr. Paul R. Hanna; Ernest J. Kump; June Noble Larkin; Dr. Robert M. Luminaksy; Angus MacDonald; Nancy Mehta; Arthur Mitchell; Dr. Franklin D. Murphy; David Packard; Edmund P. Pillsbury; Dr. George C. Roche III; Richard M. Scaife; Franklin J. Schaffner; Beverly Sills; Leonard Silverstein; Robert I. Smith; Roger L. Stevens; John E. Swearingen; Rawleigh Warner, Jr.; and Lucien Wulsin.

very least one could say that there was a diversity of membership that ranged from Henry Geldzahler to Joseph Coors and from Nancy Mehta to Robert Lumiansky. This was no peaceable kingdom of the arts and humanities, yet this diverse group quickly reached a consensus on the major points and found common ground on almost all matters. There were no dissenting statements in the report, which was said to, and in fact did, "reflect the substantial agreement of the members."[4]

Were there any real accomplishments of the Task Force? In a recent article in *Art News,* Gerald Marzorati said that "about the only real development to come out of the Task Force sessions was [Frank] Hodsoll . . . who was appointed NEA [National Endowment for the Arts] Chairman near the end of 1981."[5] There would have been neither a Task Force nor a President's Committee without Frank Hodsoll who, in his position as James Baker's deputy in the White House, could make the telephone calls that the White House always answered. It takes nothing away from Frank Hodsoll's unbeatable combination of enthusiasm, energy, and intelligence to say that there were other developments of the Task Force that will likely have some real effect on federal policy for the arts and humanities.

The Task Force called for the creation of the President's Committee, which has been in existence since 15 June 1982,[6] and consists, as of 10 June 1983, of 31 members plus its honorary chairman, the first lady of the United

4. Presidential Task Force on the Arts and Humanities, *Report,* p. ii.

5. "The Arts Endowment in Transition," *Art News,* 71: 13 (Mar. 1983).

6. Executive Order 12367, 15 June 1982, *Federal Register,* 47 (117): 26119-20 (17 June 1982).

States.[7] President's Committee members Nancy Hanks, the beloved chairman of the National Endowment for the Arts, and Sidney Brody, chairman of the Board of Trustees of the Los Angeles County Museum of Art, died in 1982. There are nine common members of the Task Force and the President's Committee: Dr. Daniel Boorstin, Armand Deutsch, Robert Fryer, Dr. Franklin Murphy, Leonard Silverstein, Roger Stevens, Daniel Terra, Rawleigh Warner, and myself.

TASK FORCE HISTORY

The deliberations of the Task Force started on a steamy Washington June day in the Indian Treaty Room of the Old Executive Office Building. The cochairman for the arts, Charlton Heston, set the tone by raising the question of the linkage between federal funding and private support, and why federal moneys so effectively generate private funding. It had been thought by some that the Task Force would question the existence of any federal funding for the arts and humanities.

Such was not the case; Heston's spirited statement in favor of federal

7. Members of the President's Committee on the Arts and the Humanities: Mrs. Ronald Reagan, honorary chair; Andrew Heiskell, chair; Armand S. Deutsch, co-vice-chair; Barnabas McHenry, co-vice-chair; Terrel H. Bell; William J. Bennett; Daniel J. Boorstin; Sidney F. Brody—deceased; J. Carter Brown; Gerald P. Carmen; Schuyler Chapin; Lloyd E. Cotsen; Charles A. Dana, Jr.; Susan Davis; Joan Kent Dillon; Robert Fryer; Nancy Hanks—deceased; Frank Hodsoll; Ignacio E. Lozano, Jr.; Gabriele Murdock—nominated, appointment pending; Dr. Franklin D. Murphy; Donald T. Regan; S. Dillon Ripley; Leonard Silverstein; Francis Albert Sinatra; Dr. Frank Stanton; Roger L. Stevens; Donald M. Stewart; Lloyd Taggart; Daniel J. Terra; Lilla Tower; Rawleigh Warner, Jr.; James G. Watt; Charles Z. Wick; and Isabel Brown Wilson.

funds for the arts and humanities may be said to have directed the first discussions of the Task Force, since it was thought that Heston was an intimate friend of the Reagans and might even speak for them on the arts. All the Task Force members found common ground in agreeing that some federal funding for the arts and humanities is necessary, that private support must be increased, and that federal matching grants should be encouraged. These three general principles were not likely to be contested by others, nor were any tremors felt from the executive branch when they were endorsed by the Task Force early in the summer and then repeated and embellished in the report.

Some journalists had suggested that the Task Force would likely criticize both the National Endowment for the Arts and the National Endowment for the Humanities and recommend radical changes in the structure of the Endowments and federal funding. Conversion of the Endowments into quasi-public corporations such as the Corporation for Public Broadcasting was a favorite assumption. The Endowments emerged from the Task Force deliberations unscathed. There was not a single substantive proposed change that captured the collective imagination of the group, a real surprise since there had been no substantial statutory change during the Endowments' decade of life, and the many members had privately agreed that there were visible stretch marks on both organizations and that some changes were desirable.

Two areas of the Endowments were vigorously discussed in the Task Force deliberations: peer panels and the roles of the chairmen and National Councils on the Arts and the Humanities. In the discussions some agreed with Kingman

Brewster that the panel system had become "a process of empowering the peerage . . . a peerage of artists and connoisseurs,"[8] resulting in a sort of subsidy by meritocracy. But those who ventured to support this view were quickly stared down by Nancy Hanks and Roger Stevens, and peer panels were thereupon heartily endorsed—in the Task Force report peer panels appear as two separate endorsements. With respect to the role of the chairman and the National Council on the Arts, it had been suggested that the council members be given a vote and thus cease being merely advisory. While the lofty corporate executives on the Task Force agreed that they would find intolerable a nonvoting role on either a business or charitable board, the former chairmen of the National Endowment for the Arts, Hanks and Stevens, scattered these protesters with a single shot, and all talk of voting councils ceased. The Task Force did, however, ask the Endowments to supply better data, which really means statistics, and I shall return to that subject.

The Task Force agreed that the president ought to have a positive role in arts and humanities leadership. While the corporate and university leaders, such as Rawleigh Warner and Hanna Gray, were expected to champion the cause of leadership, strong support came from all sides. The members who had participated in or led a significant charitable campaign, which included almost all the Task Force members in one role or another, stated in various anecdotes that without leadership any

charitable campaign, no matter how well-planned or worthy, foundered. When asked Why? the answers were identical: individual and corporate leaders prefer to be solicited for contributions to the arts or the humanities by someone with a recognizable name who is either a peer or one rung up the corporate or social ladder.

The Task Force reasoned that President Reagan, having been an artist in the movies, the favorite art form in America, and married to an artist— an actress—would be able to convince the business community that more private support was desirable and in the national interest. The president seems to have heeded this bit of Task Force advice, and he has recently begun to speak about his role as an artist and even as a partisan for the arts and the necessity to preserve the wholly American system of private support.

TASK FORCE
RECOMMENDATIONS

The Task Force made four specific recommendations plus six tax recommendations. The first specific recommendation may have seemed self-serving, or at least self-perpetuating. It called for the creation of a permanent federal organization with a majority of private members for the purpose of developing federal policies to encourage private support for the arts and the humanities, and for working within the tortuous federal establishment to protect the flanks of the Endowments. Quite separately, in the tradition of simultaneous scientific discovery, Dr. Franklin Murphy in Los Angeles, in telephone conversations with Carter Brown, and Roger Stevens in Washington in conversations with Congressman Sidney Yates, declared that the Federal Council

8. From his lecture, "Paternalism, Populism, and Patronage," at the Victoria and Albert Museum, London, 25 Oct. 1978.

on the Arts and Humanities,[9] something of a beached whale, contained all the necessary statutory equipment and could be transformed to just what was needed—a forum in which private and public members could debate, recommend, and act on a wide variety of matters related to the national policy on the arts and humanities.

Dr. Murphy brilliantly presented the proposal at the August Los Angeles meeting noting that the statutory language under which the Federal Council was created seemed almost to have been drafted with this recommendation of the Task Force in mind, since it provided virtually everything required for an advisory committee except that the Federal Council consisted only of federal members. All that was needed was to add private members and from their number to select a chairman; but that was easier said than done. Congressman Yates believed it could be accomplished without legislation; the White House counsel believed otherwise because the Federal Council contained a provision permitting a pledge of the full faith and credit of the United States, the Arts and Artifacts Indemnity Act.[10] For that reason a private, nonfederal majority on the council seemed to the White House counsel to be beyond the amendatory reach of an executive order.

New legislation was suggested and was drafted in the autumn of 1982. Congressional sponsors were located and hearing dates set for the winter of 1982 with action confidently expected in spring. But soon these plans were ended because the priority of the legislation did not seem important in Congress and because it became apparent that the

hearings would not be pro forma. One of the abiding mysteries of federal involvement in the arts and humanities is why proposals for change are bitterly opposed even when the proposals are directly related to an improvement in the very discipline or structure that is supported by the opposition. Why the arts should be burdened by this inertia factor is particularly puzzling because the arts are always innovative and adaptive and encourage organic changes. It was necessary in any event to create a new organization—the President's Committee on the Arts and the Humanities.

On 15 June 1982 President Reagan issued Executive Order 12367[11] creating the President's Committee, a radical compromise of the Task Force proposal because it created a new federal body, which is what the Task Force members had hoped to avoid. As has been shown, there was no alternative available because there was no group in official Washington that could be called on for help—the very reason that the invigorated Federal Council was needed.

There were two other Task Force recommendations that were debated and discussed. First, the lack of an effective federal-state relationship was lamented because of a variety of problems in the state arts and humanities councils. A failing often cited was the disgraceful lack of attention paid to state humanities councils by the state legislatures or anyone else. It was concluded that little could be expected to happen until a powerful member of Congress took a continuing interest in the challenge of finding or forcing state funding for state humanities councils. The recommendation for creating presidential fellows in the arts and in the humanities was a last-minute effort by Dr.

9. U.S., *United States Code Annotated*, Title 20, sec. 958.

10. U.S., *United States Code Annotated*, Title 20, secs. 971-77.

11. See note 6.

Boorstin, the Librarian of Congress. In a brief and well-argued memorandum he proposed that presidential fellows in the arts and humanities be created and privately funded. The perceived difficulties of funding and selection of the fellows have burdened the Boorstin proposal. A virtue of the fellows program, mentioned but not widely discussed, is that the continuing presence of the presidential fellows as creatures in the White House hierarchy would itself represent a visible and continuing executive endorsement of the importance of the arts and humanities.

The fourth recommendation was the reaffirmation of peer panel review systems. Again it is unclear why the virtue of removing this selection judgment entirely from the "purview of federal employees"[12] was mysteriously emphasized even though not one Task Force member argued that the peer panel system should be discarded or amended.

The Task Force deliberations on tax matters seemed initially to be destined for an agonizing discussion of a disruptive tax-revenue proposal that Ambassador Daniel J. Terra had prepared outside his own and the Task Force staff structure. The Terra proposal involved complicated tax credits, an absolute anathema to the Department of the Treasury, and was based on the assumption that the Economic Recovery Tax Act of 1981 must have the unintended effect of reducing the amount of individual charitable contributions. By virtue of the last-minute diplomatic maneuvers of the Task Force staff, the Terra proposal was revised so that it emerged neither disruptive nor controversial. The genial ambassador accepted

12. Presidential Task Force on the Arts and Humanities, *Report,* p. 17.

the revisions in good humor and a lengthy and embarrassing debate was avoided.

In the summer of 1981 increasing corporate support was viewed as a most important goal, partly because a considerable number of the Task Force members were associated with national corporations that were significant arts contributors. There were extended conversations about the desirability of endorsing corporate matching-gift programs and employee payroll deduction, even though experience had shown the same members that the resulting beneficiaries were primarily religious and educational groups rather than the arts and humanities. The arts and humanities benefited much more if the selection of the beneficiaries was made by the usual executive corporate selection methods.

Corporate giving seemed to need no additional tax incentives and was characterized as lacking in leadership more than anything else. The Task Force nonetheless recommended consideration of an incentive in the hope that something must be done to encourage the 90 percent of corporations that make little or no use of the permitted corporate deduction, which at that very moment was being increased from 5 to 10 percent of pretax profits. This increase in the permitted corporate deduction may be credited to the Task Force, since it was proposed in a Task Force research paper prepared by Peter Wiedenbach of Patton, Boggs & Blow. The references in the research memo found their way into the *Washington Post,* and an alert member of Congress took note and quickly made it a part of the Economic Recovery Tax Act of 1981.

The first and most seriously considered tax recommendation of the Task

Force was the so-called Artists and Writers Tax Act to provide better tax treatment to the creators/donors of art works and manuscripts to museums and libraries. Since 1969 the creators have been limited to a charitable deduction equal to the value of the materials: canvas and paint or typewriter and erasers for the artists and writers, respectively. This odd situation has been the subject of a number of bills in Congress; in the last session an amending provision was reported out of the Senate Committee. There has been continuing opposition by the Treasury even though they calculate that the annual revenue loss would be no more than $5 million. The Task Force thought the Artists and Writers Tax Act important because they were advised that benefits accrue not only to the artists' and writers' tax returns, but also because these creators would be able to choose where the manuscripts and objects would go, and because the museums and libraries—which were strongly represented on the Task Force by trustees and professionals—would receive an instant bounty. The Treasury continues to oppose the Writers and Tax Act ostensibly for the difficulty in securing proper—fair market value—appraisals. This does not flow logically from the legislative results because such difficulties with appraisals will always be present unless the Treasury wishes to end tax benefits for donations of all manuscripts and all art objects to publicly supported institutions.

In this regard it is interesting to note the remarks of President Reagan on 27 January 1983 at the National Gallery of Art, where he joined in the celebration of an important anniversary of the world's champion art donors, the Mellons, father and son. He said, "Our country has been blessed with great patrons like Andrew Mellon . . . [and with] the extra gift of paintings, sculpture and graphic art, that we have seen from Paul Mellon."[13] It is not likely that Congress will, because of the fair market value appraisal difficulties, remove the tax benefits from the Mellons of the art world and thus discourage the flow of donated works to public institutions. The Treasury is aware that many of these public institutions, including the National Gallery of Art, depend on private support for substantially all acquisitions. The high jinks at the Smithsonian gem collection have, however, given the Treasury appraisal arguments a second wind, and if this were not trouble enough, there is a second argument, a wretched precedent argument that goes this way: If you let artists turn the fruits of their untaxed labor into tax deductions, then why not do the same by counting every minute spent by the housewife in Ozone Park who rings doorbells for Planned Parenthood? The Artists and Writers Tax Act was a favorite of the Task Force members and remains today a favorite piece of remedial tax legislation for the numerous national arts organizations. Yet its immediate future as legislation is doubtful because of Treasury opposition.

The other tax recommendations can be summarized as being reasonably technical and concerned with mysterious limitations on private foundations and their creators, tax carry-overs, and bargain sales. The Task Force members endorsed these other tax proposals without much explanation or debate because they were assured, and rightly one must believe, that almost any tax

13. President Ronald Reagan, from his remarks at the National Gallery of Art dinner, 27 January 1983.

proposal that helps a high-income taxpayer contribute to charity will thereby increase private support for the arts and humanities. High net-worth taxpayers seem to favor the arts and humanities with their tax-deductible bounty.

The Task Force ended with the traditional White House luncheon. The members had arrived at a consensus on some important ways to continue and increase private support, but they also found themselves as a part of national and rather exalted society of the arts and humanities. They had enjoyed the meetings, particularly the opportunity of hearing anecdotes about the success and failure in various fund-raising endeavors that were the staple of the elegant receptions and dinners sponsored by members, and they were proud to be part of an effort that seemed significant and successful.

ORIGINS AND PROJECTS OF THE PRESIDENT'S COMMITTEE

The President's Committee has existed for about a year. It has selected an impressive list of projects and already has a few accomplishments. It is a fair comment to say that the President's Committee started its work where the Task Force ended. All the projects are aimed at the announced goal of the President's Committee—investigating ways to increase private support for the arts and humanities. The projects have taken a variety of forms.

One new project is community foundations, which are not known to most of the arts and humanities community.

These publicly supported foundations are growing much more rapidly than private foundations. The President's Committee is investigating ways in which these remarkable institutions can be used. First, community foundations could take a leadership role and aggressively seek increased financial support for the arts and humanities within their community. Second, corporations could use the expertise of the community foundations to distribute charitable funds so that small corporations could avoid establishing expensive grant-making mechanisms. It is hoped that the community foundations will forsake their traditional roles of using discretionary funds for social welfare and make more grants to the arts and humanities.

Leonard Silverstein, tax expert, patron of the arts, and a veteran of the Task Force, is guiding a subcommittee on taxes and information and has prepared a proposal that has the possibility of becoming legislation. The tax proposal consists of two recommendations from the Task Force: first, the extension of charitable contribution carry-over from 5 to 15 years; and second, increase from 50 percent to 75 percent the limitation on gifts to public charities. Since these proposals would generate a small loss of revenue—and thus strong opposition from the Treasury—they are artfully coupled with a proposal to extend the required holding period from one year to five years for works of art and manuscripts donated to charity. It is believed that the longer holding period will reduce the perceived pressure on appraisals by removing the temptation for speedy charitable-deduction seekers to buy for the tax investment and remove the control of this beneficial trade from the hands of the curators and return it to the connoisseurs and collectors.

The most difficult assignment for the President's Committee is the project of information, which is a search for valid statistical data on private support for the arts and humanities. The members of the President's Committee who have studied the reports that are issued by such prestigious organizations as the American Association of Fund-Raising Counsel and the Conference Board have concluded that they do not have the statistical basis that ensures the comparability required in data used to demonstrate trends, prepare forecasts, and, most important, be acceptable to the Treasury Department as the basis for needed legislative tax amendments.

The Treasury Department does not now prepare data that identify annual contributions to the arts and humanities. Until a need can be demonstrated and funds made available, it would probably not undertake an analysis of tax forms from individual citizens. Foundation, government, and corporate support is recorded; the figures are accurate for foundations and government but are estimates for even the largest publicly held corporations. Individual support is known to be the most substantial contribution to the arts; the percentage is reckoned to be at least 80 percent. The total of individual contributions to the arts and humanities can only be guessed at until a system is devised that will be capable of providing comparable data on patterns of giving within a reasonable time after year-end and at a reasonable cost.

Andrew Heiskell, the chairman of the President's Committee and a leader in the humanities, has taken an intense interest in this information project; he distrusts all existing data for the arts and recognizes that the humanities are not measured by even a reasonable estimate. It may be expected that the President's Committee will not fail to develop plans for an information program.

The President's Committee can claim to have progressed past the planning stage in three programs: city sharing and pairing, city seminars, and recognition. The Joffrey Ballet's dual residence is the best example of the successful pairing of cities—New York and Los Angeles—and it owes this life-saving graft to two members of the President's Committee, the honorary chairman and the co-vice-chairman from Los Angeles, Armand Deutsch. A theater-pairing venture has been proposed by Roger Stevens, who hopes to use the American National Theater and Academy (ANTA) to link the Eisenhower Theater of Kennedy Center and the Vivian Beaumont at Lincoln Center in order to provide for a first-rank theater company that will present the classics of the American theater, both dramatic and musical, in limited-run productions in both cities. The Alvin Ailey dance company is another active candidate for city sharing.

City seminars were given the first test run in Fort Worth on the first Friday in May 1983 and seemed to be well accepted by the participating audience. The concept, a simple one, is based on the need to share information among the private sector leaders. Board chairs and trustees know their counterparts in local arts and humanities organizations, but they rarely meet to discuss their private-support triumphs outside their own disciplines and never meet with their peers statewide.

The President's Committee began to plan ways to recognize and commend excellence in the arts and humanities from the moment it began. The White House is a splendid place for recognition of excellence, but there had never been a program or medal for the arts or the humanities. When the president awards the Medal of Freedom to someone prominent in the arts and humanities, the recipient is being recognized for a lifetime of achievement; thus the ceremonies have the aspects of a nursing home. The Kennedy Center awards are similarly gerontological.

The President's Committee resolved to recognize artists in their working prime and to pair these artists with bene-factors and thus call attention to the unique American philosophy of private support. In his remarks at the arts awards luncheon on 17 May 1983, in the state dining room of the White House, the president noted that he believed that a permanent award for the arts, similar to the National Science Medal, should be authorized by Congress. The President's Committee can be expected to use all of its abilities to urge Congress and the White House to create awards for the arts and humanities.

What will the President's Committee do in the immediate future? They will work on their outstanding projects and probably prepare a report for the president on private support for the arts and humanities in the eighties, setting forth what the federal government can properly do to preserve this marvelous American system.

ANNALS, *AAPSS*, **471**, January 1984

Culture in a Cold Climate

By CHRISTOPHER PRICE

ABSTRACT: Culture has been seen in Britain as a national institution worthy of public expenditure since the nineteenth century, but recent cutbacks in British government spending on the arts have forced the British to reexamine the place of culture in their society. The government wants the arts to raise income from private companies and individuals, but it has not provided any tax incentives for such private support. Private support of the arts in Britain poses several problems. It would blur what has been a clear distinction in the English establishment's mind between the public world of service to the community and the private world of commercial gain; and it tends to encourage popular or traditional arts ventures over innovative ones. In general, British politicians fear the economics of the arts because of its left-wing political potential. The author's parliamentary committee advocates the establishment of a ministry of culture, with national companies obtaining funds directly from the ministry, and with regional arts organizations taking responsibility for the remaining 60 percent of public cultural funding.

Christopher Price was chairman of the House of Commons Select Committee on Education, Science, and the Arts from 1979 to 1983. He has wide experience in education, both as assistant to British ministers of education and in Sheffield city government. Over the past two decades he has been editor of New Education *and educational correspondent of the* New Statesman, *for which he now regularly writes the "Diary." Educated at Leeds Grammar School, he received his degree in classics from the Queen's College, Oxford.*

T HE English don't like the word culture; but they tolerate the phenomenon. Herman Goering said whenever he heard the word, he felt for his revolver; the English don't feel for anything. They simply accept the British Museum, the National Gallery, and subsidies to their local theater as part of the national climate. Or rather, they did. As in the United States, the British cultural climate has suddenly gone extremely cold; the government is steadily reducing the tax pound that flows into museums and orchestras and theaters. By doing so, it is forcing the British to do what they have successfully avoided for 200 years—to examine the place of culture in society.

The visual arts were effectively nationalized in Britain during the nineteenth century, with avowedly nationalist, imperialist motives. An early excuse came in 1816 when the House of Commons set up a select committee to deliberate on the fate of the Earl of Elgin's collection of Sculptured Marbles. Lord Elgin had been ambassador to Constantinople in the early years of the century and, with dubious Turkish permission, had systematically stripped the Parthenon, the Erectheum, and other parts of the Acropolis in Athens—then under Turkish control—and transported his booty to Britain. After the Napoleonic War he was short of money and asked the British government to buy the Marbles for £50,000. The House of Commons eventually offered £35,000, which his lordship, with somewhat bad grace, accepted. So the Parthenon was erected within the British Museum, and the principle was established that culture, like defense, was a proper subject for substantial public expenditure in Britain.

It is this principle that the Thatcher government is now in the process of eroding. They have not yet suggested selling the Marbles back to the Greeks, who have actually demanded them back through the medium of their formidable minister of culture and ex-film star, Melina Mercouri. Melina, however, wants them to be presented free on the grounds that they were stolen in the first place; neither she nor her government is saying they could quite afford to pay for them.

What the British government is saying is that the arts in Britain must in the future raise very much more of their income from private companies and private individuals and expect substantially less from the taxpayer. This is a tall order in the middle of the recession when private companies and individuals are even shorter of liquidity than the government. But it is not just this financial stringency that has opened up a public argument. The whole idea of supporting great national institutions like the Royal Opera House has come as a shock. Implanted in the mind of even the most orthodox Englishman is a clear distinction between the public world of service to the community and the private one of commercial gain. The British Broadcasting Corporation, the British Museum, and the Royal Academy are national bodies like the police and navy. However much the English establishment admires Mrs. Thatcher's policies generally, it is uneasy about blurring the distinction between the public and private sectors in the arts.

*A parenthesis about
the United States*

This distinction seems never to have been a problem on the other side of the

Atlantic. I recently took my parliamentary committee to Houston to look at the funding of the arts. There it was accepted that public money was the junior partner, private money the senior partner in any cultural enterprise. It seemed to me all part of an American honors system. I suspect that in the United States private citizens pay for their name in lights on a museum or orchestra in the same way our nouveau riche used to buy honors from Lloyd George. The ancient Athenians financed their theater in roughly this way. There is nothing new about it. The deep reliance of the arts on the private sector in Houston will always be encapsulated for me in the story of the millionaire who was finally persuaded to sponsor a series of symphony concerts. "But on one condition!" he insisted. "Only so long as I don't have to go and listen to any of that damn music!"

RESPONSE TO DECREASED GOVERNMENT SUPPORT

So how is culture in Britain responding to the cold Thatcherite climate imposed on it? First, some parts are terminally ill. The unsubsidized London commercial theater is in dire straits, with halls closing weekly and casts getting smaller. It is mostly the general recession, made worse by mounting public transport costs to central London (another Thatcher measure) and a general drift of show-biz money into television. The government, as an election sweetener, has just announced a great leap forward into cable television.

Moreover, the authorities are fighting a losing battle in their fight to brighten up the general evening ambience of central London; in spite of a new, brighter Covent Garden area, and legis-

lation that is beginning to check the infection of Soho as a world pornography emporium, central London remains far too noisy and dirty. A stubborn refusal to make progress on the exclusion of the motor car does not help either. Other cities in Britain have made better progress, but in London the forces of Mammon are still imperceptibly gaining against those of enlightenment and culture. Our national companies—the National Theatre, the Royal Shakespeare Theatre, the four symphony orchestras, Covent Garden, and the English National Opera—survive. But the writing is on the wall.

Furious annual arguments take place with the government about the level of support national companies need; and the box office price increasingly excludes a great swathe of the lower-paid and the unemployed, whose taxes—the Thatcher government is now taxing unemployment benefits—go to support them. The government is pushing them toward private sponsorship, and for well-worn, orthodox composers and playwrights this can often be arranged; but never for anything adventurous or new.

Private sponsorship always remains a tiny percentage of the cost of the performance, 2-4 percent at present. Yet the sponsor all too often wants the sort of publicity that gives the impression they are funding the whole operation—for example, an enormous flag advertising the philanthropic beneficence of the Midland Bank, stretched across Covent Garden. This naturally annoys the British Arts Council, who feels it should take the credit for the 40 percent it funds!

Behind the row, apart from the natural English abhorrence of any mixture of trade and art, is the inability of any of our laws on taxation and advertising properly to cope with the government's new-found enthusiasm for the commercial sponsor. In the United States there is an established tax advantage for both individuals and commercial enterprises in supporting the arts. In the United Kingdom there is no similar tax concession; there are ways in which tax-free support can be given, if the artistic body in question is a charity, but they are complicated, little used, and involve long-term commitment. So most companies that invest in the arts do so as an ordinary business advertising expense. But to get that past the taxman they need their name in lights to show for it; otherwise he is liable to strike it out as an expense. Thus arts administrators waste foolish hours arguing about the size of type in which to credit the relevant company or firm—to make it just big enough to go on pretending that their particular art remains unpolluted by the vulgar world of commerce and profit.

Meanwhile the Treasury remains committed to our present tax regulations and refuses to provide any tax incentive —much less to abate value-added tax on the performing arts, which might give the London theater a bit of breathing space. With one mouth the government is saying, "Yes, we support the arts—but go to the private sector for support." With the other, "But on the other hand, we do not intend to provide a single extra incentive to make that support forthcoming."

This Janus-like ambivalence is partly attributable to Britain's lack of a ministry of culture. We have a fairly impotent junior minister in the Education Department in charge of public grants to the arts; it was ever thus. There is a deep, ingrained suspicion of any powerful cultural ministry. Dozens of arguments are used: the House of Commons is its own cultural arbiter; the Cabinet can make the important decisions; the English language is on a natural world-winning streak—we don't need to invest much thought or money in the problem. Our politicians—Left and Right—are instinctively against having any one arbiter of national taste. But this also means that there is no powerful national minister to direct the minds of the Cabinet and the Treasury to the problems faced by Britain in an age of endemic, high unemployment, euphemized as "enforced leisure," or to the economic possibilities of English culture as a money-spinner, to replace our collapsed productive industry.

The real reason that the politicians, especially those of the new philistine Right, shy away from the economics of the arts is that they are—rightly—terrified of its left-wing political potential. Like the Soviets they have always been willing to invest in a little high culture as a form of social control; but they are frightened of letting it get out of hand. The fears are compounded when they look across the channel, where Socialist governments do have ministers of culture and use them. Mitterand has doubled his spending on the arts and supposedly delegated decisions about its distribution to the regions, with the intention that it be used for political as well as cultural regeneration. The Communist regions of Bologna and Rome in Italy compete with each other in boosting their cultural budget, with the emphasis on local festivals to animate their supporters and alert them to the constant danger of imported cultural torpor. Mr. Papandreou in Greece is following much the same policy through Melina Mercouri.

Labour governments in Britain have always only gone halfheartedly into this sort of area. The Festival of Britain in 1951 was a last-minute afterthought to save a dying government; Harold Wilson's granting of the middlish official decoration Officer of the Order of the British Empire to the Beatles in 1966 was an intelligent, but ultimately implausible, attempt to cash in on the musical revolution of the time.

In a sense the Left in Britain already has its own cultural constituency. Where it has been outstandingly successful over the past couple of decades is in infiltrating the current-affairs, creative, and drama departments of the television networks. This successful incursion induces apoplexy in the British political Right, because they simply do not know what to do about it. They have even consolidated Labour's grip by instituting a fourth commercial channel and putting a well-known socialist, Jeremy Isaacs, in charge of it, with regulatory powers to reduce the influence of the advertisers and shape the whole ethos of the programs. So far its listening figures are tiny, hovering around 5 percent, but the attacks on the new channel, Channel 4, are mounting. Typically, indecorous language is being cited as an alibi for the real objection—a general irreverent and progressive tinge to the whole network.

There is not much Mrs. Thatcher can do about Channel 4. Instead she has announced an initiative, to be implemented at breakneck speed, to introduce a substantially unregulated cable television facility to about half the homes in Britain. Clearly the strategy is twofold: to swamp the progressive channels with further cable offerings of benign (and often U.S.) material that is acceptable to the advertisers; and to siphon off advertising revenue to put the other channels and eventually the British Broadcasting Corporation in difficulties. It is too early to say whether the plan will succeed. It is being commended on highly spurious employment-creation grounds; but it is dawning on our national newspapers, especially those that support the government, that it could wreck their advertising income also. The British cable revolution has not happened yet and may never do so.

A MINISTRY OF CULTURE

Finally, there is the Arts Council. Much more generously funded than the National Endowments for the Arts and the Humanities, it is a typically English device to put decisions about support of taste and culture at arm's length from the politicians and in the hands of an elite, establishment group of folk that both political parties can trust.

While funds were gently increasing, the Arts Council did its work fairly smoothly and with comparatively little criticism. When the cuts came and scrutiny began about how its mechanism operated, the edifice began to crumble. Mrs. Thatcher has put in as chairman a former editor of the *Times* to try to keep it going; but it is already under fire for being London-based, dominated by the national performing companies, narrow in its outlook incestuous in its committee appointments, and arbitrary in its decisions. Perhaps all these characteristics are inevitable in a body of this sort, but the council can operate only in unaccountable cloistered confidentiality. Once the wraps are off, it is a much more difficult task. I do not give the new chairman, Mr. Rees Mogg, much of a chance; radical reform is needed.

This is just what my parliamentary committee has proposed in its findings.[1] The conclusions would take too long to spell out here but, broadly, we want a ministry of culture—though we do not dare call it that. We do want one minister looking after the arts, national heritage, film, television, and tourism, to try to achieve a national perspective.

Second, we want to try to separate the funding of high national culture on the one hand and the seed corn for new developments, particularly in the regions of Britain, on the other. So we recommend that the national companies—from the British Museum through the orchestras, theaters and opera to the National Gallery—should get their money direct from the ministry. Let it take responsibility for the national cultural climate; on the whole the boards of trustees of those bodies are well able to look after themselves and outface any attempts at political interference.

But the other part of the public funding, about 60 percent, should go direct

1. Great Britain, Parliament, House of Commons Select Committee on Education, Science and the Arts, *Public and Private Funding of the Arts,* 3 vols. (London: HMSO, 1982).

to the regional arts organizations to provide culture as they wish. This proposal is more revolutionary than it seems. Some of these regional bodies, especially the one covering London, have very idiosyncratic ideas of how they would spend the money. Though it comes from an all-party committee with an established Conservative majority, it is the least likely of our recommendations to be accepted by the present government.

At the very least, however, Mrs. Thatcher's cuts and our House of Commons' response to them have started a debate on the arts in Britain on a level of fundamental seriousness that has hardly taken place since 1817. When Britain finally does emerge from its chilly Thatcher climate we will be in a very much better position to put together a British policy of culture, not just as a negative palliative to the so-called leisure produced by unemployment, but as a positive act for political and economic regeneration. It just might be that a consensus will emerge to plant and water flowers in what by then will almost inevitably be an even more depressing industrial desert.

ANNALS, *AAPSS,* **471,** January 1984

In the Market's Place:
Cultural Policy in Norway

By HANS F. DAHL

ABSTRACT: The arts in Norway are considered a public good and are therefore heavily subsidized, in order to make them available to the greatest number of people, to maintain Norway's national cultural standard on a par with neighboring countries, and to keep cultural traditions unbroken by preventing sudden ruptures in cultural production. The criterion for state support is art and its position in the market. The state comes in whenever the market proves insufficient, partly through direct subsidies covering production costs and partly by buying a certain amount of the cultural product. Norway advocates a policy of strong cultural decentralization. Cultural budgets are channeled through the Norwegian Cultural Fund, and individual artists' incomes tend to be a mixture of collective funds and individual royalty incomes, with a gradual shift toward individual incomes, even if still state-derived. State spending on culture has increased since the 1960s, and it has played an essential role in maintaining continuity in the quantity of cultural production, if not always the quality.

Hans F. Dahl is a historian by education and a journalist by profession. He received his doctorate in modern history from the University of Oslo in 1975. Dr. Dahl is the author of several books on continental political history and a two-volume history of the mass media and television broadcasting system in Norway. He is presently the cultural editor of Dagbladet *in Oslo—Norway's third largest daily newspaper.*

SINCE 1982, strollers on Oslo's main boulevard, Karl Johan, have been discommoded by an ugly gap in the gracious curve of buildings on the north side of the park: a yawning crater, where construction works show that a large building is being erected on what is one of the most expensive sites in town. A new bank in times of recession? A new business center in a decade of flagging economy and an alarming rise in retail prices? Neither. In this pit the Norwegian state is erecting a new theater. A brand new, $15 million theater in the center of Oslo, at a time when public budgets suffer drastic cut-downs as a result of the economic recession. Everybody seems to accept it; no political party has protested. A new theater, which must strike any foreign visitor as extraordinary these days, is to a Norwegian completely natural, thus providing a perfect illustration of the position of the arts in Norwegian public life: heavily subsidized, underpinned by long traditions of public consideration and upheld by governmental spending regardless of the tide and times of the nation's economy.

In this article I will endeavor to explain some of the mechanisms that govern the strong involvement of the Norwegian state in the arts. I shall do so with a glance at the other Nordic countries, the system being essentially the same in Sweden, Denmark, Finland, and Iceland.

A PUBLIC GOOD

In this part of the world art, like lighthouse systems and the armed forces, is considered a public good. As we know, the distinguishing mark of a public good is that it cannot be reserved for some and denied to others. One cannot impose a tax on rounding coastal lighthouses; social norms thus make the coastal guard as well as the port authorities part of the natural infrastructure of the state.

In many respects this public-good status also applies to art in Scandinavia. The works of an author, the music of a composer are said to belong to the people, in the sense that it is considered right to make them accessible at public expense so that everybody can enjoy them. Everybody, of course, does not do so. In Scandinavia, as in all other societies, art consumption is dictated by social standards of taste and habit and split into high and low cultural patterns, sharply divided according to class, age, and place of residence. Art, however, being an integral part of the public sector must in principle be publicly accessible, just like the lighthouse or the road system. The norms guiding this principle are so deeply ingrained in the system that they enable the state to erect a stately structure even at a time of crisis.

Consider the means by which public broadcasting was introduced in Norway. Radio broadcasting in Scandinavia was pioneered by private companies, but in the course of a few years ownership passed on to the state. In Norway one important step in this process was a suit brought by the authors' organization against the Oslo Broadcasting Company in 1929. The purpose of the trial was trivial enough: to increase the fees for the use of literature in the programs. The outcome, however, was of great significance. The authors got moral support for the principle that Norwegian literary works could not legitimately be broadcast to the public in such a way that shareholders in the broadcasting company earned private money on them. As the chairman of the authors' organization put it: "Our literature belongs to the people, not to the stockholders of the electric industry."[1] As a result, broadcasting had to submit to state ownership and management to prevent private profit on public property.

One might assume that the concept of art as a public good is a result of the degree of state involvement in Norway generally, but this is not the case. The public sector in Scandinavia comprises just a few percent more of the gross national product than that of the other Western nations, and the state's total involvement in the economy only slightly exceeds that of the rest of western Europe. The prerequisite for state involvement in the arts in Norway, then, is not the state, but art itself and its position on the market. The size of the market is the key issue here. The main reason behind public support of the arts is simply the absence of any sizable private demand that could support a production of any size.

The theater, for instance, is publicly run because there is no market for a serious theater in any of the Nordic countries. Let us assume that a good theater needs at least 100 employees and running and capital costs equivalent to one half of the ongoing wages. This would mean an annual budget of $1-$2 million. Even allowing for high ticket prices, this sum would necessitate between 50,000 and 100,000 visitors annually. With Scandinavian theater-going habits, this would mean a local population of at least 1 million. No town in Norway has more than 500,000 inhabitants, and only three have populations exceeding 100,000. Under these condi-

tions there can be no private market for a labor-intensive enterprise like the theater.

The fact that we do have a theater at all in Norway is due to massive public support, up to 90 percent of total running costs as a rule. Five new regional theaters have been established along the long coastline of Norway, supported by the state and the local authorities. Already established were the six institutional theaters situated in the four largest towns and the touring company comprising twelve permanent state companies, in a country where private market demand can uphold only one or two pure entertainment theaters enjoying no state support at all.

And, as if this network of official theaters did not suffice, all over Scandinavia "free groups" have blossomed. Often ideologically based, they have broken free from the established state institutions and are running low-budget, independent ventures, benefiting from municipal subsidy schemes and exploiting the private, idealistic potential. These free groups—and there are more than 150 of them all over Scandinavia—are of a high artistic and professional standard, and are a completely new element. During the 1970s they edged their way onto the cultural budgets in all the Nordic countries, but they still lead a shaky existence on the fringes of a subsidy system.

The way in which this revolution from the inside has revived and widened the choice of dramatic performances is amazing and, so far, only partly understood. One motivation has been ideological, with usually a left-wing orientation; another has been imitation. The groups get together during festivals and exchange schemes, and learn from each other in a most spectacular way. Travel-

1. Quoted in Hans F. Dahl, *Hallo-Hallo: Kringkastingen i Norge, 1920-1940* [History of broadcating in Norway, 1920-1940] (Oslo: Cappelem, 1975), pp. 125-26.

ing jesters are again to be found on the surface of Scandinavia, in addition to the heavily subsidized institutional theaters.

It must be emphasized, however, that the phenomenon of the theater boom is self-generated, springing from the companies' desire to produce and act, and not from any surplus of new natio al drama. New Ibsens and Strindbergs ·e few and far between behind the writing desks of Scandinavia. The repertoire of the theaters is usually international, with emphasis on the classics. The free groups, on the other hand, often write their own material.

STATE INVOLVEMENT IN THE ARTS MARKET

Whenever the number of consumers passes below the threshold required to uphold a meaningful production, the state enters the cultural market. This pattern, it seems, is the basic pillar of ideology carrying art support in Norway, and it applies to all forms of art and culture, stretching out even to the daily press, which is considered worthy of support for cultural reasons all over Scandinavia. The state comes in whenever the market proves insufficient, partly through direct subsidies covering production costs, as in films and the theater, partly by taking over the role of the consumer by buying a certain amount of the cultural product. In both cases market insufficiency is considered the fundamental reason for governmental funding. Art in this context fits into a general pattern of state support, covering education and communication as well. Art, knowledge, and communication apparently are considered so necessary to a small nation of 4 million people

that the legitimacy of state intervention seems self-evident.

What is not evident, however, is how all this comes about as a social process. Stating the necessity of a cultural policy, a *kulturpolitikk,* is just putting the name to an outcome of a complicated transition of money and resources. Precisely who or what tells the government that it must support regional theaters, poetry collections, or modern murals?

Imitation, sheer taking-after, seems to be important in a number of cases. Culture is by nature a prestigious venture; and a modern nation without a national theater or, say, a certain level of national film production, remains behind. The fear of staying behind is a driving political force in an area where national achievements are as easily comparable as in the arts. One of the main reasons Norway got its state opera in 1957 is the unbearable feeling of a lagging behind—in this case far behind—Stockholm and Copenhagen, which got their royal operas in the 1770s, and even Helsinki, which had one by the 1850s. If you ask why there is a certain number of art institutions—theaters, permanent galleries, museums, symphony orchestras, and so on—the answer is because of the neighbors, that is, the next town or the next country, as the case might be. On the national level the general pattern of public cultural policy in Norway seems to imitate Sweden. Beyond Sweden lies Europe and the general trends of cultural influence from abroad.

Consider once again the regional theaters in Norway. They were created during the 1970s as part of the general wave of cultural decentralization throughout Europe, originating with the late General Charles de Gaulle or, more precisely, with his minister of culture, Andre Malraux. Mr. Malraux was a pioneer in

Europe advocating the establishment of *maisons culturels,* for multicultural presentations. His idea of cultural decentralization communicated through the Council of Europe was eagerly adopted by various European governments, in Scandinavia notably by the Swedes, who during the sixties and seventies established a large number of regional cultural institutions. From Sweden, the wave hit Norway. Government spending on cultural houses more than trebled between 1972 and 1981.

The idea of regional theaters emerged as part of a general thrust for decentralization and localization. Local authorities lobbied the government with eager requests for regional theatrical stages. Actors and artists followed suit. During the 1970s regional theaters were very popular in stage culture, processing new ideas in leadership—no old fashioned directors—and team productions, but also new types of conflict between the regional authorities—who were footing the bill together with the government— and the youthful ensembles gathered around the newly established stage. Without the international context and impulses from abroad, such theaters would almost certainly never have been established in Norway. Traditionally the task of bringing the theater to audiences in the countryside and along the coast has been carried out by Riksteatret, the state touring company, now competing with the regional theaters for a slice of the budget.

MAINTENANCE OF
UNBROKEN TRADITIONS

Apart from imitation, quite a lot of state activity in the arts originates from another simple social process, the need to overcome catastrophes in the arts or,

one might say, the need to keep traditions unbroken by preventing sudden ruptures in the cultural production.

Literature is the crowning case in this context. Novelists and authors tend to enjoy an exceptionally high esteem in the country of Ibsen and Bjornson, where the idea of having a "living literature" seems crucial to the cultural identity. Apart from the polar explorers Nansen and Amundsen, there have been no greater national heroes than the towering nineteenth-century authors.

After World War II, however, Norwegian literature—having enjoyed a short patriotic spin following the liberation from the German occupation in 1945—began to shrink drastically in the number of published novels, short stories, and poetry collections. In 1963 the total number of national first editions ran to only 86 titles, while there had been 136 in 1938. No single author writing for this market could earn his living from it.

Publishers sought a solution whereby production could be increased through lower prices and greater demand. In 1965 the government struck a really original note: that of committing itself to buying exactly one thousand copies of every new first edition and parceling them out as gifts to the 1200 local libraries, thereby almost doubling the market, creating an artificial demand designed to make Norwegian novels, short stories, and poetry worth publishing once more. The reform had instant effect. The number of first editions doubled within seven years; by 1982, 230 first editions of novels, short stories, and verse were being distributed to libraries throughout the country at governmental expense. Writers could expect some income from their books—say, one or two thousand dollars per title published.

The precondition of this unique arrangement was, and still is, the existence of a strong national association of publishers, providing the government with a responsible negotiating body and also exercising a certain amount of internal control, reducing the most obvious temptations to abuse the agreement by publishing inferior titles to cash in on state money. Even so, the agreement is still controversial. The obligation of the state to buy almost any novel or poetry volume—there is a safety mechanism working post hoc—regardless of quality or contents, certainly evokes public attention every now and then. Broadly speaking, however, the agreement has been a success, even though it is commonly agreed among the critics that the number of first editions, especially of poetry, is too high measured against any reasonable standard of literary quality.

Another precondition to the 1965 agreement was, of course, the availability of public funds, the annual cost amounting to $3 million in 1982. Here too the solution was an unconventional one: the funds needed to secure a higher proportion of home production of novels and verse were raised by taxing the popular weekly magazines. Members of the Norwegian Parliament found it rather difficult, however, to levy this Donald Duck tax, as it was popularly called, to support serious literature, and after some five years the source of the funds was altered so as to flow directly from the Treasury. Taxing the lower taste of the readers goes on, however, by dropping the value-added tax on books —but now any books, not just first editions of fiction—whereas a 20 percent value-added tax is imposed on popular magazines, thus discriminating against the readers of light stuff.

Technically the budgets covering the 1965 agreement are channeled through the Norwegian Cultural Fund, established to deal partly with the sorry state of works of fiction, but partly also to pay for necessary rescue operations in all fields of the art and culture. Prior to the mid-sixties the cultural budgets, with their long-winded parliamentary routines, were not at all geared to overcoming sudden crises and unforeseen demands in the arts. Since that time, however, much has been done to make cultural funding more flexible so as to deal with unexpected events in cultural life.

State support for film production, for instance, underwent heavy changes in 1964 due to the crisis in both quality and quantity in the film production. Compared to Swedish and Danish films, the quality of Norwegian pictures was mercilessly exposed as inferior, a fact that seemed connected to the lack of predictable funds and reliable sources for Norwegian film producers. A state support system to encourage the special blend of artistic ambition and mass appeal so necessary in film production was designed and put into operation, though with little success. The number of films produced, 12 a year since the late seventies, is in fact comparable to the number in Denmark—20—and Sweden—17, but the quality is extremely uneven. Direct government funds for movies are necessary to secure their production, but not very much more. The artificial market guaranteed by the state obviously does not create an environment sufficiently vital to make Norwegian films competitive with the mass inflow from abroad, mainly from the United States.

Apart from literature and film production, government money in vast quantities is channeled directly into the Norwegian newspaper industry, with the explicit intention of avoiding an undesirable breakdown in what is considered a cultural value: the structure and diversity of the newspaper system, spread out in a great number of small local papers. The press support is not defined as part of the cultural budget. The arguments for upholding the existing structure are, however, identical to the reasons given for direct cultural subsidies, and the background is in fact the same as that of the rescue operations for literature, namely, a shrinking market.

In 1969 the Norwegian parliament passed a bill providing state subsidies to the newspaper production in addition to the tax exemption and postal levies already introduced. The reason was the by-then urgent need to secure the existing structure of papers, both geographically and politically, from apparently dramatic market development. As with literature and film, the problem was to secure a fair and predictable distribution of funds without destroying the elements of competition still lingering in the market. As is the case with novels, poetry, and films, the press subsidies are under constant discussion, the newspaper funds perhaps even more so because of political tension, because most Norwegian papers are affiliated with, if not owned by, a political party. Even here, however, the legitimacy of the rescue operation as such is hardly questioned at all.

One may ask how the cultural arguments really count against the weight of the pressure groups involved in getting state money to an established field of cultural production. The answer is that power certainly does make a difference, and that the 10,000 people employed by the Norwegian newspaper industry is a more powerful bloc than the 100 or so engaged full time in film production. They both get their money, however, for cultural reasons.

When creating a public system that automatically sponsors any given product of ideology or culture, you certainly need solid reasons for doing so. In this sense the need to smooth out discontinuities and avoid breaks in the production of values and ideas is in itself an explanation of why the government in Norway, and in any Scandinavian country, is so heavily engaged in the arts, broadly speaking.

Indeed there has been a remarkable increase in governmental financing since the sixties. Throughout Scandinavia, governmental spending on culture has almost doubled during the 1970s. The figures for Norway show a yearly increase in the Department of Culture budget of 10 percent during the period 1970-82, as against an average increase in overall government spending of 6.4 percent in the same period.

PAYMENT TO THE ARTISTS

The persons actually benefiting most from the increase were the artists themselves: writers, musicians, and, above all, painters and designers. For all of these artists the budget doubling has provided new jobs and opportunities, even if the level of income from the arts generally is very low, particularly in the visual arts. More noteworthy, however, is that the money flowing from the state to the artists seems to follow new trends and ways.

Traditionally, public support to artists in Norway passes into a foundation, one for each branch of the arts, which also collects individual rights from all the artists and distributes them in larger portions—such as scholarships, pensions, or traveling grants for which every artist of the kind can apply. The system is normally referred to as representing a "collective" way of funding.

In most cases the foundations are established by law and thereby guaranteed by the state. Thus painters and sculptors got their foundation in 1948, made up by the 3 percent tax on the purchase of art objects imposed by law that year. Composers by then already had their collective rights bureau, the Norwegian Composers' Copyright Bureau, operating on similar principles. Writers and translators got their own foundation in 1947, mainly from the state compensation of library use, whereas musicians had their foundation raised from a special levy on gramophone records.

Apart from state subsidies and taxes, most of the foundations enjoy a substantial revenue from broadcasting rights, which normally also passes into these collective arrangements. In fact the state broadcasting corporation in the Scandinavian countries represents an institution of vital importance in channeling public money from their audiences' license fees to musicians, composers, actors, and writers. As the level of license fees in all countries is decided in Parliament at par with the national taxes, broadcasting in fact may be regarded as part of the state subsidy system. In Norway the State Broadcasting Corporation for years had paid more to music than the total amount of state support.

The public money flowing into the collective foundations has furthered the growth of strong organizations on the side of the artists. "Poor writers, rich unions" is a saying in Norway.

However, the structure of publicly guaranteed foundations is gradually losing ground inasmuch as direct, individual ways of paying for rights have grown and shattered the predominance of collective funds. Writers no longer pick up their library money collectively, but are paid personally per book per capita. Painters and sculptors enjoy a direct refund from the state for each day an object is exhibited at an officially approved gallery.

Royalty incomes, it seems, tend to increase their importance over collective arrangements, be it on a private or on a governmental basis. At least this is the explicit aim of the artists themselves, who since the mid-seventies have demanded full compensation for any public use of their work—which is to say, individual compensation, according to a quasi-market ideology. The old foundation system paradoxically has created such strong artists' corporations that the demand for individual compensation for public usage is being pushed through by artists' organizations well equipped with lawyers and other professionals arguing the members' rights.

Today an average Norwegian artist is sustained by a combination of collective funds and private earnings, even if the last source also is provided by the state. In the future, however, the artist may experience a shift toward personal income, as is indeed already the case with some 500 Norwegian artists who get their state support in the shape of a "guaranteed income." That is, the state covers the difference between the artists' personal income from their art and an ideal income stipulated according to social security standards.

From this one might get the impression that state support of the arts in Norway tends to grow in importance, taking over even the small relics of a market economy relevant to the economics of art. But this is definitely not the whole story. Even as the public sector of the arts grows, so does the private market for cultural endowments. Commercial broadcasting is on its way, all over Scandinavia. Corporate funding increasingly enters the field of arts and festivals, and is sure to open up new markets for arts on a purely private basis. On the library scene the distribution of new novels by means of book clubs has created a market from which a handful or two of trendy authors actually can earn good money instantly from their writings. Beyond the realm of state support there has emerged a blossoming growth in popular music and rock—a huge and energetic software industry producing artists and original talents in scores without the use of a single public crown. All these ventures have raised heated debates in Norway during the last five years, because they all work contrary to national traditions of collective funding and public care.

Indeed the state of the arts in Norway may be said to consist of two towering ventures: on the one hand, the sustenance of a huge museum of a mainly print culture, where state money in millions helps the growth of newspapers, literature, and often written ventures piling up in public libraries, regardless of the participation of readers and listeners; on the other hand, a free-market abundance of electric music sounding from millions of loudspeakers that no longer speak, but sing and play all through the days and nights for a youthful audience whose cultural habits definitely belong to a private consumers' market. And between the two ventures: a growing traffic of exchange and mutual interests, for example, state wage-earning writers providing texts for new rock singers, or free theater groups topping the commercial record hit lists with the latest antiwar song.

State support has not suffocated artists and their creativity. On the contrary, without heavy state support we quite probably would have had no stage or book culture at all. On the other hand, creative ventures do appear from stages and podiums even outside the state support system. Public money is a necessary but not self-sufficient reason for the growth of the arts.

ANNALS, *AAPSS*, **471**, January 1984

Indirect Aid to the Arts

By MICHAEL O'HARE and ALAN L. FELD

ABSTRACT: Most government support of arts institutions is indirect—the result of charitable deduction provisions of the federal income tax, property tax exemptions extended by local governments, and other tax provisions. The money that government forgoes through these provisions must be made up by higher taxes for all taxpayers. The public, however, has little say about how these funds are spent. By its very nature, the income tax deduction places the decision-making power over arts institutions in the hands of those with high incomes. Those with high incomes receive a greater tax benefit for each dollar they contribute, increasing the amounts they donate, which increases the likelihood of their influence over those who run arts institutions, and they are allowed to place restrictions on the use of their gifts. Moreover the property tax exemption encourages arts institutions to invest heavily in real estate, which is not necessarily in the public's best interests. Replacing some indirect subsidies with direct subsidies and granting tax credits for donations in place of tax deductions would go a long way toward making the system more equitable.

Michael O'Hare is a lecturer in public policy at the John F. Kennedy School of Government, Harvard University. Trained as an architect and engineer, he has served as assistant secretary of environmental affairs for policy for the Commonwealth of Massachusetts.

Alan L. Feld is a professor of law at Boston University Law School, specializing in tax matters. He received his A.B. degree from Columbia College (1960) and his LL.B. degree from Harvard Law School (1963). He is the author of Tax Policy and Corporate Concentration *(1982) and numerous articles.*

NOTE: This article is based on *Patrons Despite Themselves: Taxpayers and Arts Policy,* a Twentieth Century Fund Report by Alan L. Feld, Michael O'Hare, and J. Mark Davidson Schuster, published in 1983 by New York University Press. For brevity, we have omitted explanations of our inferences, several chains of argument, references and citations, and some qualifications. For a complete treatment of this topic, the reader is referred to the book.

M OST American cultural institutions derive their financial support from a combination of sources. Some institutions enjoy enough income from the sale of tickets and admissions to cover the bulk of their expenses, but most art organizations rely on gifts to meet their budgetary needs. Some of these gifts are private donations of private funds; the remainder comes from government. Presumably a nation's cultural policy can be discerned in the governmental share of financial support to the arts.

Unfortunately discussions of government support for the arts have been limited to questions of the amount of direct grant-in-aid support, and to the likely effects on the arts of greater or lesser government grants. This narrow view of arts funding ignores the fact that the bulk of government aid to the arts in the United States is provided outside direct grant mechanisms. This indirect aid consists of taxes that otherwise would be payable, forgiven when the potential taxpayer behaves in a certain way. Table 1 shows the breakdown of the $458 million in indirect aid for 1973.[1] Since indirect aid comprises the majority of government assistance to the arts —direct aid for 1973 was about $200 million—it seems important to shift our attention, at least sometimes, from the question, How much money should the arts receive from government? to, How should that money be delivered? The

1. Unfortunately, it is not possible to estimate these figures for a more recent year with existing data.

TABLE 1
TOTAL ESTIMATED TAX EXPENDITURES FOR THE ARTS, 1973

Tax		Source of Tax Expenditure		Amounts in Millions of $*
Federal	Income tax:	Individual charitable deductions		182
		Capital gains tax foregone		26
		Corporate charitable deductions		64
		Capital gains tax foregone†		—
	Estate tax:	Charitable gift deduction		40
	Gift tax:	Charitable gift deduction		6
	Miscellaneous:	Gifts made through private foundations		24
State	Income tax:	Individual charitable deductions and capital gains tax foregone	24	
		Less federal tax offset‡	−13	
				11
		Corporate charitable deductions and capital gains tax foregone	9	
		Less federal tax offset	−4	
				5
Local	Property tax:	Exemptions		100
	Total estimated tax expenditure			458

*Property tax exemption is estimated with 1976 data, but deflated to 1973 dollars; all others are estimated with 1973 data.

†Data are insufficient to give a reasonable estimate.

‡As discussed in the text, part of the state tax expenditure for the arts actually inures to the benefit of the federal government, rather than arts institutions.

public should be aware of the important differences between the indirect and direct aid mechanisms, at comparable funding levels, and should have a voice in choosing particular combinations of these forms of support.

THE MAJOR TAX EXPENDITURES

The two most important sources of indirect aid to the arts are the charitable deduction in the federal income tax and the property tax exemption extended to most not-for-profit institutions by local government. In this short review we will examine these two major tax expenditures and their most important consequences.

The income tax deduction involves a third party, a donor who has resolved to give some of his or her own property to a not-for-profit institution. When patrons contribute money or property, the federal income tax allows them to deduct the value of the contributions, within certain limits that do not concern us here, from taxable income. The reduction in taxable income results in a smaller income tax liability. For example, a wealthy individual in the highest tax bracket, currently 50 percent, might write a check to the local symphony orchestra for $100. In this individual's tax bracket, the contribution reduces his or her tax bill by $50. The $100 "contribution" may be described more accurately as a private contribution that costs the donor $50—and automatically entails a $50 contribution of public money; the charity receives a total benefit of $100. The $50 provided by the public must be made up by other taxpayers— who are in effect all paying some portion of their tax dollars to charities chosen by others—or the government deficit will increase.

In like fashion the property tax exemption that enriches an arts institution does so at some public cost. The property taxes not paid by an arts institution owning its own building must be made up by other taxpayers; alternatively, if the museum and if the arts institutions were taxed in the same way as other property owners in the city, everyone else's tax bill would be slightly smaller at the same level of municipal services.

Taxes forgone for reasons extraneous to the tax are sometimes called tax expenditures. It is extremely difficult to find out the cost to the government of the various tax expenditures for the arts, or for any other charity. Governments understandably do not compile information about the taxes they do not collect. The Internal Revenue Service does not collect, much less publish, information about which types of charity receive contributions from donors at particular brackets, and municipalities typically do not bother to assess property that is not taxable. The estimates in Table 1 were compiled using a variety of survey and official data.

Charitable deduction

As with any subsidy program, the operation of the charitable contribution deduction becomes clearer when we identify the three distinct groups of people (1) who decide how the government funds will be allocated; (2) who enjoy the benefits of the activities supported by those funds; and (3) who bear the cost of allocating funds in this way. When an individual spends his or her own money for self-gratification, that person is decision maker, payer, and beneficiary, all in one; in the case of government indirect aid for the arts, these groups all differ.

The charitable contribution deduction operates to concentrate decision-making power among people with high incomes because it involves the interaction of two kinds of phenomena, only one of which results from government tax policy. The private phenomena are that wealthy people tend to contribute to cultural institutions rather more than other income groups do, and that wealthy people have more money of their own to give. Tax policy then enhances decision-making power at the upper end of the income scale by giving more weight to each dollar contributed by high-income taxpayers. A tax deduction in a graduated income tax is more valuable to higher-income taxpayers.

The wealthy contributor of $50 to an arts institution will find the government willing to match the contribution with $50, as in the previous example; but an individual with a smaller income who pays taxes at the lowest tax rate of 11 percent will find a contribution of $50 matched at most by only $6 in government funds. That is, a $56 contribution will produce a tax reduction of $6 and a cost to the low-bracket donor of $50. In some instances, when the taxpayer does not have significant itemized deductions, the government provides no matching funds. Not surprisingly the decision-making power over the charitable deduction tax expenditure is higly concentrated in upper-income groups of the population, especially for the arts (Table 2).

Society as a whole is enhanced by the benefits in the fine arts that are purchased by government tax expenditures. But some members of society derive much more in the way of direct benefits through visits to museums or attendance at symphony performances. Consumption of the fine arts in this sense can be traced by demographic group, though with some difficulty. Not surprisingly, it is concentrated among citizens with more education (Figure 1) and, perhaps because of the association of income with education, more income than the rest of the population (Figure 2). However, income's association with arts consumption is not as strong as its association with decision-making power.

The distribution of the cost of tax expenditures for the arts does not differ from the cost of any other government subsidy program: in every case, taxpayers proportionally provide necessary resources. In some instances a sudden increase in funding is accompanied by the imposition of a particular new tax, but in the absence of such action it is reasonable to assume, especially for amounts of money small in proportion to the national budget, that tax expenditures are paid for in proportion to general taxpayer burdens. These burdens rest more heavily on those at higher income levels, but the disproportion is far smaller than the disproportion associated with decision making (Figure 3).

Property tax exemption

The beneficiaries of the property tax exemption enjoyed by arts institutions are the same as the beneficiaries of the income tax deduction, with one exception. The specific consumers of art in proportion to their number of visits can be identified geographically for each institution or program. Similarly, a geographical description applies to the distribution of the costs of the tax subsidy. There is one important disparity: for the most part, arts institutions are located in central cities. The property tax exemption comes out of the city budget and is paid for by the taxpayers of the govern-

(text continues on page 140)

TABLE 2
INDIVIDUAL CHARITABLE GIVING BY SECTOR, COLUMN PERCENTAGES, 1973

Modified Income Class	Percentage of Total Households	Culture	Religion	Education	Health	Other Social Welfare	Other Charitable	Aggregate Charitable Giving
$ 1- 9,999	48%	0%	26%	7%	16%	8%	0%	21%
10-14,999	23	0.2	26	3	12	13	0	21
15-19,999	16	1	21	3	14	14	2	18
20-29,999	9	5	16	7	18	22	1	16
30-49,999	3	17	7	20	8	13	1	9
50-99,999	1	38	2	15	10	18	69	7
100,000-199,999	0.2	18	1	15	13	5	4	3
200,000-499,999	*	11	0.3	15	6	4	9	2
500,000-999,999	*	7	0.1	6	1	2	0	1
1,000,000+	*	2	0.5	8	3	1	15	1
Totals	100%	100%	100%	100%	100%	100%	100%	100%

SOURCE: The Commission on Private Philanthropy and Public Needs, National Study of Philanthropy, 1974.

NOTE: Columns may not add to 100% because of rounding. Boldface figures indicate the median income class in each column.

*Less than 0.1%.

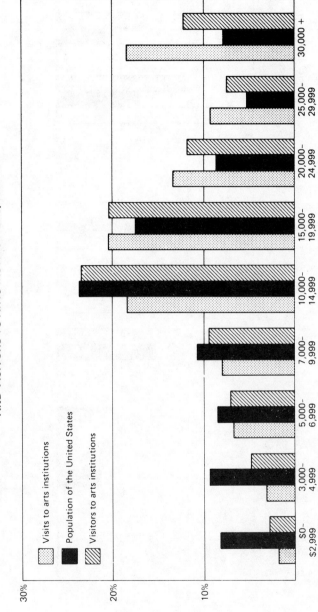

FIGURE 1

INCOME DISTRIBUTIONS OF VISITS TO ARTS INSTITUTIONS, POPULATION OF THE UNITED STATES, AND VISITORS TO ARTS INSTITUTIONS, 1974-75

SOURCE: National Research Center of the Arts, *Americans and the Arts*, 1975.

NOTE: All data include only individuals age 16 or over.

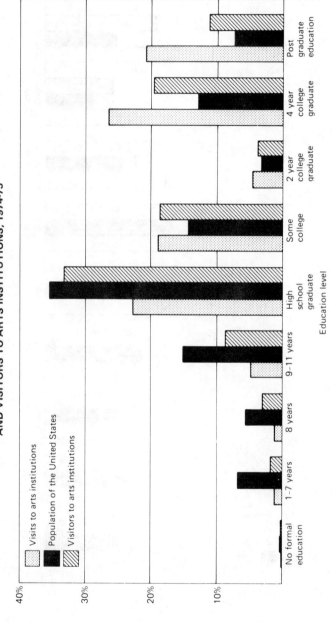

FIGURE 2

EDUCATION DISTRIBUTIONS OF VISITS TO ARTS INSTITUTIONS, POPULATION OF THE UNITED STATES, AND VISITORS TO ARTS INSTITUTIONS, 1974-75

SOURCE: National Research Center of the Arts, *Americans and the Arts*, 1975.

NOTE: All data include only individuals age 16 or over.

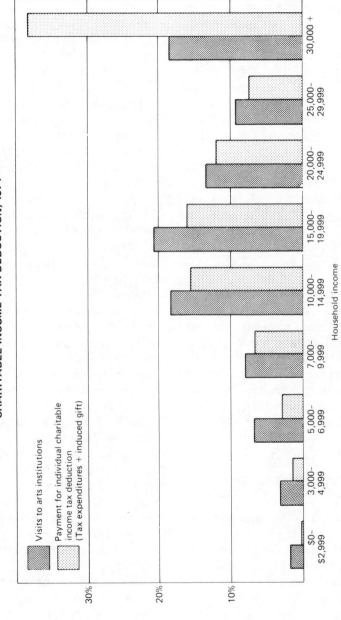

FIGURE 3

INCOME DISTRIBUTIONS OF WHO BENEFITS FROM AND WHO PAYS FOR THE INDIVIDUAL
CHARITABLE INCOME TAX DEDUCTION, 1974

Visits to arts institutions

Payment for individual charitable
income tax deduction
(Tax expenditures + induced gift)

Household income

$0–
$2,999

3,000–
4,999

5,000–
6,999

7,000–
9,999

10,000–
14,999

15,000–
19,999

20,000–
24,999

25,000–
29,999

30,000 +

30%

20%

10%

SOURCES: Based on data from National Research Center of the Arts, *Americans and the Arts*, 1975; and from Commission on Private Philanthropy and Public Needs, *National Study of Philanthropy*, 1974.

ment in which the exempt institution is located. Visitors to the arts institutions, on the other hand, are widely spread across the metropolitan area. This geographical distinction may imply other demographic differences: to the extent that suburban arts consumers on average are better educated or wealthier than inner-city residents, the less well-off will be paying for activities enjoyed by those better off. However, the incidence of the property tax is difficult to assess, especially when secondary effects are taken into account.

Decision-making power over the property tax subsidy differs from control over the income tax charitable deductions. Every dollar of public funds provided to an arts institution by the charitable deduction was delivered as the result of a conscious decision by a donor to favor that institution. The property tax subsidy flows, insofar as the institution owns real estate, after a general entitlement to this form of tax expenditure is made once and for all by the legislature. As to the latter decision, a further gap between decision making and cost bearing may exist: the state legislature mandates the tax exemption, but it is the locality, not the state, that must bear the cost.

CONSEQUENCES OF INDIRECT AID MECHANISMS

Although indirect aid augments the resources available to arts institutions, it is a mixed blessing. Tax expenditures alter the ways in which donors and institutions behave, thereby changing the arts experience enjoyed by the visitor to the institution, or even the visitors who experience the art. The property tax exemption has particularly unfortunate

side effects. Aside from the poor matches between payers and beneficiaries and costs and benefits discussed earlier, it encourages institutions to invest more heavily in real estate, providing the experience of art relatively more through the use of buildings and relatively less through the use of other economic inputs. This result bears no relationship to any public policy principle.

The property tax exemption is restricted to institutions that own real estate, and is given in proportion to the amount owned and rented. Thus, when the Opera Company of Boston stopped renting a downtown theater and bought its own, it suddenly began to receive a significant municipal subsidy—about a third of the annualized capital cost of its real estate—that had no relation to the quality of its performances or to the public benefits provided by the opera company. The subsidy began on the company's purchase of the building and would not have been affected by a sharp decline in the quality of productions or a sharp fall in attendance.

Obtaining real estate for two-thirds of the price that other users of real estate pay makes this form of expenditure look artificially cheap to the managers of arts institutions, relative to other production costs. As an inevitable consequence of this perception, the institution's manager will use real estate, which is subsidized, whenever possible; for example, a museum may substitute real estate for labor, exhibiting the entire collection at once in a larger building rather than, with the same economic resources, spending money on the staff needed to cycle work through traveling exhibitions or improving the quality of the consumers' experiences by providing extension, education, and lecture programs.

The charitable deduction, in contrast to the property tax exemption, imposes almost no legal conditions on the behavior of the recipient of the funds, other than that they be for charitable or educational purposes. Instead, the individual donors who decide to which institutions they will contribute and how much they will contribute have enormous control over the behavior of those institutions.

A principal drawback of the charitable contribution deduction derives from its separation of decision making from those who bear the costs. The form of the deduction ties the amount of public tax support for cultural institutions to choices made mostly by wealthy donors. A donor normally does not contribute to charity or to culture as a whole; instead, the donor selects a particular institution—and often a particular program within that institution—because he or she favors it and its activities. The choice may or may not flow from pure altruism or from the highest aesthetic refinement; it reflects the particular and sometimes idiosyncratic values of the donor. Of course, to the extent that the contribution reflects an expenditure of the donor's own resources, this is highly appropriate; but to the extent that it also allocates public funds, it creates a disturbing picture. In effect, the tax system has delegated to wealthy donors important aesthetic choices that determine what cultural institutions show to the public.

It might seem that a responsible director of an arts institution could pursue the program that seemed best for the institution, no matter what donors wanted; a contributor cannot force an institution to accept a gift. But this expectation ignores several important facts about institutions and the people who run them:

1. The board of trustees appoints the director; in particular, they appoint a director who will guide the institution as the trustees intend.

2. Many trustees are elected precisely because they are—or might be—large contributors.

3. An unwillingness on the part of patrons to contribute can prevent an institution from implementing new programs. If the resources are not available, the program cannot be put in place.

4. Directors who want to keep their institutions solvent must not only respond to present offers with their various conditions, but also anticipate what sort of future philanthropic response their present programs will induce. They must also consider how a refusal of a poorly conceived offer now will affect the likelihood of future charitable gifts from that donor's friends and business associates.

If the desire and intentions of the wealthy donors who control the lion's share of the charitable deduction tax expenditure were known to be the same as those of the nation as a whole, this would not be a problem. But there are many reasons to believe that their interests might be different. To choose only one example, wealthy people have much more experience and familiarity with the arts from childhood than do working-class people. What a prep school, Ivy League college graduate who grew up in a home with paintings on the walls wants from his or her first visit to a museum is quite different from what a high school graduate working in a steel mill who has no family experience of this particular form of culture wants or needs. Furthermore, to the extent that arts institutions reflect upper-class tastes, the enthusiasm of upper-class patrons for programs that would make the arts intellectually and aesthetically accessible to the less wealthy may be quite muted.

A second effect derives from a sub-rule of the charitable contribution deduction. In general a gift to charity of property whose value has increased gives rise to a deduction based on the value at the time of the gift, without any tax liability—at capital gain rates or otherwise—on the appreciation. This rule, favoring gifts of appreciated value to charity, has particular importance for gifts of artwork to museums. While other charities derived about a tenth of their deducted charitable gifts in kind, over half of such gifts to cultural institutions were in kind.

The combined tax benefit of an ordinary deduction for the current value and no tax on the appreciation may reduce to the vanishing point the out-of-pocket cost to a donor, and correspondingly enlarge the public portion of the gift. Yet in such cases the donor may impose express or implied conditions on a gift that render it less valuable to the public. Thus a donor may require the work to be displayed in a particular way or may require the museum to accept, in addition, works in which it otherwise would have little interest. The museum accepts the gift because, even with conditions, it is better than nothing at all, but the donor's power to impose conditions derives from the leverage of indirect public funding.

In the simplest case, the donor may require only that the museum not sell the work. While there is much to be said in support of the view that a work of art owned by a public institution should not be sold back to the private market, a retention condition may limit the public benefit of the gift. For example, such restrictions usually prevent museums from selling or exchanging works of art with other museums, thereby barring any reallocation of the works to better serve the viewing public.

RECOMMENDATIONS

This brief look at two important tax subsidies that affect the arts suggests the need for several different kinds of remedies. One factor limiting appropriate analysis is the absence of reliable data from which conclusions can be drawn. The Internal Revenue Service and other tax-collecting agencies should begin to assemble data concerning tax-exempt institutions so that informed policy decisions are possible.

For the property tax exemption, and other similar tax subsidies that tie public support to the use of a particular production input, the best remedy is to sever the tie and provide the subsidy without the condition. In the case of the property tax exemption, this would mean repeal of the exemption and application of the same number of dollars to the cultural institutions based on the particular activities from which the public benefits. After an appropriate transition period, the subsidy so provided should become subject to the normal political process, increased or decreased like any other public grant. If the recent New York experience, which ended in enthusiastic public support of property tax exemptions for cultural institutions, is any indication, the institutions might well gain appreciably in dollars through full participation in the political process. But at the same dollar level of subsidy the absence of a requirement that the institution invest in real estate to get the grant would enable it to order its affairs more efficiently.

Two changes in the tax rules governing the charitable contribution deduction follow from the earlier description of the deduction. First, the proportion of public funds carried by each dollar of private donation should be equalized and not weighted heavily toward wealthy individuals. One way to achieve such a result is to substitute a tax credit at a uniform rate for the present deduction.

Second, the full-deduction rule for gifts in kind of appreciated property, which further distorts the public cost and private decision-making balance, should be eliminated.

Institutions currently labor under express and implied conditions imposed by donors. We propose two changes. First, a "sunset" provision should prevent enforcement of donor restrictions after a reasonable period of time, such as 25 years. Second, museums should be encouraged to sell or exchange artworks among themselves to eliminate misallo-cations of unique works. This might be done by requiring that gifts on which a tax deduction or credit is claimed be offered at reserve auction to other museums. The museums initially receiving the gift might still refuse all offers received and keep the work, but the cost of that decision would be known, as would the value of the work, to the bidding institutions.

It is not possible to prevent donors from expressing their desires about the maintenance or use of gifts, but with these legal restrictions the museum could defend its interest, and that of other museums, much more vigorously.

Indirect distribution of aid to charities generally has virtues that no direct grant system can provide. But particular indirect aid programs also have drawbacks that are not widely known. Wider discussion and understanding of this two-thirds of the cultural public support system will enable us to adjust these mechanisms for a better balance of virtues and defects.

ANNALS, *AAPSS*, **471**, January 1984

Arts Funding: Growth and Change
Between 1963 and 1983

By KENNETH GOODY

ABSTRACT: Between 1963 and 1983, not only was there a tremendous growth in the amount of money given to the arts by foundations, corporations, and government, but a substantial shift in the mix of these funds as well. While corporate support has remained a solidly important source, government funding has become increasingly important to the arts as foundation support has become less so. Given the dependence of arts organizations on these sources, the range of focus and purpose of their programs and their expectations for the future are important. A survey of private and corporate foundations and corporate giving programs highlights the hesitation of both of these groups to support artistic projects directly, experimental work, or newly established organizations. Additionally, both foundations and corporations have become more likely to fund administrative projects and arts service organizations. This range of focus of government support is very broad, but the purpose of this funding has been controversial. The short-term future of arts funding does not appear as dim as recently expected, and may bring increases.

Kenneth Goody consults on public policy issues pertaining to corporate, government, and foundation funding of the nonprofit sector. His research and analysis has included the arts, humanities, international education, international relations research, and international agricultural development.

NOTE: This article is excerpted from work in progress commissioned by the Arts and Humanities Division of the Rockefeller Foundation. A more complete analysis of arts funding, together with a section on funding for individual creative artists, will be complemented with an investigation of the funding of humanities activities, including advanced humanities research and fellowships, humanities in the schools, and international education.

Many social and political forces have combined, at this moment of history . . . [and] provide an unparalleled opportunity for the arts and the nation. . . . Wisely applied, all these factors can lead to an environment more conducive to distinguished performance and to a higher level of artistic accomplishment . . . one thing is immediately clear: The potential for successful development of the performing arts is tremendous.[1]

Viewed in quantitative terms, the great potential for the arts in the United States, as recognized in the preceding passage from the 1965 *Rockefeller Brothers Panel Report on the Performing Arts,* has been met. In the nearly 20 years since the report was issued, not only has the number of arts organizations increased at a phenomenal rate— major symphony orchestras doubling; resident professional theaters quadrupling; professional dance companies increasing by a factor of ten—but so has the size of the American audience. Perhaps the clearest indicator of how the arts have become a central part of American life can be seen in the vast increase in money spent for artistic purposes nationwide. Money given to the arts by local, state, and federal government, foundations and corporations has increased by more than 2000 percent, from approximately $40 million in 1963 to approximately—and conservatively —$940 million in 1982. Even if inflation is considered, the increase is nearly 800 percent.

Although most observers have noted the tremendous growth over the past two decades in arts funding, an examination of arts literature indicates that

this is an area that has received little systematic study. This assessment of the support provided to the arts by federal, state, and local governments, corporations, and foundations is not meant to be a follow-up to the broadly conceived Rockefeller panel report. Rather, utilizing data that the panel had collected for 1963 as a starting point, this article will attempt to analyze the growth in aggregate funding levels over the past 20 years, and through an extensive survey of private and corporate foundations and corporate giving programs attempt to describe the range and purpose of support provided by these sources to the arts.

THE GROWTH OF ARTS FUNDING

The tremendous expansion of arts funding could not have been better timed. The health of the professional arts community when studied by the Rockefeller panel was precarious. Theaters were decreasing in number; symphony orchestras and opera companies were few; professional dance was nearly nonexistent. Problems cutting across discipline lines included extremely low pay for artists and long periods of unemployment or underemployment; poor quality of professional training; "woefully inadequate" performing arts spaces; lack of sponsoring organizations; the constant specter of "crisis financing"; and a lack of service and information organizations. There existed, the panel concluded, a pressing need for substantial new funding.

This increase in arts funding not only strengthened preexisting institutions but, bolstered by an ever expanding audience, enabled many new organizations to be established. The growth in

1. *The Performing Arts: Problems and Prospects,* A Rockefeller Panel Report on the Future of Theater, Dance, and Music in America (New York: McGraw-Hill, 1965), p. 8.

the number of arts organizations, however, may have been too great for the increasing pool of money to reasonably support. Many of the problems that plagued the arts universe 20 years ago are still pressing: low pay and unemployment for creative and interpretive artists; the ever present reality of crisis financing, and the lack of effective central sources of information and dialogue.

Federal government

In 1963 almost all arts income, besides that from individual giving and earned sources, came from corporations and foundations. The National Endowment for the Arts had not been established, and only a few states had instituted formal arts programs. Figures for governments at all levels must certainly have been low and were not specifically recorded. The Rockefeller panel estimated that foundations gave about 1.5 percent of their total grants that year, or almost $12 million, to the performing arts. Corporate support was estimated to be about $20 million, or 3 percent of their total giving. The actual figure would be slightly higher if visual arts and the few incipient government programs were factored in.

Recognizing that diversification was one way to increase substantially the funds available to the arts, the panel wrote,

[we] stress the value of broadening the base of financial support. This can only be accomplished if the organizations are imaginative and effective . . . and if the public is made fully aware of the significance of the work being done.[2]

2. Ibid., p. 4.

While the panel reminded corporations that a healthy cultural environment was clearly in their best interests, and foundations that the arts are a natural area for the bold and venturesome projects for which foundations are designed, it was from government that the panel hoped for the most support. Although the history of the development of the National Endowment for the Arts, and the role of the Rockefeller panel, are beyond the scope of this assessment, the following quotation from the panel is telling of the period.

More and more voices propose that the performing arts turn to the government for aid. They say very simply that the arts should be made far more widely available to the many than it is possible to make them by private support alone. It is therefore necessary to explore the present and potential roles of government in support for the arts.[3]

Direct federal funding of the arts was unfolding as the panel's report was released. The creation of the National Council on the Arts in 1964 was followed in 1965 by the establishment of the National Foundation on the Arts and Humanities, and its components, the National Endowment for the Arts (NEA) and the National Endowment for the Humanities (NEH). These acts generated controversy, largely centered around the issue of the potential impact of government on the quality of the arts. The panel wrote,

Perhaps an even greater danger of support by any level of government is the encouragement of mediocrity. If public funds for the arts were spread among all the arts organizations regardless of quality . . . then improvement in the quality of the arts would be negligible—no matter how much is spent.[4]

3. Ibid., p. 112.
4. Ibid., p. 145.

TABLE 1
NATIONAL ENDOWMENT FOR THE ARTS GRANTS EXPENDITURES

	1966	1968	1970	1972	1974	1976	1978	1880	1982	1983	1984*
Millions of dollars	1.8	8.5	10.4	28.8	59.6	81.3	114.6	142.4	132.1	131.3	148.9
Biennial percentage change		+377	+23	+176	+107	+36	+41	+24	-7	-6	+13

SOURCE: National Endowment for the Arts, Annual reports 1966-84.
NOTE: Table does not include administrative costs.
*Congressional appropriation.

Although the debate on the role of the government in the arts was never settled, direct federal support grew rapidly. In 1966 the NEA made grants totaling $1.8 million, a figure that by 1980 had increased to $142.4 million, decreasing somewhat in 1983 to $131.3 million, as shown in Table 1.

State government

Appropriations by state governments to the arts also increased rapidly. In 1963 only New York, North Carolina, and California had developed programs of arts funding. Spurred in part by the existence of the NEA, mandated by legislation to make block grants to the states, and in part by both a general awakening of interest by state legislators and a realization of the economic impact of the arts on local economies and tourism, in 1974 each state had an arts council supported by both NEA grants and legislative appropriations. As Table 2 shows, funding increased from $2.7 million in 1966 to $125 million in 1983.

Local government

Although there are no national aggregate data for local government arts support, funds given by cities and towns may have increased at a rate similar to that of states. Data for local support have not been collected systematically for many reasons, including differing accounting procedures, variation in definitions used, and the lack of a centralized information source. It may be estimated, however, that there are over 2000 local arts councils, most of which receive municipal funds and make grants to support a variety of local organizations.

A 1982 study of 24 large city arts agencies estimates that they spent approximately $80 million in 1981.[5] While this figure may not be a reliable indicator of total local giving, the study highlights the nature of much city support: 60 percent went to operate city-owned cultural facilities, usually museums. This is certainly the case in New York City, as operating expenses of city-owned museums claim over 90 percent of the Department of Cultural Affairs' budget.

Indirect governmental support

Local support highlights the importance—and obscurity—of indirect gov-

5. David Cwi, *City Arts Support: Status and Issues* (Baltimore: Cultural Policy Institute, 1982).

TABLE 2
ARTS EXPENDITURES BY STATE GOVERNMENTS

	1966	1968	1970	1972	1974	1976	1978	1980	1982	1983
Millions of dollars	2.7	6.7	7.7	24.1	30.3	57.4	69.2	102.8	128.5	125.0
Biennial percentage change		+153	+14	+214	+26	+89	+20	+49	+25	−3

SOURCE: American Council for the Arts.

ernmental funds and services for the arts. New York City itemizes energy as a form of support, and estimates its cost as 25 percent of its arts support for 1981. Federal and state support, other than the NEA and state arts agency totals, have not been estimated, although one may assume they are significant. The 1979 edition of *Cultural Directory: Federal Funds and Services for the Arts and Humanities* lists over 300 programs of support.[6] Federal agencies such as the Departments of Commerce, Housing and Urban Development, Transportation, and Energy do not have formal arts programs. However, there are staff who coordinate the arts activities of agencies. These programs, which include financial aid in the form of grants, contracts, commissions, and loans; employment and training; and management advice, information, and statistical data, were particularly substantial in the late 1970s.

Foundations and corporations

Giving by foundations and corporations has increased from 1966 to 1982— both in terms of dollars and percentage

of total giving—but is not comparable to the rate of government funding.

Corporate giving increased from approximately $24 million in 1966 to approximately $336 million in 1982 or 1300 percent—nearly 600 percent if inflation is considered.[7] Overall corporate giving for the same period increased only about 260 percent, with support for the arts comprising about 3 percent of their total giving in 1966, and about 11 percent in 1982, shown in Table 3.

The Foundation Center reports that foundation giving to the arts has increased from roughly $38 million in 1966 to about $349 million in 1982, a jump of 950 percent. In 1966 the arts received about 2.6 percent of foundation giving; in 1982 the figure was 11.1 percent; overall foundation giving had increased by about 110 percent, as shown in Table 4.

The mix of funding sources

Not only has there been tremendous growth in the amount of money given to the arts by government, foundations, and corporations, but there also has been a substantial change in the mix of

6. *Cultural Directory: Federal Funds and Services for the Arts and Humanities* (Washington, DC: Smithsonian Institution, 1980); this is the last volume of this book that was printed.

7. Based on figures reported to the American Association of Fund Raising Counsel, Inc., by the Conference Board.

TABLE 3
CORPORATE GIVING TO THE ARTS

	Total Corporate Giving (millions of dollars)	Corporate Giving to Arts (millions of dollars)	Estimated Percentage of Total for Arts
1966	805	24	3
1968	1005	50	5
1970	797	40	5
1972	1009	70	7
1974	1200	96	8
1976	1487	134	9
1978	2084	210	10.1
1980	2359	257	10.9
1981	2600 (est.)	309	11.9
1982	2950 (est.)	336	11.4

SOURCES: Business Committee for the Arts; American Association for Fund Raising Counsel, Inc.; Conference Board.

NOTE: Definitions of "the arts" may vary among these sources.

TABLE 4
FOUNDATION GIVING TO THE ARTS

	Total Foundation Giving (millions of dollars)	Foundation Giving to Arts (millions of dollars)	Estimated Percentage of Total for Arts
1966	1250	38	3.0
1970	1900	114	6.0
1973	2000	200	10.0
1976	1900	247	13.0
1980	2810	289	10.3
1981	3060 (est.)	315	10.3
1982	3150 (est.)	349	11.1

SOURCES: Foundation Center; American Association for Fund Raising Counsel, Inc.

NOTE: Due to the availability of new data, the Foundation Center has recently revised upward data from 1976 to 1982. In 1981 this represents an increase in reported foundation giving of 17 percent, and shows that corporate giving has not surpassed that of foundations, as was previously thought.

these funds, as shown in Table 5. State and federal money, once representing about 5 percent of total contributions, now make up nearly 30 percent of arts giving. Foundations, which in 1966 led the field by giving 57 percent of all arts money, now account for about 37 percent of that total. The relative importance of corporations has remained constant; since 1966 funding from that sector has ranged from about 25 to 36 percent of the total.

RANGE OF PURPOSE AND
FOCUS OF ARTS FUNDING

Given the dependence of the arts on government, foundation, and corporate sources, it is important to understand the range of purpose and focus of their

TABLE 5
SUPPORT GIVEN TO THE ARTS, IN MILLIONS OF DOLLARS: 1963-82
(percentage of total)

	1963	1966	1970	1976	1980	1981	1982
Foundations	12	38	114	247	289	315(est.)	349(est.)
	(35)	(57)	(66)	(48)	(36)	(36)	(37)
Corporations	20	24	40	134	257	309(est.)	336(est.)
	(59)	(36)	(23)	(26)	(33)	(35)	(36)
State government	1.5	2.7	7.7	57	103	114	129
	(4)	(4)	(5)	(11)	(13)	(13)	(16)
Federal government	.5	1.8	10.4	81	142	147	132
	(1)	(3)	(6)	(16)	(18)	(17)	(14)
Total	34	66.5	172.1	519	791	885	946

SOURCES: 1963: The Rockefeller Panel; 1966-82: National Endowment for the Arts; American Association for Fund Raising Counsel; Conference Board; Foundation Center.

NOTE: Definitions of "the arts" vary among individual funders and information centers. Aggregations of data should be viewed as an approximation more than fact; this is particularly the case when data are compared over time.

giving, and how this may have developed.

Although it would be impossible to characterize the giving of groups as diverse as foundations, corporations, and government programs in generic terms, similarity of purpose and structure allow for comparison of like programs. An analysis of the giving patterns and future plans of a broad range of private and corporate foundation programs and corporate giving programs surveyed for this assessment sheds some light on general characteristics of each group, and their expectations for the future.

Foundations

Foundations, which exist solely to foster education, scientific and cultural purposes, and which are restricted only by charter and board sentiment, are often afforded great latitude in which to operate. The Rockefeller panel noted this when it wrote that foundations are able to "give particular encouragement

to the bold and the venturesome—an encouragement they are especially equipped to provide." The response of a diverse group of foundations,[8] however,

8. The 226 corporate and private foundations surveyed between December 1982 and February 1983 were selected randomly from a group of arts funders provided by the Foundation Center. They were asked to supply information on a range of topics, including substantive area of arts giving; program rationales; dollar figures; purposes of grants; changes in program structure; grants to individuals; type of arts organizations supported; funding for the experimental or avant-garde; funding partnerships; and expectations for the future. Thirty replied that they did not have an arts program; 20 replied that due to a lack of staff they could not complete the questionnaire. Of the remainder, 94—57 percent—replied. The respondent group is broad and encompasses foundations of all sizes and locations: 13 percent make over $10 million in grants per year; 16 percent make $5-10 million in grants; 43 percent, $1-5 million in grants; and 29 percent make less than $1 million in grants. Surprisingly the respondent sample over-represents smaller foundations. The Foundation Center reports the following statistics for size of foundation grants: 16 percent of the foundations listed in the Foundation Directory make over $10 million per year; 13 percent make $5-10 million; 56

would suggest that most do not operate in that way when giving to the arts. Considering the purposes of foundation grants and the types of organizations funded, foundations—for many reasons, but particularly for lack of staff—tend not to fund artistic projects directly or emerging experimental work.

The survey offered a range of possible funding options in the arts: general support; administrative/income development/capital expansion projects; direct funding for specific artistic purposes; arts services organizations; and the study of policy issues. Preliminary analysis of responses shows that only half the respondents have at some time or another, over the past 20 years, given direct support for an artistic effort. One-third have given money for general support, and the remainder—20 percent—have given exclusively for administrative costs or to service organizations. This apparent unwillingness to fund direct artistic costs is stronger among corporate foundations: only one-third of corporate foundations have funded artistic projects, as opposed to 60 percent of the independent group.

Although a hesitancy to fund art programs directly is not surprising, over the past 20 years an increasing number of both private and corporate foundations have begun funding non-art-related activities, largely, it appears, at the cost of artistic projects. Of the 80 percent of survey respondents who have changed the format of their arts giving programs over the past 20 years, about 70 percent

have begun funding non-performance projects. Data from the Foundation Center support this trend, as shown in Table 6: between 1978 and 1981 total foundation giving to the arts increased by 68 percent. However, giving to what is labeled "general culture," a broad category of which administrative/service support is a major component, increased by 450 percent. Arts professionals appear successful in securing foundation grants.

Another indication of what may be called foundation cautiousness is the type of organization funded. When asked if their giving included any support for the avant-garde, only one-third responded positively, and about one-half of these responses can be considered qualified. This group tends to consist of foundations with arts programs of over $150,000. The following statements of respondents not funding the avant-garde are illustrative:

1. "Our directors prefer to support traditional art forms accepted and supported by the community."

2. "[We have] no money to waste as venture capital."

3. "[We] do not see [ourselves] as an arbiter of artistic taste for the community. Therefore, decisions regarding funding in the arts tend to be made on the basis of management/fiscal considerations rather than artistic merit."

4. "[The] risk [is] greater than [the] reward."

5. "No [we do not fund the avant-garde]. Grantees must meet requirements of the IRS."

Similarly, when asked if they tend to support organizations of "proven reputation," or "those of promise, but not established achievement," 65 percent indicated that they support established organizations exclusively.

---

percent make $1-5 million; and 14 percent make less than $1 million. Fifty-two percent of respondents are located in the 20 largest U.S. cities, and 48 percent in smaller cities and towns. The respondent population is somewhat biased toward large city foundations: 40 percent of those not responding are located in big cities and 60 percent are not.

TABLE 6
FOUNDATION GIVING TO ARTS AREAS
(percentage increase from 1978-81)

Art and architecture	80
General culture—service organizations	450
Media and communication	3
Music	5
Theater and dance	6
Total increase	68

SOURCE: Foundation Center Data Bank.

NOTE: 66.2% of the overall increase went to the category General Culture Service Organizations.

Corporations

In almost all areas of corporate giving, the goal is to be widely recognized as a good citizen through efforts geared toward improving the overall environment of corporate locations. The arts lend themselves well to these purposes: the arts can be highly visible, relatively noncontroversial, enjoyed or even participated in by employees and the public, and they are usually high on the public's agenda. Corporate support represented 36 percent of all giving to the arts in 1982.

Similar to foundations, survey responses indicate that corporations tend to hesitate to fund direct artistic costs or making grant decisions based on artistic criteria.[9] This reflects a sensitivity to

9. The 97 corporate giving programs surveyed were selected randomly from those listed in *Guide to Corporate Giving in the Arts,* published by the American Council for the Arts. Nine replied that they did not give to the arts; of the remainder, 38—43 percent—replied. Thirty-four percent of respondents give more than $3 million away each year, 24 percent give $1-3 million; 21 percent give $500,000-$1 million per year; and 21 percent give less than $500,000 per year. Fifty-one percent of the respondents are located in the 20 largest U.S. cities, and 49 percent in smaller cities and towns. Respondents are biased toward large city programs just as are foundation respondents: 40 per-

staff inexperience in the arts. Most corporate grants are not for project support, and perhaps reflecting a business bias, most support administrative projects and service organizations. General support is given only by about one-third, and it would seem that usually the best-known local arts group receives corporate attention.

Many corporations engage in forms of support other than the outright giving of money. In-kind services, donated materials and use of corporate facilities, purchases of art, and matching employee gifts are employed by at least one-half of the respondents. Many corporations choose to maximize an alternative method of giving to the arts: considering grants as advertising efforts and treating them as a business expense. This represents a growing area of support that is usually not included in dollar figures for corporate donations, an area that arts organizations should be aware of as they approach corporate grant makers.

Major factors in how corporate giving differs from foundation giving are the importance of the chief executive officer and the emphasis on local giving.

cent of those not responding are located in big cities and 60 percent are not.

Although most corporations tend to support established organizations, many also support amateur groups that encourage employee participation. Corporations in cities—usually with larger programs and staff—are more likely to support newly established groups and the avant-garde. Indeed, of the 23 percent of all corporate programs that support experimental work, roughly 65 percent are located in large cities.

Federal, state and local government

The impact of government support for the arts has been a center of controversy for the last 20 years. Although this is a complex issue, concern registered by the Rockefeller panel in 1965 highlights the question:

Popularization in any realm often leads to a reduction of standards. In our effort to broaden the audience base, we must not be led to accept imitation as a substitute for creation, mediocrity as a stand-in for excellence. Democratization carries with it a peril for the arts.[10]

Government programs for the arts exist, essentially, for three reasons:

—to facilitate overall excellence in artistic creation and performance;

—to increase public access to the arts; and

—to nurture art forms that tend not to be funded by private sources.

Total direct state and federal support for these purposes has increased since 1963 from perhaps $1 million to approximately $260 million in 1983.

The purpose and focus of government support for the arts is very broad

and beyond the scope of this assessment. To be sure, organizations ranging from the most established, to the avant-garde, to the ethnic and regional receive government support. That support comes in many forms, ranging from matching capital expenditure programs to commissioned experimental choreography.

As government programs are funded by tax revenues, factors are considered in grant making that are not necessarily considered by foundations and corporations. This has led in part to intense competition for government funds by numerous groups. A resolution passed by the Forty-second Annual Conference of Mayors in 1974 makes this clear.

That city governments working together with the public at large shall help to effect a new national goal: "That no American shall be deprived of the opportunity to experience (or to respond artistically to) the beauty in life by barrier of circumstance, income, background, remoteness or race."

An example of this is consideration of geographical location or "remoteness." The National Committee for Cultural Resources presents one argument when it states,

Although the arts are nationwide in scope, and although even small communities have their own arts organizations, there is a strong tendency toward centralization of the arts in the larger cities. This makes some of the arts inaccessible, both geographically and economically, to large numbers of people.[11]

The contradictory argument is made in a 1980 report entitled *Public and Private Support for the Arts in New York City*. Concerning federal funding, the report takes note of

10. *The Performing Arts*, p. 207.

11. *National Report on the Arts* (New York: National Committee for Cultural Resources, 1976), p. 25.

[the] increase in political pressure, as congressmen and senators . . . look for support for their constituents—support that is based on geographic distinctions, not simply artistic merit. As far as New York City and New York State are concerned, this has meant that a decreasing portion of Endowment support has been coming here over the past few years. . . .

with more and smaller grants, the impact of the program might well be dissipated. . . .

emerging arts organizations of quality, wherever they are located, deserve encouragement and financial support, but those organizations that serve strictly local audiences should be first supported by their own communities.[12]

Each factor in government decision making involves its own set of arguments and factions. One outgrowth of this is what some have referred to as politicization of the arts. As *Public and Private Support* states, "an increasing number of arts organizations have begun to look to the political process for . . . means of support."

Development of the service sector

An additional result of government funding, states a report published by the Center for Arts Information, has been

a sudden growth in the nonprofit arts field in the United States. "Arts administration" has now emerged as a recognized profession. The arts service field has directly paralleled this growth.[13]

The arts service field has indeed paralleled this growth. The number of organizations may number over 500 nationwide, with probably 100 or so based in New York City. The range of services provided by the group is very diverse—fund raising, management help, coordination of volunteers, and information. In addition, many groups serve special constituencies, and look after the interests of a particular type of arts organization.

The potential importance for such a sector was recognized by the Rockefeller panel in 1965 when it noted that

there is a need for the creation of new organizations . . . a wide variety of service and information organizations is necessary to collect statistics and to provide guidance on the general direction of growth and change, and to bring together those responsible for the direction of arts organizations to exchange ideas about the solution of common problems.[14]

Funding for the service sector has apparently been plentiful. Although data are incomplete with regard to the funds available to this sector, as they are for the arts overall, foundations and governments have increased their funding for this group. Foundation funds for the category "general culture," of which service organizations are a large component, increased 450 percent between 1978 and 1981, as compared to an increase of 68 percent for total foundation arts giving. This comprises one-third of foundation funds to the arts. Although available figures for corporate giving are not itemized, survey responses would suggest strong corporate support for these purposes. The NEA has been

12. *Public and Private Support for the Arts in New York City* (New York: Cultural Assistance Center, 1980), pp. 115-17.

13. Ellen Thurston, *A Preliminary Survey and Study of Management Assistance Programs* (New York: Center for Arts Information, 1979), p. 7.

14. *The Performing Arts,* p. 15.

supporting this group, largely through its Services to the Field Program, which represents about 7 to 10 percent of its budget. It would appear that this service sector is an entrenched part of the arts community in the United States.

CONCLUSIONS AND PROSPECTS FOR THE FUTURE

In considering the overall condition of the arts universe, and the changes that have occurred over the past 20 years, one is struck by the tremendous increase in public interest in the arts, in the number of arts organizations, and in the number of dollars given for artistic purposes. A closer examination of the three major sources of funds is necessary to appreciate the full scope of the increase in funding.

Foundations, although possessing the potential for bold and venturesome giving, have acted cautiously in the arts area. The results of a survey conducted for this assessment indicate that only one-half fund direct project costs; most fund, to one extent or another, administrative projects and service organizations. Furthermore, only one-third of the group fund avant-garde activities or newly emerging groups. Foundation funds represent about 35 percent of total money received by arts organizations, down from about 60 percent in 1966.

Corporate giving programs, geared to presenting the corporation as a good citizen, tend to reflect the interests and taste of the community that the corporation hopes to influence. The survey data show that most corporations fund nonperformance-related costs and are not inclined to support the avant-garde or emerging organizations. Corporations

provide a major portion of arts funding—approximately 36 percent, which, although there was a proportional drop in the early 1970s, has remained constant over the period under review.

The aims of government funding for the arts, on both state and federal levels, which is supported by tax revenue and tied to the political process, has generated controversy for two decades. Some claim that the general purposes of promoting excellence are in contradiction to promoting less recognized art forms and expanding the overall arts audience. Funding criteria include nonartistic or institutional considerations. Total direct government funds make up about 30 percent of the total, up from 7 percent in 1966. Giving by local government and the indirect state and federal services and funds are probably an important, somewhat hidden, source of arts support.

An outgrowth of both the need for management advice and the politicization of the arts, has been the emergence of the service organization. Although not serving the full need as a central source of information and dialogue, the service sector claims an increasing share of arts funding.

Predicting future patterns of grant makers is imprecise at best, but survey responses shed light on short-term prospects. Will the trend for foundations and corporations to devote increasing portions of their funds to the arts continue?

The prospects for increased foundation funding of the arts in the short term probably are not bright. Respondents were asked to give dollar figures for their arts giving for the years 1964, 1970, 1976, 1979, 1980, 1981, and 1982 and estimates for 1983. From those figures it is clear that a full 50 percent gave their largest amount during 1981 or before. Only 20 percent of the respondents intend specifically to increase their giving to the arts in 1983. The overwhelming reason cited for this is perceived greater need in social service, education, and health areas. It appears that many foundations consider the arts something of a luxury in the face of intense competing demands.

Responses from corporate giving programs present a different picture. About 75 percent of the respondents plan to increase their giving to the arts in 1983. This response is tempered, however, as nearly 60 percent of respondents replied in a somewhat negative fashion when they were asked for their "own personal sense for the future of [overall] corporate support for the arts." The following quotation is illustrative: "[We] anticipate that the bulk of our contribution dollar will go to welfare organizations. Quality of life is important, but basic human needs must be met first."

It also appears that corporate giving programs may become increasingly cautious, as these responses indicate.

1. "Corporate support will tend to be more and more restricted to established major institutions—recession environment works against creative and original new funding in favor of greater assumed community social needs."

2. "Corporations will be more concerned to receive direct public recognition . . . the 'community good' will no longer be a reason that is easily condoned by shareholders."

3. "Corporations are going to closely scrutinize the nonprofit organizations . . . small inefficient organizations will not survive and community impact will be an important ingredient in reviewing requests for corporate funding."

4. "[There should be] more focus on good management and possibilities for earned income."

The most important factor determining the level of corporate contributions is corporate profits. This may, in fact, explain the large number of respondents who, although able to increase giving in 1983, expressed doubts about the future. In fact, as the following quotation makes clear, an unknown, but probably not insignificant, number of corporations have sharply reduced or ceased their giving programs.

[we] recently reported [our] second consecutive loss year. Since funding of our contributions program is based on a percentage of pretax earnings for the prior year, we have been extremely limited in considering contributions to the arts as well as social and educational programs.

In considering overall corporate support for the arts, survey data show that while corporate giving programs plan to increase support for the arts, data on corporate foundations indicate that they are not going to increase support.

Current political pressures on federal, state, and local governments to reduce deficits will probably preclude large increases in government support for the arts and may lead to decreases, particularly in the form of indirect support. Although the NEA's budget was cut by approximately 10 percent in 1982, the reduction in 1983 was only 1 percent. Indeed there will probably be an increase in 1984 in direct federal support in the arts, as the congressional appropriation for the agency for 1984 shows a 13 percent rise over the 1983 level. Congress apparently has decided that Endowment funds are worth fighting for, and, given the relatively small amount of funds and great public support, the administration has decided not to continue early attempts to cut the arts budget in half.

One may look forward to an increase in overall state arts support. Figures recently released by the National Association of State Arts Agencies estimated that total state giving will increase about 9.5 percent for 1984.

It is very difficult to gauge local arts giving. Taking into consideration the financial state of many municipalities, however, prospects for greatly increased funding are dim. Any cuts that are to be made in local giving will most likely be reflected not in operational budgets for city-owned arts facilities, but in grant programs to arts organizations.

It seems clear that the fear that government support for the arts would be slashed has been unfounded. In fact, the arts may enjoy slightly increased support from government sources in the short term and, perhaps if the case for the arts can be made well enough, greatly increased support in the long term.

BOOK DEPARTMENT

INTERNATIONAL RELATIONS AND POLITICS

CASTLE, EMERY N. and KENZO HEMMI, eds., with Sally A. Skillings. *U.S.-Japanese Agricultural Trade Relations.* Pp. xvii, 436. Baltimore: Johns Hopkins University Press, 1982. $35.00. Paperbound, $14.95.

This is a very useful, highly integrated, and valuable contribution to the overall analysis of U.S.-Japan relations. Not only scholarly and well written, the book is also timely, particularly in view of intense foreign demands of wider access to Japan's agricultural market and the unabating urges to make greater efforts to open Japan for key farm products, especially beef and oranges, for which the United States is strongly demanding import liberalization, and against which Japan's powerful Ministry of Agriculture, Forestry, and Fisheries argues that there is a limit to what it can do. This work succeeds admirably in dispelling some of the crudest assumptions of Japanese intransigence and American aggressiveness in agricultural trade.

This volume, written by a team made up of several American and Japanese contributors, is probably the most systematic and penetrating comparative study yet completed on this important topic. The work's underlying premise is that the two agricultural economies are basically complementary and interdependent, yet not without vexing aspects, which have led to misperceptions in Japan and the United States.

Part I offers an overview of U.S.-Japanese agricultural trade problems, an outline of the editors' policy prescriptions, as well as a discussion of the world food situation and the prospects in general. Part 2 analyzes the general domestic setting of agriculture and agricultural policy in Japan and the United States. Part 3 presents a detailed study of each Japanese and American agricultural policymaking, and examines their linkage to the overall bilateral relationship. Finally Part 4 deals with the basic components and dynamics of U.S.-Japanese agricultural interdependence.

One of the major strengths of this volume lies in its analytical framework, which helps immensely in the understanding of the complexities and intricacies surrounding U.S.-Japanese agricultural trade. Indeed the entire work is resolutely comparative in its conception and presentation; Japanese and American contributions are mutually reinforcing and complementary. Rather than merely recording national differences, the work as a whole explains a great deal about similarities of Japanese and American politicoeconomic forces, their institutional arrangements, organization, and processes, and their impact on the agenda setting of agricultural policy and trade, all of which adds intrinsic value to this cross-Pacific endeavor.

Some minor critical remarks seem in place. For one, the Liberal Democratic Party has been in power continually since 1955 and not, as the book states, 1948. More important, the pursuit of common interest and similar world objectives should not be extrapolated from the basic complementariness of the two agricultural economies. No doubt Japan and the United States are close in a political, security, and economic sense, but, as this volume clearly shows, they are still far apart in terms of their agricultural trade preferences and policies, which, by and large, may be seen as a function of Japan's food scarcity dilemma and the fundamental differences between Japan's position on the world's future food situation and policy, and that of the United States.

This notwithstanding it is hoped this important work gets the attention it deserves by specialists and nonspecialists alike.

WALTER ARNOLD
Miami University
Oxford
Ohio

CROSS, HARRY E. and JAMES A. SANDOS. *Across the Border: Rural Development in Mexico and Recent Migration to the United States.* Pp. xix, 198. Berkeley: Institute of Governmental Studies, University of California, 1981. $12.00.

Cross and Sandos have written a generally informative, accessible, and sensible book on Mexican-U.S. migration. They provide good historical perspectives, particularly regarding the Mexican sending region—not surprising, since both authors are historians with previous work on Mexico. They usually show sensitivity to data problems, which are very important to recognize in order to have any hope of understanding the activities and impacts of illegal immigrants; for example, data collected on illegal migrants within a

day or two of entry may not provide much insight about the longer-run activities and impact of illegal immigrants. Cross and Sandos often are reasonable in their use of simple economic models to gain insight in the face of incomplete information.

The book is organized into three parts. The first part—the first five chapters—provides historical context on the sending and receiving regions, the sizes and composition of the migratory flows, and the major Mexican and U.S. policies that have affected the migratory flows. Focus is on the dominant sending region constituted by the poor rural areas of the five north central—not border—states of Durango, Guanajuato, Jalisco, Michoacán, San Luis Potosí, and Zacatecas. Cross and Sandos survey historical developments from 1880 on, with emphasis on the severe dislocations experienced during the revolution (1913-20) and the religious uprising of the Cristeros (1926-29); the limitations of land reform; biases of the green revolution in agriculture in favor of irrigated wheat cultivation—and, thus, relatively against poorer dryland maize producers; and the nature of agricultural price policies.

While much of the discussion is plausible, at times Cross and Sandos's explanations seem only to push questions back one step. For example, in the postrevolutionary period, they claim, *haciendas* cut drastically their permanent labor force to rely on sharecropping and renting in order to shift some of the investment and risk burden to peasant farmers, while at the same time labor supply expanded rapidly due to accelerated population growth. But why did the advantages of investment and risk sharing come into existence only after the revolution? And why did population growth rates double?

The second part, Chapter 6, considers the contemporary impact of illegal Mexican migration on the United States. This chapter primarily is comprised of a thoughtful survey of previous studies relating to the size of illegal Mexican immigration, with numbers in the mid-1970s estimated to be in the two to five million range; the labor market impact, with conclusions dependent upon assumptions about the extent of substitution of lower-priced migrant labor for higher-priced citizen labor; and participation in income taxes, social security, welfare benefits, unemployment compensation, and education and health facilities, with estimates varying widely, but suggesting a strong positive association with duration of stay.

The third part, Chapter 7, makes policy proposals. For the United States, Cross and Sandos recommend a five-year program to admit migrants on one-year temporary visas—subject to health, literacy, and age requirements, and a $300 deposit refundable upon exit within a year—with visa holders basically incurring rights and responsibilities comparable to those of citizens. The rationale for this proposal is that while there are no likely changes that will reduce sharply the immigration in the near term, such a procedure would permit acquisition of more reliable information about the phenomenon and a sounder basis for policy at a later time. For Mexico they recommend increased rural employment opportunities and other policies that would direct more resources to the lower end of the income distribution. The details of their recommendation, however, are not unquestionable. For example, they claim that "at the very least, the price of maize should reflect the cost of maize farming" and that "for small farmers, credit is the greatest single stimulus to agricultural innovations." But the pricing recommendation is ambiguous or a recipe for disaster. For example, should the price of maize be sufficient to cover cultivation costs in the desert? And the role of credit as a magic stimulus is a myth that long has been discarded by most scholars of developing agriculture. Finally, they presume that it is in the Mexican government's interest to cooperate in lessening migratory flows, but it may not be, particularly in periods of substantial readjustment such as the de la Madrid administration faced upon its inauguration.

Despite some questions about some dimensions of the analysis, I recommend this book to those interested in Mexican history and development, U.S. labor markets and social service demands—particularly in the Southwest—Mexican-U.S. relations, and international migration.

JERE R. BEHRMAN
University of Pennsylvania
Philadelphia

MITCHELL, C. R. *The Structure of International Conflict.* Pp. 355. New York: St. Martin's Press, 1981. $35.00.

The Structure of International Conflict was written to be a comprehensive introduction to conflict research, primarily intended for undergraduates in the social sciences. Although the primary focus is on conflict among nation states, the book is based on the assumption that conflict among human beings, groups of humans, and human organizations is a generic phenomenon, such that there are similarities among conflicts at the various levels. As with a medical textbook concerning a disease, Mitchell's clear purpose is to suggest how conflict can be resolved or at least contained and managed. He summarizes previously published research findings and theories of others; his contribution is synthesis rather than new ideas or findings. The book is a good summary of the state of knowledge in the field.

Criticisms of this book are thus more directed toward the state of knowledge in the field of conflict research than at the book itself: that the book is in some measure unsatisfying is more the fault of the field than of the author. It is full of maxims about the sources of conflict, how conflicts develop, and methods for resolving or managing and containing conflicts. There can be no question that the understanding of all of these matters is more substantial and more systematic than it was before conflict research became a popular field. Yet the book contains very few solidly based generalizations about the conditions under which the various maxims might apply. This is especially troublesome since several of the maxims suggest contradictory courses of action. For example, threats may increase the willingness of an adversary to negotiate, but they may also have exactly the opposite effect. Until more is known about the circumstances in which the several maxims are likely to be applicable, even though the potentialities of conflicts may be clearer, little practical guidance will have been provided concerning the courses of action that should be chosen.

Another problem with the book is the implicit overriding goal of conflict resolution. In the nuclear-missile era, when unprecedented and unimaginable destruction could be the consequence of international conflict, this goal is widely shared, but it is not the only goal either of those who seek to preserve the existing distribution of values or of those who aspire to change this distribution. The book seldom deals with these other goals and consequently seems disembodied from the reality of conflict.

Perhaps these flaws are conditions of the progress conflict research has made. Correcting them, however, will be the precondition if conflict research is to make the contribution to which its practitioners aspire. *The Structure of International Conflict* accurately reflects both the progress and the shortcomings of the field.

HAROLD K. JACOBSON
University of Michigan
Ann Arbor

ONEAL, JOHN R. *Foreign Policy Making in Times of Crisis.* Pp. ix, 358. Columbus: Ohio State University Press, 1982. $27.50.

International crises are spectacular and perhaps unique events. Some can change the course of world history; and almost by definition crises can have substantial impacts for either good or ill upon the nations involved. An attempt to understand the dynamics of crisis behavior, therefore, could yield important results both for explaining nations' activities in the international arena, and for developing policy prescriptions about how to handle crisis situations. In this book John R. Oneal, a political science professor at

Vanderbilt, presents three historical case studies of international crises. He argues that while crises present direct threats to a state's interests and perhaps even to its existence, they also create an opportunity for innovative decisions and institutional changes that are ordinarily not possible in the humdrum world of incremental policymaking. Thus he chronicles three crises in the hope that an understanding of them might suggest better means for handling future international upheavals.

The case studies concern the Truman administration's response to three major instances of perceived Soviet aggression during the opening of the Cold War: (1) the reluctance of Soviet forces to withdraw from northern Iran after World War II; (2) the rising fortunes of the communists in the Greek Civil War in late 1946 and early 1947; and (3) the Berlin blockade. Each of three crises is described historically in terms of three phases: destabilization, the central phase of decision and response, and restabilization.

The crises are then analyzed according to their impact on four theoretical variables. The first is the prevalent image of the enemy. Iran and the Greek Civil War changed American perceptions of the USSR quite significantly, as the Soviets came to be viewed as implacable enemies on the verge of initiating a major military confrontation. The Berlin blockade, in contrast, changed images in the opposite direction, suggesting a Soviet reluctance to set off armed combat. The goals of the United States toward the Soviet Union, such as the development of military containment and nonmilitary policies designed to rebuild the West, form the second dimension. The third variable is change in decision-making coalitions and participants; and Oneal charts the ups and downs of various political figures, although some of these personnel changes seem only marginally related to the crises themselves. Finally, crises can also stimulate changes in organizational structure. The onset of the Cold War and America's growing involvement in international affairs stimulated the growth of coordinating bodies in the foreign policymaking realm, such as a unified Department of Defense and the National Security Agency. The book concludes with a balanced assessment of the efficiency and effectiveness of U.S. policymaking during these crises and with an attempt to draw implications from the case studies for making decisions under crisis conditions.

This book has done a laudable job of integrating historical description with theoretical and conceptual analysis to help our understanding of crisis behavior. The study still could be extended in several ways. First, a much wider variety of cases would obviously be necessary to support broad generalizations. Second, the observation that crises generate a need for policy coordination and oversight could be applied to explain the growing power of irregulars in American foreign policymaking at the expense of regular bureaucracies and agencies. Third, Oneal's conclusions about ways for better processing information and evaluating options during crises seem somewhat timid in view of his goal to "suggest how these confrontations might best be managed so that war can be avoided." In sum, *Foreign Policy Making in Times of Crisis* is a solid piece of research and suggests several paths for future study concerning this important topic.

CAL CLARK

University of Wyoming
Laramie

*AFRICA, ASIA, AND
LATIN AMERICA*

BRAUN, OTTO. *A Comintern Agent in China, 1932-1939*. Translated by Jeanne Moore. Pp. xii, 278. Stanford, CA: Stanford University Press, 1982. $25.00.

Otto Braun's memoirs of the Long March, now available for the first time in a fine English translation, are an important addition to the literature on Mao Tse-tung and the rise of Chinese communism. A German Comintern agent, he was the only westerner to accompany the Communists from Kiangsi to Shensi and to witness the rise of Mao to party leadership. Identified in the West only in the late sixties, he published his memoirs in book form in German a decade ago, shortly before his death.

The initial reaction to this rich and absorbing book may be incredulity—that the phantom China expert has struck again from the Honolulu jail. For Braun's daily associates were the great, near-great, or ex-great of Chinese communism—Chou En-lai, Chu Teh, Mao Tse-tung, Lin Piao, Chiang Ch'ing —and their names dot these pages with heady regularity. This, however, is not a document designed to drop names, for Braun was at best a truculent and disapproving observer of the making of some important Chinese and world history.

Braun was nothing if not the perfect Comintern agent. Cut off from Moscow and instructions during the whole journey, he never wavered in loyalty or purpose, and indeed, in the 30 years between the experience and the writing, seems not to have given an inch. In his words,

all my life I have considered the touchstone of every Communist, regardless of nationality or situation, to be his posture towards the Soviet Union. I let myself be guided by this in China and always championed the interests of the Soviet people (which are embodied in the policies of the Soviet government) . . . I believe I can say with satisfaction that I have withstood this test.

This bias permeates his every word; and although it does nothing to diminish the value of his memoirs, it makes him seem an odd robot of the precomputer age, whose mindset was locked into place very early and quite permanently. The contrast with the pragmatism and flexibility of most of his companions on the march is stark, and it is of course that very pragmatism and flexibility that he saw as absolute evils.

Braun's account of the march is nearly impersonal, although the rigors must have been even more excruciating for the westerner than for his Chinese companions. Only an occasional reference to sleeping in a squatting position to avoid freezing, or to feet too infected for walking shows that the robot was human. His view is wholly political and ideological; it delineates the failure of Chinese communism to follow Comintern directives to cooperate with Chiang K'ai-shek in a true United Front and thus protect the motherland of communism from the Japanese threat. Mao is the villain; and Braun's Mao is a petty one indeed, moved only by personal ambition, void of principle or true ideological underpinning. His memoirs end, of course, before Maoism moved to real success, so there is no reason for acknowledgement that the long string of ideological faults and failures that he catalogs added up in the end to dramatic victory.

Strangely, Braun's undeviating perspective makes him almost as fascinating as his account of the march. Together Comintern agent and Long March provide a compelling document with a place in the basic bibliography of Maoism. Thanks to Stanford for making it easily available.

R. KENT LANCASTER
Goucher College
Towson
Maryland

CHALIAND, GÉRARD, ed. *Guerilla Strategies: An Historical Anthology from the Long March to Afghanistan.* Pp. xii, 353. Berkeley: University of California, 1982. $28.50.

Guerilla warfare is not new in the history of military—and indeed, more accurately, political—conflict. Guerilla movements in all of their aspects have been quite well studied, from insurgency to counterinsurgency, through political mobilization, military strategy, and so on. Chaliand gives us in this anthology an overview of modern guerilla strategies, from the Long March (1934-35) to current operations in Afghanistan. In his own words, this book is concerned "less with

the history and more with the strategy of this kind of war, analyzing its underlying principles and their connection with the ultimate goal, political change." The book begins with a 30-page introduction in which Chaliand offers an assortment of sometimes superficial, and at other times sharp, observations about the nature and conditions of guerilla—or what he also calls "revolutionary"—warfare. He also draws the lessons it teaches and comments on the types of counterinsurgency movements that it generates in the opposition. The introduction is followed by 300 pages of excerpts grouped into "Stories" narrated by participants in the struggles, and "Analyses" drawn up by participants and witnesses.

Reading the excerpts in the "Stories" category, I wondered at times about the basis of Chaliand's choices. As he states in the introduction, "with the exception of a few classic pages, the texts that follow are generally not very well known. Many are published here for the first time in English." I fail to see the usefulness of many of these texts, and to publish them for the first time in English does not necessarily justify their presence in this anthology.

For example, I cannot see how 15 pages from a 1948 work by Camille Rougeron could give us anything new concerning the "historical dimension of guerilla warfare," even if Rougeron was "one of the major French theoreticians of the past few decades." As for the building up of the Chinese People's Liberation Army during the Yenan period, is there no better source than the 10 pages from Agnes Smedley's biography of Chu Teh? The "Story of a Guerilla in Algeria" is well written but does not tell much of anything about the National Liberation Front. Moreover, except for its last sentence, the entire text by B. Fall simply does not seem to belong in this anthology. After describing at length the French mop-up operation along the famous Street without Joy, Fall concludes that no operation against the enemy could be successful unless "the proportion of attackers to defenders was 15 to 1 or even 20 to 1, for the enemy had in its favor an intimate knowledge of the terrain, the advantage of defensive organization, and the sympathy of the population." The other excerpt concerning the Franco-Vietnamese war comes from "a sympathetic but independent observer," and is "also the only testimony not published through the regular Vietnamese propaganda service." And so. What is wrong with propaganda? A judicious use of a propaganda piece could have introduced us to another dimension of revolutionary warfare. Does not Chaliand himself assert that "propaganda has been an important aspect of their [nationalist movements] struggle"?

The reasons behind the selection of the texts in the "Analyses" category are more apparent, and better founded. The excerpts themselves are interesting, some because they are of recent vintage, such as the piece written by Chaliand about Afghanistan in 1980; others because they are analytically incisive, such as the piece by Eqbal Ahmad, or because they convey a note of authenticity, such as the autocriticisms of H. Bejar for the failure of the guerillas in Peru, and of Aby Ayad for Al Fatah's crucial mistakes.

I am an admirer of Gérard Chaliand's earlier writings. I am disappointed by this anthology.

TRUONG BUU LAM

University of Hawaii
Honolulu

DEEB, MARIUS K. and MARY JANE DEEB. *Libya Since the Revolution: Aspects of Social and Political Development.* Pp. xi, 156. New York: Praeger, 1982. $21.95.

Colonel Muammar al Qadhdhaffi has ruled Libya for more than a decade. His radical approach to foreign policy and Libya's role as a major petroleum exporter have preoccupied our interests and also obscured our understanding of the changes in Libyan economy, polity, and society that have taken place since 1969. Marius K. Deeb and Mary Jane Deeb have attempted to fill this void by analyzing those aspects of the structure, institutions, ideology, and foreign policy of Libya that, in their judgment, have undergone the greatest change since the revolution yet have received the least attention in scholarly works. They have selected six aspects of development, ranging from general issues of rapid urbanization and educational reform to the social emancipation of Libyan women, the role of Islam in Libyan politics, the socioeconomic basis of the revolution, and Libya's Arab policy. In each case they have tried to analyze the relationship between traditional Libyan structures, institutions, and values and the policy of the state.

The book falls short of all its promises. The analyses of the six aspects of development vary in length and quality. The treatment of the general issues is the most disappointing. The analysis of rapid urbanization, which focuses too narrowly on the Tripoli region, is of little use in understanding fundamental problems of population distribution in Libya. The chapter on education chronicles educational change in a clinical manner, with nearly as much space devoted to education prior to 1969 as to changes in the past decade. By contrast, the analysis of the emancipation of Libyan women is a thorough and incisive treatment of the dilemma that they face in a society that continues to expand opportunities for them while holding back achievement. The remaining sections are a political analysis of Qadhdhaffi's efforts to construct radical ideologies of popular democracy and precapitalist socialism, and to translate them into domestic socioeconomic policies and foreign policies toward other Arab states. These sections are particularly useful in explaining the way in which conflicts with fundamentalist Islam and traditional socioeconomic and political systems of tribal nomadism and small provincial towns are reconciled with the influence of wealth from petroleum and western technology in Libya.

Deeb and Deeb state that understanding the interrelationships among the major aspects of Libyan development is necessary to understanding economic, social, and political change since the revolution. Yet they rarely meet their responsibility to define and explain these relationships, perhaps depending on the reader's ingenuity or some other knowledge of Libyan affairs to provide the links. The book ends on page 139 without the benefit of either a summary or a conclusion. In this sense the authors, who are obviously well informed about their subject, are also presumptuous.

GARY L. FOWLER

University of Illinois
Chicago

KEESING, R. M. *Kwaio Religion.* Pp. xi, 257. New York: Columbia University Press, 1982. $28.00. Paperbound, $14.00.

The Kwaio are a Melanesian people, numbering about 7000, who live on the island of Malaita in the Solomons. Their territory extends across the island, and consists mainly in a rugged mountain range. Dr. Keesing has worked among them in a series of visits over the past 20 years.

Kwaio religion is dominated, like many others, by the contrast between *mola*—secular—and *abu*—the local version of *tabu,* forbidden or sacred. Keesing, following Mary Douglas, observes that abu is not a quality that inheres in objects or places; it depends upon the right of persons of particular categories or in particular conditions to approach the objects or places without causing pollution. He also cites schemes of symbolic opposites of the type constructed by Needham.

Unlike most anthropologists, Keesing treats magic, very briefly, before the forms of communication with the ancestors which constitute the typical rituals. He rejects, as most of us have, Durkheim's sharp distinction between religion and magic, and remarks, as Mali-nowski did, that magic does not replace but complements practical activity.

Like most Melanesians, and some Africans, Kwaio propitiates other ancestors besides their direct lineal forebears. Hence Keesing's definition of a descent-group, each of which has or should have its own priest, is not unilineal. His most interesting chapters are devoted to the rituals of birth and death, which, he says, mirror each other. The latter is illustrated by a detailed account of the mortuary rites of a descent-group priest, the custodian of its ancestral shrine. They are seen as accomplishing the desacralization of the group, all members of which have been rendered abu by the death. Their "plunge into sacredness" is also a "quest of powers for worldly success," since it is for that above all that the Kwaio look to their ancestors. Keesing sees here a contradiction in juxtaposing the "most spiritual" and "most materialistic moods." Is not this an introduction of the western values that he has elsewhere repudiated as a distortion?

The comment, however, points ahead to a discussion of the politics of religion and its function as an ideology. Men's success in the pursuit of power depends on "extracting the labour of women for male ends," and it it is this, and not some fundamental fear of women as dangerous, that leads to their portrayal as polluting. Keesing observes that the matrilineal peoples of the Solomons do not have such an ideology, and suggest that in some remote past the Kwaio may have made the switch to patriliny which entails it.

LUCY MAIR

London
England

MARCUM, JOHN A. (for the Study Team of the United States-South African Leader Exchange Program). *Education, Race and Social Change in South Africa.* Pp. 251. Berkeley: University of California Press, 1982. $25.00.

Unlike the 33 earlier titles in the University of California Press's Perspectives on Southern Africa series, this volume is simply a 75-odd-page report with 160-odd pages of appended documents collected in South Africa in August and September of 1981. Marcum, the only Africanist in the group constituting an exchange program of six "senior American university administrators," wrote the report of the tour, whose apparent purpose was to put supposed American expertise in managing peaceful racial change at the service of liberal South African educators.

The report contains much interesting detail: "Total African secondary enrollment rose from 35,000 in 1955 to 209,000 in 1974, then leapt to 658,000 in 1979," for example, and the likelihood that over half the tertiary student body in South Africa will be black—that is, nonwhite—by 1990. The 18 documents, all emanating from academe except for a government response to a report on university education, range from Es'Kia Mphahlele's plea for a Soweto Community College to a copy of the document one must sign to gain access to prohibited books in South African university libraries—including the one at the university of the supposedly independent republic of the Transkei. The documents are useful to those interested in higher education in South Africa, and particularly in academics' response to the 1976 Soweto explosions, but they say very little about the grand subject hinted at by the collection's title.

The overall assumption of the volume—and apparently the tour group, whose stay in South Africa was in part funded by Nedbank of South Africa—seems to be this: the universities—together with corporate liberals serving their own enlightened interests by encouraging wider educational opportunities for blacks, which will enable them to take places in the private sector for which there will be insufficient whites—constitute a force which, guided by American educators' constructive engagement, stand a good chance of changing the mistaken direction of the *apartheid* regime. The corporate/academic alliance, one infers, can stand against the threatening tides of Afrikaner intransigence and African desperation. Neither the African freedom fighter nor the Afrikaner reactionary speaks in this collection or appears prominently in Marcum's report on the group's findings. The result is that the book's tenor largely reflects the hitherto ineffectual voice of white Anglophone liberalism, not those of the earthier and less reasonable forces that will shape the future in South Africa; the forces of the future are not those the group talked with, however much its members seem to think they did.

RICHARD SIGWALT
College of William and Mary
Williamsburg
Virginia

NWABUEZE, B. O. *The Presidential Constitution of Nigeria.* Pp. xvii, 558. New York: St. Martin's Press, 1982. $45.00.

The promulgation of the Nigerian Constitution of 1979 is potentially an event of tremendous significance for much of the Third World. Like many of the states formed from the British Empire, Nigeria adopted a Westminster-type government at independence; and like many of these new states the Nigerian government proved unable to master the multiple stresses and cacophony of demands that followed independence. In 1966 Nigeria lapsed into military rule. Through rhetoric that had become familiar in much of the world by the 1970s, the military rulers of Nigeria frequently promised a speedy return to civilian rule.

Here the common pattern ended: while the frustrations of government often led military regimes to create weak and impotent civilian governments only to see them quickly fail, the Nigerian junta seemed determined to analyze and solve the problems that had instigated the coup of 1966 and to develop organically a tenable civilian political system from the local to the national level. In October of 1977 a Constituent Assembly began meeting; in the summer of 1979 a series of elections were held, and in October of that year Nigeria's first president under the new system, Alhaji Shehu Shagari, took office. This was a bold and courageous move with implications for military regimes throughout the world.

Given the Nigerian experiment's importance as a model for democracy in the Third World, this experiment should be the object of study and analysis by scholars throughout the world. Unfortunately this has not been the case. While the studies that have appeared have frequently been of high quality, they have been of limited quantity. Thus the appearance of *The Presidential Constitution of Nigeria,* which was written by eminent legal scholar and jurist B. O. Nwabueze, seemed timely. But while the book is satisfying in its depth, its narrowness relegates it to the specialist.

To some degree Nwabueze has been trapped by his own logic. Utilizing an Austinian type of legal positivism, Nwabueze underlines the inherent weakness of constitutions that are purely political documents—such as that of the Soviet Union—and points out that the essence of a constitution is the creation of law that is above politics. What Nwabueze has done in this book is to explore the legal precedents and relationships of the Nigerian constitution in the most minute detail while avoiding the political reality that generated them. This is done through continual references to the development of American constitutional thinking, since the U.S. Constitution was the model for the Nigerian one. Only in the last chapter are the political underpinnings of the constitution confronted. Here Nwabueze is at his most cogent as as he argues that the success of the

constitution is predicated on the prior creation of a national ethic, which includes the sacrosanctity of the constitution. But this notion of a national ethic, on which the success of the constitution rests, is explored in under 10 pages.

What results is a book doomed to sterility both by the absence of criticisms of the constitution and by the isolation of the legal content of the document from its political environment. One learns much about constitutionalism but little about Nigeria. If the purpose of the book is to codify the legal underpinnings of the constitution, and thus to provide a source of quick reference for Nigerian jurists, then it may prove to be a successful effort. If, on the other hand, the purpose is to capture and distill the processes that led to the Nigerian experiment, then the book must be counted as a failure.

Thus the separation of the legal aspects of the Nigerian Constitution from its social and political mileu makes *The Presidential Constitution of Nigeria* useful primarily for legal scholars and students of constitutionalism. One additional shortcoming—which should be shared equally by publisher and author— is the failure to include the constitution itself in an appendix. It is more than simply a nuisance when over 500 pages are used to analyze a document that is not provided.

STEVEN METZ
Towson State University
Maryland

PHARR, SUSAN J. *Political Women in Japan: The Search for a Place in Political Life.* Pp. xiv, 233. Berkeley: University of California Press, 1981. $16.95.

This study helps to advance our knowledge not only of how women gain the first step to political power by achieving the vote, but of how they manage to "translate their newly-found legal rights into power"—that is, how they gain important positions in the political system. In doing so the book also throws light on the ability of women to move into positions of power in other male-oriented careers, such as business. The complex process by which this occurs has as yet been little studied except in the United States.

The study was based on intensive interviews with a sample of 100 Japanese women between the ages of 18 and 33, who had been active in voluntary political groups such as citizen, student, and women's movements, trade unions, and consumer protection groups. Twenty-five percent of the sample had held leadership positions in these organizations. This special group of women was chosen because women of their age had grown up in an era when the first step toward political power for women had been achieved, for Japanese women acquired the vote in 1945.

From her findings Pharr concludes that although women's entrance into political activity is influenced in the first instance by the same psychological and situational variables as for men, in addition they must undergo the kind of gender-role change that will enable them to compete successfully with men for the high positions. This change has social and psychological costs, such as role strain, particularly for the older women. However, there are also satisfactions, such as being able to engage in new types of behavior, and enhanced feelings of self-esteem. The satisfactions will gradually outweigh the costs as this redefinition of women's role becomes more acceptable, and an increasing number of women will be able to move into the top political positions.

An extensive account of the design of the study is given in Appendix A, and Appendix C contains the questions used in the interviewing schedule. Pharr's knowledge of Japanese and her participation in the lives of the Japanese with whom she worked undoubtedly accounts for the solidness and depth of the study.

This is a clearly written, innovative study. It has an impressive bibliography that includes Japanese studies. Perhaps its greatest contribution is that it demonstrates the importance and efficiency of the participant observation method in studying society.

AILEEN D. ROSS

McGill University
Montreal
Quebec

WOLPERT, STANLEY. *Roots of Confrontation in South Asia: Afghanistan, Pakistan, India, and the Superpowers.* Pp. x, 357. New York: Oxford University Press, 1982. $30.00.

Historian of many talents—political biographer, novelist, lecturer, and author of a text on India from prehistoric times to the present—Wolpert here turns to American foreign policy in South Asia. Two implicit arguments that underlie his effort seem to me irrefutable. First, Americans today face foreign policy choices that demand widespread public consideration, but the public knows very little about many world areas toward which we must make policy, so that scholars have a responsibility to engage the general reader and enter policy debates. Second, history provides an effective means for this engagement, not only because the supposed lessons of history figure so prominently in ideology, but also because American thought normally spins within tightly constricted temporal bounds. To broaden the time frame for foreign policy thought helps better to fit America into its global context, and helps thereby to open avenues to alternative policy conceptions.

Wolpert thus writes for the general reader, who knows little or nothing about South Asia, whose interest in this region, piqued by the Soviet invasion of Afghanistan, centers squarely on American foreign policy options. He takes this reader on a brief, engaging tour of regional history from classical times, though Muslim conquests, and through the colonial period, when Great Britain ruled India, when Russia pushed south across Central Asia, and when nationalist movements generated the internal dynamics of emergent polities from Kabul to Calcutta. Most of the book concerns internal and external sources of international conflict in South Asia since 1880; half the book treats events since the independence and partition of British India in 1947.

Straightforward yet provocative, his conclusion is that American policy, trained myopically on the Soviets, has lurched along since 1947 without any real understanding of the region. Inconsistent and counterproductive, past policy should be abandoned for one designed to promote cooperative resolutions to the many outstanding problems between nations in the region. Any improved policy would require more superpower cooperation, and less confrontation. When they simply play power games there with one another, superpowers exacerbate conflict in South Asia, and subvert their own regional interests at the same time.

Scholars of South Asian history and of American foreign policy will bicker with many points of fact and interpretation. But the readers for whom it is intended will find this book a little feast of information, ideas, and optimism. Unfortunately its cost as a hardback may keep the book from many of its most appropriate readers.

DAVID LUDDEN
University of Pennsylvania
Philadelphia

YOUNG, CRAWFORD. *Ideology and Development in Africa*. Pp. xvii, 376. New Haven, CT: Yale University Press, 1982. $29.95.

This book was written under the auspices of the Africa Project of the Council on Foreign Relations. Its chief aim seems to be to bring a detailed knowledge of African issues and connect them with broader questions that concern Americans in general and policymakers in particular.

Young's central concern is to determine the relation between ideology and economic performance in the African context. He undertakes a macro analysis of the African continent by drawing, first, a typology of the prevalent ideologies in the area: Afro-Marxism, the regimes that declare Marxism-Leninism as their official doctrine; populist socialism, a broad anticapitalist socialist posture; and African capitalism, a general acceptance of the rules of the market economy. He then tests the nexus of these three ideologies with a set of six criteria: economic growth, equality of distribution, autonomy and self-reliance, human dignity, political participation, and societal capacity.

Young takes 20 African countries—for instance, Somalia, Mozambique, Angola (Afro-Marxist); Tanzania, Algeria, Guinea-Bissau (populist socialist); Kenya, Nigeria, Zaire (Afrocapitalist)—and explores the interrelationship between their ideological preference and economic performance. He refers to his methodology as a "discursive" analysis and admits that his indicators have not been adequately "operationalized" and are susceptible to imprecision and subjectivism.

Some of Young's conclusions can be summarized as follows: in terms of growth, aside from the oil-producing states, the Ivory Coast and Kenya have done quite well, but the Afro-Marxist and socialist states do not show a dynamic expansion. Young feels that the success or failure of Mozambique in building a strong economy will have profound repercussions in Africa. Much credit is given to the Afro-Marxists and populist-socialists for enforcing an egalitarian commitment and inhibiting accumulation of wealth, unlke their capitalist counterparts. Young does not find a close correlation between the degree of autonomy and ideology and cites examples of socialist countries having ties with Western capitalism, such as Gulf Oil in Cabinda, Angola, and South African involvement in Mozambiqan railroads and port installations. On the overall level, he argues that ideological preference has a significant influence on economic performance and that it ought not be dismissed as "simple evanescent rhetoric." He recommends natural resources, climate, strategic and geopolitical location, food prices, and environment as additional factors that must be explored in the shaping of developmental processes in Africa.

Almost all of Young's data consist of secondary monographic and statistical sources. He does promise interview data in the early pages, but it does not appear.

For an informed but nonspecialist audience, this study offers a swift journey through 20 African countries, providing a resumé on their ideological choices and their developmental implications, and could be added to the list of recommended reading for students of African politics.

RUKHSANA A. SIDDIQUI
University of Pennsylvania
Philadelphia

EUROPE

BOGGS, CARL. *The Impasse of European Communism.* Pp. xiii, 181. Boulder, CO: Westview Press, 1982. $23.50. Paperbound, $10.75.

WOODALL, JEAN, ed. *Policy and Politics in Contemporary Poland: Reform, Failure, Crisis.* Pp. xix, 200. New York: St. Martin's Press, 1982. $25.00.

The major communist parties in Western Europe claim a commitment to a "democratic road to socialism." Often this is a genuine evolution of traditional Marxist-Leninist ideology based on the assumption that political and economic power can be secured through gradual change rather than by revolution, and through the utilization of democratic processes. Boggs concludes that this strategy is not working very well.

Boggs bases his analysis on a theoretical assessment of the historical and strategic development of Eurocommunism; of those parties and movements, notably in France,

Italy, and Spain, that seek a transition to socialism based on the democratization of existing political and economic structures—the so-called parliamentary road to socialism. After examining the logic and premises of this conception, he moves to a critique of the major Eurocommunist theoreticians—Togliatti, Berlinguer, Ingrato, Napolitano, Carrillo, Marchains, Elleinstein, Poulatzas and Claudin. His conclusion is that their ideas fail to resolve the historic Marxist conflict between democratization and rationalization, comprehended here in terms of the drive toward statism, bureaucratization, and further refinement of the social division of labor under capitalism. In fact, Boggs concludes,

Eurocommunism will probably represent a sort of historical resolution of legitimation and production crises within Mediterranean capitalism that extends rather than overturns hierarchical social and authority relations, the capitalist state, and the social division of Labor. Such a resolution might broadly parallel the function of social democracy in Northern Europe in a previous phase of capitalist development.

Each chapter is heavily documented by notes ably supporting Boggs's conclusions.

Woodall's symposium is focused on the fate of the communist Poland, offering some logical explanation of the turbulent sequence of events there since the summer of 1980; and it evaluates those events' significance within the framework of the political reform and policy experiments that took place in Poland after December 1970, when Edward Gierek became first secretary of the Polish United Workers' Party (PZPR).

Although there is by no means complete agreement among the editor and eight contributors on the causes of the events in Poland, they do all concede the complexity of a situation that is due not simply to the ineffectiveness and lack of vision on the part of the PZPR and the government, but rather to an overambitious blueprint for reform designed to embrace all aspects of social and economic life—a reform that fell increasingly out of step with material reality.

All collaborators, as well as the editor, are British. The nine chapters were completed at different times and therefore do not all take account of the events between July and September 1981. They also differ in their uses of notes and references at the end of each chapter. On the whole the symposium is an intelligent contribution to contemporary thought and debate over the fate of contemporary Poland.

JOSEPH S. ROUCEK

City University
of New York

BOURNE, KENNETH. *Palmerston: The Early Years, 1784-1841.* Pp. xiv, 749. New York: Macmillan, 1982. $24.95.

Bourne's formidable work on probably the most famous foreign minister in British history comes within 20 years of studies of Palmerston by Donald Southgate and Jasper Ridley, who themselves built upon the 1930s two-volume biography by H.F.C. Bell. Bourne's study differs, however, in the massiveness of its research into every detail not only of Palmerston's life but also of every institution with which he was associated and every aspect of any foreign or domestic policy or issue he influenced. The resulting book, the first of a projected two-volume study, requires some 638 pages, exclusive of notes and index, at 600 words per page in small print to bring Palmerston only to the year 1841. As Norman Gash observed in the *Times Literary Supplement,* 22 October 1982, "This is a book that is difficult to read and even more difficult to assimilate."

To a certain extent the excessive detail obscures Palmerston the man, and for the reader who wishes a clear, succinct assessment of that man, this reviewer suggests Ridley's biography. On the other hand, Bourne's wealth of information provides a clear and entertaining picture of almost every facet of upper-class life in early nineteenth-century Britain. One may discover how the aristocracy conducted its amours; the physical

dimensions and appearance of the war and foreign offices, and the duties, personalities, and problems of their staffs; the variety of issues an able administrator such as Palmerston confronted; the confounding perplexities of settling Belgian independence; and a host of other matters. The information is stupendous, almost staggering.

The picture of Palmerston that emerges shows a docile, cheerful, obedient, decent child and young man—diligent in his studies and especially good in languages—growing into a very hardworking and capable politician, administrator, and foreign secretary, who slowly gains confidence and ability as a parliamentary orator. He has matured fully by 1841, but we must await the next volume for Palmerston as prime minister.

Palmerston: The Early Years rewards the scholar who has the time and interest to read it through. It is not a work either a scholar or a general reader can easily skim. But it is so rich in detail and scholarship that it can stand as a reference work, almost an encyclopedia, for those people who wish to inform themselves on almost any political, social, economic, and administrative aspect of British upper-class life in the first half of the nineteenth century.

FRANKLIN B. WICKWIRE

University of Massachusetts
Amherst

JOES, ANTHONY JAMES. *Mussolini.* Pp. 405. New York: Franklin Watts, 1982. $18.95.

Many claims have been made regarding the best vehicle for the exposition and understanding of history. "History is biography" has been one claim. Anthony James Joes, in this work on Benito Mussolini, seems to accept this concept as his guiding principle. His is indeed an account of both the life and the times of *Il Duce.*

Joes thoroughly and clearly relates to his subject practically every major and many minor political, socioeconomic, intellectual, and cultural aspects of Italian history from the Congress of Vienna until 1945. Given a limit of 378 pages, that is quite an achievement.

Both the times and the life are excellently done, and are used to illuminate each other. We see how the human being, Benito Mussolini, was formed by the Italy existing before and during his lifetime. We also see how that human being succeeded for decades in dominating and shaping his national environment according to his will. Joes can write Italian in English. At times his prose, which is clear and flows easily, almost reaches the poetic and dramatic levels that can be attained so easily and naturally in the Latin languages. He can also think in Italian. He is so completely at home in the intellectual, ideological, and emotional world of nineteenth- and twentieth-century Italy that he succeeds in translating into American English the ideas and motivations that grew into a coherent ideology called *fascismo*. He makes comprehensible the reasons the March on Rome was such an immediate success in the Italy of 1922, and why it found so many admirers and imitators all over Europe. This is an unusual achievement for an American scholar.

One reason may be that Joes takes Benito Mussolini seriously. This attitude stands in strong contrast to much that has been written in English about the Duce during and since World War II. It is in a way a revival of an attitude toward Mussolini held in the English-speaking world before the war, including, at various times, Lloyd George, Winston Churchill, James A. Farley, and Franklin Roosevelt. Another reason for Joes's success in translating Mussolini into American is his own obvious deep personal familiarity with Italian life and humanity. This gives him the ability to present Mussolini honestly in terms of his own national culture and origins. *Io sono passionamente Italiano*. We are presented not with a cardboard Caesar, but with a powerful and shrewd personality with considerable abilities. He was not only *Il Duce* but also exemplified Machiavelli's *Principe,* both for good

and evil. Although the liberal bourgeoisie and the conservative monarchists thought they could coopt Mussolini for their own ends, he actually used them for his own national and social revolutionary purposes.

Joes emphasizes what has been little understood, especially in American writing on the subject, that fascism "was not a counterrevolution but *another* revolution." Basic to this insight is the emphasis upon Mussolini's socialist origins. He quotes Togliatti, "Let us not forget that Mussolini was a Socialist party leader."

The word *bios* means "life" in Greek. This biography reproduces Benito Mussolini in three-dimensional form. He is shown and explained with all of his contradictions—the ceaseless energy, the iron-jawed determination combined with endless vacillations of will; the egocentric megalomania projected onto and through a whole nation; and the social revolutionary ardor combined with love of his own nation and its rich traditional heritage.

HEINZ F. MACKENSEN
Fairleigh Dickinson University
Teaneck
New Jersey

KREJCI, JAROSLAV and VITEZSLAV VELIMSKY. *Ethnic and Political Nations in Europe.* Pp. 279. New York: St. Martin's Press, 1981. $27.50.

Of the making of books about nationalism there is no end. The subject is infinitely varied, and the variations consist not only in differences between nations, but also in differences between authors writing about nationalism.

The study by Krejci and Velimsky starts with the premise that national consciousness is important, and observes that there is some divergence between state boundaries and the territories of nations. In other words, not all nations are states, and some states are more or less multinational. The authors explicitly reject the assumption of Marxists and many non-Marxists that economic relations are of primary or exclusive importance in the formation and maintenance of states. Their approach is comparative, differentiating between empire-building nations and those nations isolated, dispersed, or submerged in another state. The definition of nation is said to be elastic, involving political, cultural, territorial, and linguistic concerns.

A distinctive feature of this book is its very wide coverage of nations. Europe is defined in its pre-1914 sense as running from the Urals to Connacht. Minority nations, such as the Kalmyks, Lusatians, and Furlanians, are noted, as well as the relatively better-known Bretons, Latvians, and Macedonians. Comparative chapters and tables, complemented by 12 chapters reviewing minorities in specific European countries, give the authors ample opportunity to display their detailed knowledge of national minorities throughout Europe.

The strength of the book is in the breadth of its coverage, and the readiness of the authors to differentiate between nations, and to see nations in dynamic terms, including an allowance for the death or disappearance of nations by coercion or assimilation.

The weakness of the book arises from Krejci and Velimsky's conscious decision to redress the balance of historical writing, which is mostly about states. To emphasize nations that by their own figures constitute only a very small proportion of contemporary Europe's population is to view Europe through a very peculiar kind of telescope, in which the smallest parts are much magnified, and the largest parts much reduced in scale. The nations that have been the winners historically, that is, secured control of states on their own behalf, should never be overlooked.

RICHARD ROSE

University of Strathclyde
Glasgow
Scotland

MITRAKOS, ALEXANDRE S. *France in Greece during World War I. A Study in the Politics of Power.* Pp. xviii, 258. New York: Columbia University Press, for East European Quarterly, 1982. $20.00.

In the past decade France's opening of its diplomatic archives has allowed a reexamination of twentieth-century French foreign policy. Alexandre Mitrakos's *France in Greece during World War I,* which studies the objectives and conduct of French diplomacy in Greece, relies heavily on the French foreign ministry archives to correct outworn generalizations about Franco-Greek relations. Since Greece's key strategic location made it the focus of intense and prolonged Allied military and diplomatic concerns, this book also illuminates the complexities of France's wartime diplomacy and aims in the Balkans.

Mitrakos's book focuses on Aristide Briand's ministry—October 1915-March 1917—when France was most deeply involved with Greece and generally dictated Allied decisions for that nation. Mitrakos argues the inaccuracy of the traditional view that the Allies sought Greek adherence to the Entente. On the contrary France considered a Greek alliance undesirable and tried to render it impossible. Furthermore France repeatedly used forceful tactics that ignored neutral rights and inflicted suffering on the Greeks. French agents in Greece, with governmental cognizance, created a crisis atmosphere to justify Allied intervention. They sought thereby to undermine Greek sovereignty and to foster the establishment of a French protectorate. Traditionally King Constantine has been viewed as a blind Germanophile and Prime Minister Venizelos as systematically pro-Entente. But, Mitrakos argues, Constantine was as patriotic as Venizelos and equally torn between neutrality and support for the Entente. Policy toward Greece, which became a divisive issue among the Allies, also reflected the pervasive influence of military developments as well as domestic political requirements and the ambitions of wartime leaders.

French policy toward Greece was linked to Great Power political and strategic considerations and long-standing French commercial interests in the Near East. Although Greece held little political or economic value for France, its significance lay in its strategic proximity to the Dardanelles and Asia Minor. Rather than an alliance with Greece, France preferred a neutral but docile state that would accept French military and political demands without making any counterproposals. Thwarted both by Greek groups determined to avert French domination and Allied opposition to French initiatives, France essentially failed to achieve this control. Furthermore French policy lacked coherence and clear directives. Responsibility for France's complex and devious policy with its inevitable confusion and mistakes rested with Briand. French claims that military considerations—protection of Sarrail's army—dictated control were not sufficiently proved to justify drastic French measures. Mitrakos argues that the French naval attache, Commandant de Roquefeuil, was responsible for most of the coercive measures, in opposition to official Quai d'Orsay policy, but with Briand's awareness. France's objective was to establish a virtual protectorate over wartime Greece in order to secure its postwar diplomatic position in the Balkans. Thus this wartime history can be understood only in the larger context of contemporary Franco-Balkan relations.

Mitrakos has done an excellent job of sifting through a large volume of diplomatic correspondence to produce a clearly written analysis of Franco-Greek relations. Although he has dealt with a confused and complex subject, he has mastered the details and fitted them into the broader outlines of French policy. This well-written study not only illuminates the details of the wartime disputes but also places them in a larger context. It is therefore an important contribution to contemporary European diplomatic history.

MARJORIE M. FARRAR
Chestnut Hill
Massachusetts

ROSTOW, W. W. *The Division of Europe after World War II: 1946.* Pp. xii, 212. Austin: University of Texas Press, 1982. $19.95. Paperbound, $8.95.

In this brief study, half of which consists of documents, political economist W. W. Rostow, assistant chief of the Division of German and Austrian Economic Affairs in the State Department until September 1946, embraces the view, attributed sometimes to *Annales* historians, that events are signs and that some few such signs are paradigmatic. The matrix-event of Rostow's tale is the decision of the United States not to withdraw from Europe after World War II but rather to promote the economic unity and actively contribute to the political security of Ciselbian Atlantic Europe. Essential to that matrix was the recommendation by the U.S. chargé d'affaires in Moscow, George F. Kennan, on the eve of the Yalta conference of February 1945, that Europe be divided into two spheres of influence, Soviet and American, with the purpose of limiting Soviet —or, to use Kennan's term, Russian—expansion; that the United States pursue a policy of containment instead of seeking a One Europe postwar settlement.

Opposition to the recommendation was strong in other American governmental circles, at least until the middle of 1946. By his long cable of February 1946, however, Kennan softened resistance to his Two Europe scheme by avoiding specific reference to it, stressing instead the two premises upon which his Two Europe solution depended: that the Soviet Union seeks the destruction of "the internal harmony" of American society, but that "Soviet power, unlike that of Hitlerite Germany, is neither schematic nor adventuristic." It is rather "highly sensitive to logic of force," therefore ready to withdraw "when strong resistance is encountered at any point." Kennan thus implied that the Soviet Union would probably yield in the face of American determination to use force if necessary in order to achieve its One Europe solution.

But the United States probably did not possess "the will 'to go whole hog' and oppose with all its physical and diplomatic resources Russian domination of the area"— Kennan's presumption in 1945; this was precisely because it was a democracy and not a totalitarian state—Charles E. Bohlen to Kennan, 1945. And so it had to acquiesce in practice to a Two Europe policy, or lose the whole of Europe to the Soviet Union, even while continuing to pursue a One Europe policy in rhetoric. Thus on 24 September 1946, President Truman's special counsel Clark Clifford submitted a top secret report recommending a Kennan-like policy—"to build up a world of our own which will pursue its own objectives and will recognize the Soviet orbit as a distinct entity with which conflict is not predestined but with which we cannot pursue common aims." The logical consequence of this matrix-event/idea was the Truman Doctrine, the Marshall Plan and NATO.

We may concede that neither the United States nor the Soviet Union "pursued a predetermined, deliberate, sophisticated strategy to achieve postwar global domination." We may admit even that

the ultimate Cold War confrontation between the two powers resulted less from any firm conscious design on either side than it did from incremental increases in tension caused by individual episodes of miscalculation and misunderstanding, flowing, of course, from differing presuppositions but not from firmly fixed purposes.

Such concessions should not divert the reader, however, from Rostow's more important thesis: acceptance in practice by the American government by September 1946 of the idea that if one cannot successfully apply one's goals to a large external area—One Europe—it may be preferable to apply them to a reduced external area than to no external area at all.

The major weakness of the book probably stems from the Rostow's own decision to write precisely the kind of book that neatly deals with an important cluster of events and ideas. To achieve a more comprehensive understanding of the beginnings of the Cold War, we need the kind of analysis that

George Kennan has recommended and that Rostow himself theoretically espouses: an analysis based on the principle that it is not the diplomat who makes foreign policy, or not the diplomat alone, but that every national policy presupposes certain military, political, and economic capabilities and often produces unexpected results. Once such an analysis has been effected, we still may be able to agree on the fundamental importance of the matrix-event of 1946. Not however as the beginning of the cold war but as method—as the identification of a method of waging it more successfully! For the Cold War itself we may have to go back to 1945, 1944, even 1917.

TRAIAN STOIANOVICH
Rutgers University
New Brunswick
New Jersey

VAN CREVELD, MARTIN. *Fighting Power: German and U.S. Army Performance 1939-1945.* Pp. xi, 198. Westport, CT: Greenwood Press, 1982. $27.50.

Putting aside weapons or other resources, some armies fight better than others. The essence of fighting power is relatively constant: discipline, courage, morale, cohesion, readiness to fight and die. The question is, How is that instilled? Van Creveld seeks an answer by examining an example, the German army in 1939-45. He expertly probes a long list of possibly relevant factors, using the U.S. Army for comparison.

He concludes that the German army was obsessed with operations, with combat effectiveness, in its approach to war. This was seen to require cohesive units led by highly respected officers of proper character for waging war, with officers and men exercising a great deal of responsibility and initiative. Everything was designed accordingly. Men trained together in the units in which they later fought, and under the same officers; replacements and rotation were by unit;

wounded men who recovered went back to the same units. Officers were selected primarily on the basis of character—leadership, courage, initiative, competence—particularly when displayed in combat, and were trained in part at the front. Most officers were in combat units, pay was generally better for combat personnel, decorations were primarily for combat achievements, and promotions were most rapid for combat distinction. Orders were concise and left details to subordinates, responsibility was widely delegated, paperwork was minimized. In most instances the American practice was quite different, undermining the U.S. Army's fighting power.

The conclusions seem quite sound, though not entirely novel, and Van Creveld's presentation is very clear and concise. It is likely that fighting power results from organizational practices, a management style, training regimes, and so on that mesh well with the nature of the society, the nature of the opponent and the war, and the strategic context. If so, the essence of fighting power remains the same, but the ways it is achieved may—indeed must—vary to some extent. Thus this book is a fine study of how the Germans did it, but only suggestive about how it can be done elsewhere, in our time.

PATRICK M. MORGAN
Washington State University
Pullman

UNITED STATES

DILGER, ROBERT JAY. *The Sunbelt/Snowbelt Controversy: The War over Federal Funds.* Pp. 240. New York: New York University Press, 1982. $27.50.

The demographic and industrial shifts to states in the south and the Carter and Reagan administration's readjustment of federal appropriations toward the south has exacerbated both political and economic competition between the Northeast-Midwest and the South. During the past decade, northeastern and midwestern states have been significantly affected by harsh economic conditions. Most northeastern-midwestern states have suffered high unemployment and deterioration of their physical and economic infrastructure. In contrast, many southern states have grown prosperous as a result of population shifts and the relocation of many northern-based industries.

A number of economists and urbanologists have documented how these shifts have affected areas in the north and the south. *The Sunbelt/Snowbelt Controversy* provides a detailed examination of the geopolitical battles between legislative representatives of the north and the south. As a result of this competition, sophisticated political coalitions came into being. Dilger describes what he considers a new and unique way in which geopolitical interests achieve specific objectives, how the Northeast-Midwest Coalition functioned during the Carter presidency, and how political coalitions use think tanks, notably the Northeast-Mideast Research Institute. What was unique about this collaborative effort was the effective use of computer politics—providing key legislators with detailed information and analysis to support legislative lobbying.

In this book Dilger provides a comprehensive and cogent treatment of the rise and impact of regional political caucuses. In each chapter he presents an analysis of how the Northeastern-Midwestern Congressional Coalition interceded in the federal policymaking process. He examines the political machinations surrounding a number of key pieces of federal legislation which include debates over the Housing and Community Development Act of 1974 and the Elementary and Secondary Education Act of 1978. Dilger not only includes a detailed description of the legislative involvements by members of the coalition to increase or maintain funding for their region; he also dispels the notion that politicians representing a geographic region are in agreement over policies. He emphasizes that political gamesmanship still plays an important role in the legislative process, which cannot be easily overcome by regional coalitions. Therefore, perceived members of a coalition may vote as a regional, subregional, or party block.

In the final chapter, Dilger concludes,

The coalition's efforts at altering legislative outcomes were responsible for providing the Northeast-Midwest region with hundreds of millions of dollars that would have otherwise gone to the sunbelt. While this outcome represents a substantial amount of federal revenue, the coalition's efforts fell short of its goals of changing the balance in the regional distribution of federal funds (200).

The book represents an important contribution to the literature on public policy and should be widely read by students of political affairs as well as by policymakers.

STUART W. ZISOOK

DePaul University
Chicago
Illinois

IPPOLITO, DENNIS S. *Congressional Spending, A Twentieth Century Fund Report.* Pp. 286. Ithaca, NY: Cornell University Press, 1981. $22.50. Paperbound, $7.95.

Dennis S. Ippolito, a political scientist, performs two useful services in this book, but he also makes the serious error of assuming that the rhetoric of politics is not only important but also a statement of truth, and this badly mars an otherwise readable and admirable account of how Congress formulates budgets.

In Part I, Ippolito traces the history of attempts to control Congress's alleged inability to control itself as it controls the purse, and places the reforms of 1974 in this historical context. In Part II, he describes congressional budgeting processes as they have been worked out since passage of the Congressional Budget and Impoundment Act of 1974. This is done with sufficient detail to allow the reader who begins knowing little about the actual processes to understand the ways in which individual congressmen as well as political issues have influenced the development of the procedures now being used.

As Ippolito describes it, we have alternated between periods of expanding expenditure, when previous attempts to build in rules to limit congressional expenditures have been undermined, and periods characterized by new efforts at congressional reform designed to curb spending. On his own evidence the periods of expansion have been associated with war or with socioeconomic change, and Congress has acted as agent, not cause, of the shifting attitudes toward the public purse. Nevertheless, the retrenchment phase seems always to be justified by abuse of a spendthrift Congress.

The central flow of Ippolito's book is that, although he describes this pattern, he does not appear aware of his own participation in it. Even though his survey of history should serve as a warning not to do so, Ippolito takes political rhetoric for objective fact and assumes that this time around the federal budget is truly out of control. In support of his proposition that federal spending is excessive in the eyes of "many experts," he cites Gerald Ford and Jimmy Carter; he shows government expenditure plus transfer payments as a growing percentage of gross national product (GNP) but makes no mention that government expenditures without transfers added remained remarkably constant, at approximately one-fifth of GNP throughout the 1960s and 1970s. There is no mention that government expenditures are a much larger percentage of GNP in other industrialized nations that have posted better economic performances over recent years.

Ippolito assumes, as Americans appear to have done over the years, that there is some inherent flaw in congressional procedures that allows or causes Congress to avoid the fiscal restraint we allegedly want. In writing about the 1890s he tells us that the declining power of the Appropriations Committee was accompanied by a sharp increase in veterans' pensions, and that in fiscal 1894 the federal budget registered the first deficit since the Civil War. There is no mention of the depression of the 1890s, no mention that expenditures fell sharply in 1894 along with revenues, no mention that an increase in veterans' pensions in the 1890s was an inevitable result of the aging of Civil War veterans. In what sense then was Congress irresponsibly responsible for the deficit?

Ippolito continues in the grand American tradition and in Part III of his book advocates a reform that will, he hopes, comes close to being a reform to end all reforms: a constitutional limit on expenditures. Fortunately, Parts I and II of the book are sufficiently well done that no reader will fear that the cycle that allows us periodically to shout at Congress for its profligacy is likely to come to an end.

ANNE MAYHEW
University of Tennessee
Knoxville

KETTL, DONALD F. *Managing Community Development in the New Federalism.* Pp. xi, 156. New York: Praeger Publishers/ CBS Group, 1980. $21.95.

The Reagan administration has not yet defined what its program of New Federalism means. But concurrent with current economic problems in the economy in general, and the critical conditions of cities and urban areas, something will be done in the future in the area of community development. Donald F. Kettl's work was published at the end of the decade when the Nixon-Ford-Carter versions of New Federalism were at issue, and the Reagan people were putting forth only hints of what they had in mind as part of a political campaign.

The value of Kettl's work is that it puts forth not any new theories, but an explanation of the old theories and policies, including those that worked and those that did not work. Others may not share this view, of course, because this work is not exotic; it merely begins with a summary of the evolution of the two developments of American federalism of modern times.

One development, dating from the 1930s, was the bypassing of the states through direct grants to local governments; the other, dating from 1966—the City Demonstration Act, or Demonstration Cities Act—provided for the enlargement and self-determination of local citizens to determine how funds would be used. Nixon's congressionally approved Community Development Block Grant program of 1974 incorporated both programs, putting more power back into the hands of local government elected officials at the expense of citizen participation groups— and cut the funds, though Professor Kettl does not make this point.

Kettl's analysis is based upon examining national policy, and the effect of block grants in four Connecticut cities: New Haven, New London, Bridgeport, and Norwich. Despite this localization he manages to end up with a product that has both national and local application. His analysis was careful to include the interdependencies of all federal, state, and local governmental units—bringing such entities as the Army Corps of Engineers, Environmental Protection Agency, and others into the picture.

Kettl is also careful to not get caught up in the politicized bias toward citizen participation groups. He notes, for example, that the so-called failure of Model Cities was a refrain picked up from consulting organizations, who were criticizing unrealistic and counterproductive planning requirements, a matter that got turned around and used to change the programs and reduce funding.

The only two drawbacks to this book are weakness in design, and the price. The publisher put the volume together with a sturdy binding, but the typesetting and layout are the most economical—cheapest—for a trade-text book. The price defeats the purpose of adoption as a supplemental text in upper-level undergraduate as well as graduate courses. Perhaps the publisher had in mind that it would only be used by specialists. The irony is that Dr. Kettl is good writer, with a clear and simple prose style; and this book was published by a unit of CBS, a company that has a lot of money and is always on the lookout for profit makers.

Donald F. Kettl is assistant professor of government and foreign affairs at the University of Virginia, and was previously assistant professor of political science at Columbia.

FREDERICK M. FINNEY
Sinclair Community College
Dayton
Ohio

MILLER, ARTHUR SELWYN. *Toward Increased Judicial Activism: The Political Role of the Supreme Court.* Pp. xi, 355. Westport, CT: Greenwood Press, 1982. $29.95.

How many books advertise the political role of courts in their subtitles? Answer: too many that do not deliver what they promise. How many authors explain in dust jacket blurbs that they began with the intention of justifying Supreme Court policymaking but found that "free-hand constitution-making" forced them to write a sharp criticism instead? Answer: virtually every author who purchases the propaganda of pluralistic democracy. Fortunately Miller's latest book on the Supreme Court does deliver all that it promises; and Miller defends with aplomb an activist court.

Apparently it is Miller's belief that we already have enough doctrinal analyses of American constitutional law and too many studies of the Supreme Court, which, in the end, cannot cope with the theoretical tension between an appointed court and the principles of democracy. The real question, he asserts, is who wins when the Supreme Court decides. The answer, invariably, is the moneyed and the propertied. Even those decisions that appear to assist the disadvantaged merely preserve the status quo by defusing social discontent. The purpose of this book, then, is to recommend a "new normative posture"—used interchangeably with "synthesis" and "theory"—for the Supreme Court.

In Part I, Miller presents a history of judicial activism and a summary description of its modern critics. In Part II, under the title "The Bankruptcy of Politics," he argues that because Americans have come to believe the "incessant propaganda" about pluralistic democracy, there is no one to speak for national values or the national interest. In Part III, he paves the way for his prescriptions by showing that because the Constitution is always in a state of becoming, we have already tacitly accepted the role of the court as a "Council of Elders," a national faculty of political theory. Finally, in Part IV, Miller presents his central argument for reform: judicial activism that furthers the attainment of human dignity is both necessary and desirable.

Miller rejects the notion that the intentions of the framers should guide modern decisions. He asserts that each generation of Americans writes its own constitution, and it is within this context that the Supreme Court, because it is the only existing governmental organ that can articulate national values, should pursue an activism of a particular kind, that which enhances basic human dignity. He admits that this involves "openly being a 'superlegislature,'" and proceeds to defend his position against activism's many critics—from neoconservatives to the legal profession to those who believe simply that the justices are inadequately prepared or equipped to do what Miller wants. Would the justices have time for a more active role? Yes, if they were to hear cases in panels of three and do away with written opinions. But is it not the case that opinions explain their reasoning processes? No, nobody really believes that, and decisions without opinions would, for the better, make lawyers more outwardly result oriented. Would it not be the case that Miller's court would be a less democratic institution? No, because that criterion depends upon the validity of that which never was—a true majority rule. But would Miller's prescription not make the Constitution a mere artifact cut adrift from the courts? Yes, but that is precisely where we are now. I agree with Miller: why not recognize that fact and move forward?

WILLIAM C. LOUTHAN
Ohio Wesleyan University
Delaware

ROSSI, ALICE S. *Feminists in Politics: A Panel Analysis of the First National Women's Conference.* Pp. xxvii, 411. New York: Academic Press, 1982. $29.50.

This book was prepared and written by a member of the Social and Demographic Institute of the University of Massachusetts, Amherst. The work rests upon the results of an extremely detailed questionnaire on the biographical facts, political and social beliefs, and actual participation in political life of the 1300 feminist leaders and activists who attended the First National Women's Conference in 1977 in Houston. The chairperson of the conference was Bella Abzug.

Rossi approached her task with the unspoken assumption that nowadays underlies so much statistical research and analysis in the social sciences. If sufficiently detailed questionnaires can be devised and presented to a delimited target group for answers, and if their answers are analyzed and interpreted with the statistician's methods, it will be possible for the social scientist to draw conclusions about human behavior, which will be as valid as those derived by the natural scientist from observing the instinctive behavior patterns of rats or baboons. There is a basic fallacy here.

Rossi launched a truly heroic effort to obtain the raw data from the conference delegates, and then to classify them and interpret them. The book includes 27 charts and 93 tables of figures to report her statistical discoveries. She devotes two chapters to the design of the questionnaire and what it was intended to measure. The charts and tables include such items as "Table 6.5—R^2 in Regressions on Selected Affect Scales with the Same Set of Political and Demographic Predictor Variables: October versus February," and "Table 6.11—Belief/Affect Constraint: Average within-Individual Variability across Thirteen Feminism Measures, by Organizational Membership Type."

Rossi is at her best when she forgets her statistics and simply reports her own interpretations of the feminist movement and its many facets and sectors. It is when she reports, here and there, what real, individual women she encountered at the conference had to say, that she produces her best, most informative writing. Her brief historical sketch of the origins and growth of the American feminist movement since the early nineteenth century is especially clear and valuable. Many other parts of the book are readable only with the greatest effort since they are written in language that bristles with the statistician's technical jargon.

Judging from Rossi's comments in her chapters on the actual governance of the conference itself, the gathering was run by the chairperson in a fast-paced, strongly controlled manner.

One heard charges from some delegates that they couldn't get to a microphone in time or without the permission of a floor manager; that message passing and signals were widely used to instruct groups and delegations how to vote on a substantive or procedural issue.

The book is a valuable source of information, both historical and statistical, on the American feminist movement during the administrations of Ford and Carter.

H. F. MACKENSEN

Fairleigh Dickinson University
Teaneck
New Jersey

SCHULTE NORDHOLT, JAN WILLEM. *The Dutch Republic and American Independence.* Translated by Herbert H. Rowen. Pp. xii, 351. Chapel Hill: University of North Carolina Press, 1982. $29.95.

This is a timely book. Published in Holland in 1979, it appeared in this country last year, on the bicentennial of the establishment of diplomatic relations between the Netherlands and the United States. Jan Willem Schulte Nordholt, who teaches American history at the University of Leiden, tells an important story here. While not denying France's paramount role in the founding of the United States, he shows that the Netherlands made a much more significant contribution to American independence than most histories of the Revolution and general textbooks give it credit for. The Dutch Republic was in fact the second European state to grant official recognition to the rebellious 13 colonies; it was the first anywhere in which an American embassy was set up; and it was moreover the exclusive holder of the foreign debt of the United States during this country's formative years.

Schulte Nordholt develops a number of major historical themes. He first highlights the crucial role of the Dutch merchants in the early and most critical phase of the Revolutionary War, as they supplied the American colonists with the wherewithal to fight the British forces. This huge and immensely profitable contraband trade in armaments was conducted on St. Eustatius, a speck of an island in the West Indies, at grave risk to the home country's neutrality.

He next describes in considerable detail the Herculean task of securing the Netherlands' recognition of the United States, of concluding a treaty of friendship and commerce between the two countries, and of coaxing a loan out of tightfisted Amsterdam bankers. The Dutch Republic's slowness in coming round to American recognition was due to its visceral attachment to the traditional neutrality, to the clash of opposing economic interests within the country, to the eruption of party conflict between the pro-American Patriots and the pro-British Orangists, and not least to the dilapidated condition of its navy. Schulte Nordholt shows simultaneously how the American Revolution began to impinge on the Dutch public consciousness from the late 1770s onward, as the leaders of the Patriot movement held it up as a paradigm for effecting a limited democratization of Dutch political and social structures.

The hero of the book is unquestionably John Adams. His aggressive diplomacy, unflagging zeal, and realistic judgment as the American envoy and minister in the Netherlands from 1780 until 1782, and intermittently thereafter until 1788, brilliantly fulfilled his government's aims in the Dutch Republic. Scarcely less significant, though largely unrecognized, were the protean labors of C.G.F. Dumas, the first American agent in Europe and a man who displayed an unstinting devotion for the welfare of the United States.

The last few chapters relate how aging Patriots and younger Dutch conservatives reinterpreted the American political experience in the light of the more radical French Revolution, either by praising the stability and elitism that, they thought, derived from the Federal Constitution, or else by citing the American experience as a warning against the dangers of unrestrained popular rule. The author makes clear that no matter how

Dutch politicians and intellectuals looked upon the United States, their interest in its form of government continued unabated until the turn of the nineteenth century.

Schulte Nordholt has succeeded in renewing the subject of the Dutch recognition of the United States because, unlike earlier writers, he stresses the interrelations of two peoples rather than the links between two governments. He surpasses previous historians by his greater insight into human character, and by his warm sympathy for the many political and intellectual figures who promoted the American cause in the Netherlands. The book has been rendered into English so flawlessly by Herbert H. Rowen that, but for a few literary allusions and philosophical asides, one can scarcely tell that it originally came out abroad. It deserves a wide readership in the United States.

PAUL ROSENFELD

Rutgers University
Newark
New Jersey

VIGUERIE, RICHARD A. *The New Right: We're Ready to Lead.* Pp. 191. Falls Church, VA: Viguerie Company, 1981. $8.95.

BELKER, LOREN B. *Organizing for Political Victory.* Pp. xi, 194. Chicago: Nelson-Hall, 1982. $16.95.

GREEN, MARK. *Winning Back America.* Pp. xi, 354. New York: Bantam Books, 1982. $3.95.

SIMON, PAUL. *The Once and Future Democrats: Strategies for Change.* Pp. 182. New York: Continuum, 1982. $12.95.

Richard Viguerie, author of *The New Right,* is well known for first using direct mail techniques to raise money for political causes. Himself a zealous New Right conservative, his successful mail solicitation business with its computerized lists of millions of names serves conservative causes. Viguerie believes that the New Right is about to triumph at the polls and take over the Republi-

can Party. His book is a political manifesto that pinpoints conservative issues and explains the importance of the new techniques of persuasion and money raising. The groups he hopes to unite in a conservative coalition are a disparate lot—those opposed to abortion, gun laws, pornography, detente, welfare spending, Panama Canal treaties, affirmative action, and so on. Their members believe in God, school prayers, hard work, thrift, honesty, chastity, and motherhood, and they pledge allegiance to the flag and proudly sing our national anthem. The core of this conservative alliance is the Moral Majority. Viguerie alleges that Jerry Falwell has uncovered 50 million conservative born-again Protestants and 30 million conservative Catholics and Jews. He advises President Reagan to lead these people in a great national religious revival, to proclaim national days of fasting and prayer, and to encourage good citizens to visit the sick, prisoners, and the dying.

Viguerie is the soap-box demagogue who strings together pious slogans and catchy clichés to appeal to the frustrated who do not know the cause of their unhappiness. If such people become desperate they will respond to myths, and Viguerie is a myth maker. But the evidence is reasonably clear that the American people are not that desperate—yet. The conservative tide receded in November 1982, and the issues seem to be the real ones of jobs, inflation, and the arms race. The inflamed language of this little book does not convince that the New Right is likely to take over the country soon.

Loren Belker, author of *Organizing for Political Victory,* is a Nebraska insurance man who managed the successful campaign of the Nebraska senator, J. James Exon. His very prosaic how-to book avoids all mention of issues and offers purely technical advice useful in those low-key campaigns where there are no real differences between the candidates. Belker assumes that a person decides it would be fun to be an elected official and throws his hat into the ring. Belker's book tells such a candidate how to choose a campaign manager, how to hold dinners and cocktail parties, and especially how to project the right image: hire a good public relations agency, take a Dale Carnegie course in public speaking, keep your hair cut, shake hands firmly, and look voters directly in the eye—but be careful here, because a long look into the eyes of a member of the opposite sex has a dangerous sexual connotation. No mention here of Viguerie's sophisticated direct mail methods.

Politics for Belker is a pleasant game for amateurs. The candidate must of course address some issues. Belker advises appointing an issues committee that will come up with a maximum of three issues that will appeal. Perhaps this sounds worse than it is: Belker is a liberal Democrat who probably cannot imagine a Nebraska candidate choosing sham issues. But the reader is left with the scary impression that Belker thinks that one popular issue is as good as another in the American political game.

Mark Green is a successful public-interest lawyer and political commentator. His book, *Winning Back America,* is offered as a "positive program of electable liberalism." It is an encyclopedia of facts and issues for progressive candidates. Green pays tribute to the campaign skills of Viguerie, but he focuses on the issues. He is an aggressive spokesman for political and economic democracy and believes that Reagan Republicanism can be defeated.

I am not unsympathetic to Green's point of view but was bored by his book. A paperback of 350 pages with small type, gray paper, and almost no margins is unappealing. Within this drab format, Green manages to crowd some discussion of nearly every important issue of the day. His solutions are bland, simplistic, overoptimistic, and unconvincing. The financial problems of Social Security, he says in two pages, are easily solved in the short run, and in the long run who knows what may turn up, so why worry? Similar short and facile discussions cover inflation, jobs, nuclear war, a national health system, multinational corporations—the United Nations should send these a questionnaire to find out what they are up to—and so

on. The only thing missing is any policy for education, science, and the arts. The reader is left with the impression that there are no real problems, but only apparent ones created by Ronald Reagan and David Stockman.

Paul Simon, a liberal Democratic congressman from conservative southern Indiana, survived the Republican surge in 1980 and was reelected in 1982. His book is good reading. Simon is a student of history and literature as well as of politics and economics and comes through as an educated person. His qualities are intelligence, common sense, tolerance, and a respect for excellence. He has those habits of rationality that become a leader.

He has damning things to say about politicians who do not lead but follow public opinion polls—like Belker's clients; wise and temperate things to say about the Moral Majority, whose demagoguery he exposes but whose appeal to troubled people he makes credible. Unlike Green, he has ideas about education and culture, citing a Chinese saying, "They had no poets so the city died," and he is not afraid of the charge of elitism when speaking of excellence in the arts and sciences. On health care, instead of the utopianism of Green, he comments that a program of national health coverage similar to Canada's is not likely to pass Congress in the next 10 years, but that we can do a lot to meet the most pressing needs of our society; and then outlines a possible program.

Simon has sensible things to say on other issues—energy, defense, inflation, foreign policy, and so on. He is cautiously optimistic but promises no millennium. The human condition is improvable, he assumes, but not perfectible. Viguerie and Green believe it is perfectible; Belker has no thoughts on the matter. Simon concludes his book with a quotation from Walt Whitman: "It is provided in the essence of things that from every fruition of success, no matter what, shall come forth something to make a greater struggle necessary."

RICHARD SCHLATTER
Rutgers University
New Brunswick
New Jersey

SOCIOLOGY

ENGRAM, ELEANOR. *Science, Myth, Reality: The Black Family in One-Half Century of Research.* Pp. xviii, 216. Westport, CT: Greenwood Press, 1982. $27.50.

The thesis of this book is that propositions derived by social science research about the black family in the United States are so tainted by white middle-class biases as to comprise a body of myth—indeed of scientific racism—which perpetuates the stereotype that lower-class black families are deviant entities without redeeming social value.

Engram, a Duke University Ph.D. and now a businesswoman on the West Coast, begins by identifying biases presumably inherent in the institutional, structural-functional, and interactionist schools of sociology—she omits consideration of conflict/radical thought—and concludes that only anthropology's enthographic approach, with its tradition of avoiding censure of exotic peoples' ways, is sufficiently free of value orientations to get at the realities of black life. Next, Engram reports in 93 pages her evaluations of a selected body of research, published mostly after 1959, pertaining to black mating, unwed motherhood, marriage, child rearing, and marital disruption. The researches scrutinized were not chosen by systematic sampling of her nearly 800-item bibliography, but were, I think, selected because in her view they reveal either lingering racist feelings in their authors or an ignorance of the humanistic values in black culture. Thus, for example, sociologists perpetuate the myth of black hypersexuality, but seem unaware that "potence is stimulated by tenderness and caring," qualities she asserts to be abundantly present among poor blacks.

The book closes with a brief consideration of the methodological problems Engram feels are peculiarly encountered in researching black life, and a short conclusions chapter. Engram here broaches, but regrettably does not develop, the very interesting idea that if race is indeed an untenable biological concept, as Ashley Montagu and others have long insisted—a position she seems to agree with—then social scientists who carve off a race for study will assuredly discover traits, such as black male irresponsibility, which feed back into a racial mythology. Less prejudicial joints at which to carve, Engram suggests, would be along a society's socio-economic lines, whatever might be the racial distribution within the strata.

This book is much too light a vehicle for the heavy burden of its thesis, but it does deliver, in a voice of despair and anger, a more blunt and personal message: white social scientists, after decades of research, still do not understand blacks; their eyes are blinded particularly to the compassionate, loving, caring altruism that is an enriching part of African heritage, and that permeates and gives authenticity to even seemingly pathology-ridden black ghetto families.

RALPH W. ENGLAND, Jr.
University of Rhode Island
Kingston

KUPER, LEO. *Genocide: Its Political Use in the Twentieth Century.* Pp. 255. New Haven, CT: Yale University Press, 1982. $15.00.

Genocide: Its Political Use in the Twentieth Century, by sociologist Leo Kuper, gives a systematic analysis of the massacres of 800,000 Armenians in 1915, six million Jews between 1933 and 1945, three million Bangladeshis in 1971, and 100,000 Huter between 1972 and 1975.

Kuper begins his work by placing genocide within its most usual contexts: religious, racial, and ethnic. He further presses the notion that historical evidence supports Arthur Koestler's position "that the trouble of our species is not an excess of aggression but an excess capacity for fanatical devotion."

This "fanatical devotion," Kuper points out, is really a "warrant for genocide" and becomes, in fact, not only a necessary condition but its justification. In other words, the genuine fanatic constructs a legitimating ideology behind which to put into motion the operations for murder. He develops a theory that genocide in the twentieth century becomes workable in plural societies—that is, in societies that contain "persistent and pervasive" cleavages between the racial, ethnic, and/or religious groups that compose them. He concludes, properly, that genocide becomes the one possible means whereby the political and/or religious and racial elite can maintain its power.

Kuper's work is provocative and bold, showing how the great political powers have encouraged genocide by supplying the contending parties with sophisticated arms for mutual destruction, yet he remains hopeful that his analysis will ultimately be used by those great powers as a plea for restraint.

JOSEPHINE KNOPP

Harcum Junior College
Bryn Mawr
Pennsylvania

LÉVI-STRAUSS, CLAUDE. *The Way of the Masks.* Translated by Sylvia Modelski. Pp. x, 249. Seattle: University of Washington Press, 1982. $18.95.

This short book is especially recommended to those who have heard of Lévi-Strauss and French structuralism, but who have been reluctant to read the larger works. It presents a straightforward analysis, in simple language, of ceremonial masks and associated myths found among the Indians of the Northwest Coast. This is the English translation of an essay originally published in 1975 with the title *La Voie des masques,* plus three journal articles published between 1975 and 1979. With the exception of one article devoted to Kwakiutl social organization, the other parts of the book all deal with the masks and myths of the American Indians who lived along the Pacific coast from Alaska to Vancouver Island.

The problem with which Lévi-Strauss begins is how to explain the peculiar shape of a mask used in ceremonies by several Salish-speaking tribes of the area. Lévi-Strauss proposes that masks and other works of art should be analyzed using essentially the same methodology that he has long applied to myths.

In the case of the Salish mask, he argues that it is impossible to understand the mask if it is considered only in the context of the society in which it is found. The true meaning of the mask will appear only if it is compared with masks found in other societies. In the present instance, Lévi-Strauss assumes that all of the Northwest Coast tribes have had intensive contact with one another and have borrowed myths, masks, and beliefs to the extent that they share a common ideological structure and it is in terms of this structure that masks or myths will have meaning. Once Levi-Strauss has found a mask among the Kwakiutl that contrasts both in physical characteristics and associated beliefs with the Salish mask, he maintains that he has explained the masks by showing how they have complementary roles in this larger system of ideas.

The remainder of the book deals with the myths associated with wealth objects called coppers and attempts to show how these myths are part of the same ideological structure that includes the masks.

At several points in his analysis Lévi-Strauss pauses to consider criticisms of his earlier work. However, he does not deal with the most basic criticism—that this method of determining ideological structures is essentially arbitrary. In the present work it may also be questioned whether he has not exaggerated the extent to which the tribes of the Northwest Coast shared a common culture.

SETH LEACOCK

University of Connecticut
Storrs

LIGHTFOOT, DAVID. *The Language Lottery: Toward a Biology of Grammars.* Pp. xii, 224. Cambridge, MA: MIT Press, 1982. $17.50.

Lightfoot explores the relation between genetics and grammars, using child language acquisition to connect them. A basic problem for linguists is how children learn language even though exposed to very fragmentary stimuli. As part of their genetic endowment, children have a rich set of innate grammatical principles enabling them to create a grammar for their language. The grammars linguists write attempt to reflect the language universals children inherit and use to master their language. This book ably introduces some of the concepts that guide this kind of research.

Lightfoot studies genetics not just to shed light on language acquisition but to advance certain grammatical descriptions over and against their rivals. Many, however, balk at equating the grammars children create with those that linguists write. Accordingly they will find unjustified Lightfoot's claim of genetic sanction for his favorite analyses, viewing it as a gratuitous attempt to establish a legal monopoly for some pet theories.

Lightfoot implies that parallel order between determiners and nouns and between auxiliary and main verbs is genetically determined, making language easier to learn. If the orders differ, as in any Dravidian language where determiners precede—that man —but auxiliaries follow—he gone has—they hinder language acquisition and will evolve to conform to the genetic template. Yet the Dravidian languages have steadfastly maintained this pattern for 2000 years. Lightfoot suggests that subject-object-verb word order causes perceptual difficulties, impeding language acquisition, and tends to change to subject-verb-object word order, as in English. Of the 23 Dravidian languages, 21 have preserved subject-object-verb word order for two millenia, oblivious to the strain they put on children's ability to learn Tamil, Kannada, or Telugu. If we take the link between genetics and grammars seriously, we must either segregate Dravidian speakers as a genetically distinct population or, preferably, revise the putative universals their languages are supposed to violate.

Fear of arbitrariness in grammars makes linguists invoke notions to reduce it—simplicity, psychological reality, and, now, genetics. But such arbitrariness is a global property of whole grammars, not of isolated pieces. No one would deny genetics a central role in explanations of holistic language acquisition. But then to conclude that it supports one's particular analysis of modal auxiliaries or phonological features is logically suspect. Notwithstanding these reservations, Lightfoot's well-written, engaging book raises exciting, important issues and deserves to be carefully read.

SANFORD B. STEEVER

University of Chicago
Illinois

PERRY, RONALD W. *The Social Psychology of Civil Defense.* Pp. 127. Lexington, MA: D. C. Heath, 1982. No price.

Disaster research is a relatively new specialty in the social sciences. The author of this well-written little book deals with the issue of what can be expected of civil defense programs and how citizens will respond to warnings of nuclear attack.

How are people likely to behave in connection with a crisis-relocation program? Past experience of natural disasters does provide, in the absence of prior experience of nuclear attack, some data on human responses to evacuation programs. Perry points out that several assumptions regarding crisis relocation planning (CRP) require examination.

The book concentrates on the issue of citizens' likely response to warnings to evacuate under CRP. How can studies of evacuation in natural disasters be utilized in increasing our knowledge of citizen response to nuclear attack warnings? Four relevant issues are examined as a means of answering this question:

(1) the theoretical bases in social science for civil-defense programs; (2) the logic that underlies

comparisons of nuclear attack with natural disasters; (3) the extent and nature of comparisons that can be made based upon warning-response in natural disasters; and (4) the implications of these comparisons for the design and implementation of crisis-relocation planning [p. 3].

After a masterly summary review of civil defense efforts and the philosophy of emergency managements, Perry devotes three chapters to these specific issues. He stresses emergent-norm theory, which explains collective behavior on the basis of spontaneous search for meaning by persons faced with an unstructured situation, and points out its applicability as a theoretical standpoint.

The book shows a sophisticated awareness of the problems of comparing natural and nuclear disasters, in particular by reference to three variables inherent in the emerging decision-making processes. This is followed by a competent review of research conclusions, and the connection between other variables. Perry affords a model specifying the variables that are significant in personal decisions to relocate or evacuate.

The work manifests a thorough acquaintance with the relevant literature and is marked by clarity of style. Within a short volume Perry has provided a wealth of material that adds appreciably to our understanding of an increasingly crucial area of social science research. On any applicable criterion, this is a scholarly and informed contribution.

JOHN E. OWEN

Arizona State University
Tempe

ECONOMICS

PINDER, JOHN, ed. *National Industrial Strategies and the World Economy.* An Atlantic Institute for International Affairs Research Volume. Pp. ix, 302. London: Allanheld, Osmun, Croom Helm, 1982. $34.50.

This volume attempts to analyze the sources and potential solutions to the glaring shortcomings of industrial policies in advanced countries. Eight commentators offer their analyses. The first, by Saunders, examines changes in the distribution of world production and trade. It offers a useful, tight summary of the transformation of industrial sectors in the world economy over the past two decades. The second contribution, by Pinder, examines how policy changes are viewed not just as a threat to the international order, but as a necessary response to imperfections of modern industrial markets. Pinder sees the problem of modern industrial policy as one of accommodating and encouraging positive and efficient, rather than negative and inefficient protective industrial policies.

The first two articles set the stage for the following sectoral and country analyses. The third selection by Woolcock looks at the steel sector. He asks how countries have reacted to the stagnating demand for steel since the early 1970s. The answer, as we know, is disquieting. The response has mainly been one of increased public intervention. These interventions have unfortunately been short-term palliatives rather than long-term adjustments to supply and demand and comparative cost. Following steel, Edwards launches into an analysis of four other sectors—textiles, man-made fibers, shipbuilding, and aircraft. His is an ambitious attempt to explain the differential developments in these sectors, and he largely succeeds.

Hosomi and Okumura, in the first of four country analyses, document the widespread acceptance of industrial policy in Japan. It is actively used as a tool to promote Japanese firms in key areas of research and development, energy conservation, small-firm development, and recession cartels. Japanese activism is to be sharply contrasted to the U.S. case discussed by Diebold. The United States has had no explicit industrial policies. While industries may be rocked by unintended actions of government, for example, there is a strong antiindustrila policy bias in the United States—a bias still intact as of late 1982. Diebold explains why this has historically been true. But he adds that the international position of the United States has slipped, so that an intelligent and comprehensive U.S. policy is needed. Diebold next examines the Canadian case. In Canada numerous dilemmas of industrial policy revolve around more restrictive versus more open foreign investment, as well as freer versus more protectionist trade, and the structural mix of industry. Diebold usefully restricts himself to developing a series of insightful policy questions rather than seeking definitive, obviously premature answers.

Hager focuses on the common roots of industrial policy in western Europe, where industrial policy is often and willingly used to keep the peace between social classes. He raises the key question of how Western Europe can beneficially—for itself—favor international competitiveness. Generally, the European Community is on the defensive over time in competition with nonindustrialized countries. Since the community cannot allow its industries to be eroded, the question boils down to what the necessary degree of incremental protection is, given that we want trade to be as large as conditions permit.

In the final chapter, Pinder rejects cynicism and sees real possibilities for positive nonprotective industrial policies that offer the benefits of specialization and division of labor while minimizing world political conflict. He finds many examples among the pioneering European Community countries, which have been joined in a ladder of economic convergences. Pinder finds growing integration despite the divergences during world recession. He puts the final outcome in the form of a challenge for industrial and developing countries.

In my judgment this collection is both important and contributory. It offers us a careful analysis by knowledgeable observers. Admittedly it is only a beginning, considering the challenge of dissolution that we face. Much is to be done to avoid the potential disasters that lurk in uninformed nationalism and protectionism. The United States is merely beginning to look at the unintended repercussions of its own unplanned actions. The controversy here still rages, however, as

a recent *Wall Street Journal* front-page column doubting the wisdom of industrial policy still indicates. However, some small victories are being scored. One example is *The Global 2000 Report to the President*. The report points up the complete lack of basic statistical coordination between such major departments of the U.S. government as Energy and Agriculture. The mere fact that the report was published, under the auspices of the U.S. government, despite tremendous opposition of entrenched ideologues, indicates the slow but definite progress we have made. Pessimism and cynicism may be fashionable, but the collection under review offers a positive and constructive antidote to do-nothingism.

DONALD HUDDLE

Rice University
Houston
Texas

SHINOHARA, MIYOHEI. *Industrial Growth, Trade, and Dynamic Patterns in the Japanese Economy.* Pp. x, 243. Tokyo: University of Tokyo Press, 1982. Distributed by Columbia University Press. $17.50.

Readers of these 14 articles will learn why Japan has become an industrial giant in Asia and how Japanese economic growth helped to industrialize South Korea, Taiwan, Hong Kong, and Singapore, the newly industrialized countries (NICs). This book sparkles with insights and contains many valuable tables showing important economic relationships for the Pacific Basin countries.

According to Shinohara, Japanese postwar economic growth must be understood in terms of rapid structural change. The constant pattern underlying this process, however, was one of new industries expanding with new technology, exporting, and yet stimulating the growth of domestic production, while always lowering unit costs. These new blocks of industries fitted deeply into the domestic structure through subcontracting, even monopsonistic arrangements, and they exported to high-income markets where demand was rising. Government agencies like the Ministry of International Trade and Industries (MITI) greatly assisted the evolution of these industrial structures by encouraging industrial mergers and helping certain industries like textiles to exit from the market.

Just as Japan has now caught up with the United States as a world economic power, so too are the NICs of Asia striving to catch up with Japan by similar state-guided politics that promote export-led industrial growth at home. As Japan also invests and transfers advanced technology to those NICs, their industrial structures become similar to Japan's. Without Japanese exports of capital goods to the NICs and Japan's importing more goods from the Pacific Basin community, this region would never have grown as rapidly as it did in the 1970s. Shinohara predicts that this pattern will continue through the 1980s and beyond, with the Association of Southeast Asian Nations countries gradually joining today's NICs. The big question mark, of course, is China, for it is still not clear if sufficient economic modernization will occur to permit that huge country to develop the same export-led industrial growth pattern as that of the Pacific Basin states.

Shinohara believes world trade expansion must continue if Japan and the Pacific Basin are to prosper as in the recent past. For this goal he advocates policies in Japan of limiting exports of automobiles to the United States until the American auto industry can be revitalized. He urges such fine tuning policy to deter protectionist policies from Washington, which could disrupt the complex trade and growth mechanism in the Pacific Basin.

There are also other interesting articles that explain why Japan's ratio of savings to gross national product is so high, why key industries like steel and automobiles rapidly became modernized and captured high market shares in the advanced countries, and why investment cycles of 24 months or 10 or 12 years are still important for policymakers. These excellent, high-quality articles ought to be read by policymakers in Washington. It is hoped that many of them will learn about how Japan overtook the United States, how Pacific Basin trade and industrialization developed so rapidly, and why Japan and the United States must cooperate and find policies to solve their current economic difficulties rather than engaging in conflict through trade protectionism.

RAMON H. MYERS

Hoover Institution on
    War, Revolution and Peace
Stanford
California

OTHER BOOKS

ABRAHAMSON, MARK. *Social Research Methods.* Pp. xvii, 413. Englewood Cliffs, NJ: Prentice-Hall, 1983. $21.95.

ALBERTONI, ETTORE A., ed. *Studies on the Political Thought of Gaetano Mosca: The Theory of the Ruling Class and Its Development Abroad.* Pp. x, 205. Milan, Italy: Gaetano Mosca International Committee for the Study of the Ruling Class, 1982. Paperbound, $12.00.

ALDOUS, JEAN, ed. *Two Paychecks: Life in Dual-Earner Families.* Pp. 248. Beverly Hills, CA: Sage, 1982. $22.00. Paperbound, $10.95.

ALEXANDER, YONAH and KENNETH A. MYERS, eds. *Terrorism in Europe.* Pp. 216. New York: St. Martin's Press, 1982. $25.00.

ALLAN, J. A., ed. *Libya since Independence: Economic & Social Development.* Pp. 184. New York: St. Martin's Press, 1982. $22.50.

ATWATER, EASTWOOD. *Psychology of Adjustment: Personal Growth in a Changing World.* Pp. xvi, 426. Englewood Cliffs, NJ: Prentice-Hall, Inc., 1983. No price.

BAILY, MARTIN NEIL, ed. *Workers, Jobs, and Inflation.* Pp. xiv, 365. Washington, DC: Brookings Institution, 1982. $31.95. Paperbound, $12.95.

BAK, JANOS M. and BELA K. KIRALY, eds. *From Hunyadi to Rakoczi: War and Society in Late Medieval and Early Modern Hungary.* Pp. xiii, 545. Brooklyn, NY: Brooklyn College Press, 1982. Distributed by Columbia University Press, New York. $27.50.

BARDO, JOHN W. and JOHN J. HARTMAN. *Urban Sociology: A Systematic Introduction.* Pp. vii, 401. Itasca, IL: F. E. Peacock Publishers, Inc., 1982. No price.

BERLINER, ARTHUR K. *Psychoanalysis and Society: The Social Thought of Sigmund Freud.* Pp. x, 205. Washington, DC: University Press of America, 1983. $20.75. Paperbound, $10.50.

BIKLEN, DOUGLAS P. *Community Organizing: Theory and Practice.* Pp. xii, 321. Englewood Cliffs, NJ: Prentice-Hall, 1983. No price.

BLANTZ, THOMAS, E., D.S.C. *A Priest in Public Service: Francis J. Haas and the New Deal.* Pp. xi, 380. Notre Dame, IN: University of Notre Dame Press, 1982. $25.00.

BLUHM, WILLIAM T., ed. *The Paradigm Problem in Political Science: Perspectives from Philosophy and from Practice.* Pp. 227. Durham, NC: Carolina Academic Press, 1982. $19.95. Paperbound, $9.95.

BRECHER, CHARLES and RAYMOND D. HORTON, eds. *Setting Municipal Priorities, 1983.* Pp. vii, 252. New York: Columbia University, 1982. $27.50.

BROWN, ARCHIE and MICHAEL KASER, eds. *Soviet Policy for the 1980s.* Pp. xiv, 282. Bloomington: Indiana University Press, 1983. $19.50.

BURGHARDT, STEVE. *Organizing for Community Action.* Pp. 120. Beverly Hills, CA: Sage, 1982. Paperbound, $7.00.

CARSTEN, F. L. *The Rise of Fascism.* 2nd ed. Pp. 279. Berkeley, CA: University of California Press, 1982. $18.50. Paperbound, $7.95.

CASSEN, ROBERT et al., eds. *Rich Country Interests and Third World Development.* Pp. 369. New York: St. Martin's Press, 1982. $32.50.

CATES, JUDITH N. and MARVIN B. SUSSMAN, eds. *Family Systems and Inheritance Patterns.* Pp. 124. New York: Haworth Press, 1983. $19.95.

CHALIAND, GERARD, ed. *Guerilla Strategies: An Historical Anthology from the Long March to Afghanistan.* Pp. 353. Berkeley: University of California Press, 1983. $28.50. Paperbound, $7.95.

CHILCOTE, RONALD H., ed. *Dependency and Marxism: Toward a Resolution of the Debate.* Pp. xi, 179. Boulder, CO: Westview Press, 1982. $18.95. Paperbound, $9.95.

CHURCH, GENE and CONRAD D. CARNES. *Brainwash.* Pp. viii, 164. Glendale, CA: Great Western Publishing Co., 1982. $5.95.

CLARKE, PRESCOTT and J. S. GREGORY. *Western Reports on the Taiping: A Selection of Documents.* Pp. xxx, 454. Honolulu, HI: University of Hawaii, 1982. $25.00. Paperbound, $15.95.

CORTADA, JAMES W. *Historical Dictionary of the Spanish Civil War, 1936-1939.* Pp. xxviii, 573. Westport, CT: Greenwood Press, 1982. $67.50.

CRABB, CECIL V., Jr. *American Foreign Policy in the Nuclear Age.* 4th ed. Pp. x, 614. New York: Harper & Row, 1982. Paperbound, $18.50.

CRAIG, GRACE J. *Human Development.* 3rd ed. Pp. xv, 587. Englewood Cliffs, NJ: Prentice-Hall, Inc., 1983. No price.

DEVLIN, JOHN F. *Syria: Modern State in an Ancient Land.* Pp. xi, 140. Boulder, CO: Westview Press, 1983. $16.50.

DOBKOWSKI, MICHAEL N., ed. *The Politics of Indifference: A Documentary History of Holocaust Victims in America.* Pp. xii, 473. Washington, DC: University Press of America Inc., 1982. $29.75. Paperbound, $17.25.

ELCOCK, HOWARD. *Local Government: Politicians, Professionals and the Public in Local Authorities.* Pp. xi, 330. New York: Methuen, 1982. $25.00. Paperbound, $10.95.

ELLISTON, FREDERICK and NORMAN BOWIE. *Ethics, Public Policy, and Criminal Justice.* Pp. xvi, 495. Cambridge, MA: Oelgeschlager, Gunn and Hain, Publishers, 1982. $30.00.

FISHBEIN, LESLIE. *Rebels in Bohemia: The Radicals of the Masses, 1911-1917.* Pp. xv, 270. Chapel Hill, NC: University of North Carolina Press, 1982. $24.50.

FITZPATRICK, FATHER TOM. *The Barrio God.* Pp. xiv, 127. Glendale, CA: Great Western Publishing Co., 1981. Paperbound, $7.°̄

GAPPERT, GARY and RICHARD V. KNIGHT, eds. *Cities in the 21st Century.* Pp. 352. Beverly Hills, CA: Sage Publications, Inc., 1982. $25.00. Paperbound, $12.50.

GARRATY, JOHN A. *The American Nation: A History of the United States.* 2 vols. 5th ed. Pp. xvi, 835. New York: Harper and Row, 1983. Paperbound, $18.50 each volume. 1-vol. ed., $24.95.

GIDDENS, ANTHONY and GAVIN MACKENZIE, eds. *Social Class and the Division of Labour: Essays in Honour of Ilya Neustadt.* Pp. xvi, 337. New York: Cambridge University Press, 1982. $34.50. Paperbound, $11.95.

GILBERT, MARTIN. *Winston Churchill: The Wilderness Years.* Pp. 279. Boston: Houghton Mifflin, 1982. $16.95.

GODSON, ROY, ed. *Intelligence Requirements for the 1980's: Clandestine Collection.* Pp. x, 231. New York: National Strategy Information Center, Inc., 1982. Paperbound, $8.50.

HAGUE, ROD and MARTIN HARROP. *Comparative Government: An Introduction.* Pp. xiv, 266. Atlantic Highlands, NJ: Humanities Press, 1983. $22.95. Paperbound, $9.95.

HAREVEN, TAMARA K. and KATHLEEN J. ADAMS, eds *Aging and Life Course Transitions: An Interdisciplinary Perspective.* Pp. xviii, 281. New York: Guilford Press, 1982. $24.50.

HERNANDEZ, ERNIE, Jr. *Police Handbook for Applying the Systems Approach and Computer Technology.* Pp. viii, 231. El Toro, CA: Frontline Publications, 1982. Paperbound. No price.

HERZ, JOHN H., ed. *From Dictatorship to Democracy: Coping with the Legacies of Authoritarianism and Totalitarianism.* Pp. xii, 311. Westport, CT: Greenwood Press, 1982. $35.00.

HOOD, NEIL and STEPHEN YOUNG. *Multinationals in Retreat: The Scottish Experience.* Pp. xi, 193. Edinburgh, Scotland: Edinburgh University Press, 1982. Distributed by Columbia University Press, New York. Paperbound, $20.00.

HOPPLE, GERALD W., ed. *Biopolitics, Political Psychology and International Politics: Towards a New Discipline.* Pp. xiii, 195. New York: St. Martin's Press, 1982. $22.50.

HOSMER, STEPHEN T. and THOMAS W. WOLFE. *Soviet Policy and Practice toward Third World Conflicts.* Lexington, MA: Lexington Books, 1983. $23.95.

HUMMEL, RALPH P. *The Bureaucratic Experience.* 2nd ed. Pp. xv, 282. New York: St. Martin's Press, 1982. $16.95. Paperbound, $8.95.

HUMPHRY, DEREK and ANN WICKETT. *Jean's Way.* Pp. 116. Glendale, CA: Great Western Publishing, 1981. $5.95.

JACKSON, DOUGLAS W. and SUSAN C. PESCAR. *The Young Athlete's Health Handbook: A Guide to Sports Medicine and Sports Psychology for Parents, Teachers, Coaches, and Players.* Pp. 317. New York: Everest House, 1981. $9.95.

JAFFA, HARRY V., ed. *Statesmanship: Essays in Honor of Sir Winston Spencer Churchill.* Pp. viii, 279. Durham, NC: Carolina Academic Press, 1981. $22.95.

JANIS, IRVING L. *Groupthink: Psychological Studies of Policy Decisions and Fiascoes.* 2nd ed., rev. Pp. xii, 351. Boston, MA: Houghton Mifflin, 1983. $14.95.

JULIAN, JOSEPH and KORNBLUM WILLIAM. *Social Problems.* 4th ed. Pp. xv, 606. Englewood Cliffs, NJ: Prentice-Hall, Inc., 1983. No price.

KAHN-HUT, RACHEL, ARLENE KAPLAN DANIELS, and RICHARD VOLVARD. *Women and Work: Problems and Perspectives.* Pp. xi, 327. New York: Oxford University Press, 1982. $19.95. Paperbound, $9.95.

KATZ, BARRY. *Herbert Marcuse and the Art of Liberation: An Intellectual Biography.* Pp. 234. London: NLB, 1982. Distributed by Schocken Books, New York. $22.50. Paperbound, $8.50.

KEGLEY, CHARLES W., Jr. and EUGENE R. WITTKOPF. *American Foreign Policy: Pattern and Process.* 2nd ed. Pp. xv, 661. New York: St. Martin's Press, 1982. $19.95. Paperbound, $12.95.

KENDALL, PATRICIA L., ed. *The Varied Sociology of Paul F. Lazarsfeld.* Pp. xiii, 417. New York: Columbia University Press, 1982. $35.00. Paperbound, $17.50.

KIRBY, ANDREW. *The Politics of Location: An Introduction.* Pp. xvii, 199. New York, NY: Methuen, 1982. $28.00. Paperbound, $13.95.

KNORR, KLAUS and PATRICK MORGAN, eds. *Strategic Military Surprise: Incentives and Opportunities.* Pp. vi, 265. New Brunswick, NJ: Transaction Books, 1983. Paperbound, no price.

KOSECOFF, JACQUELINE and ARLENE FINK. *Evaluation Basics: A Practitioner's Manual.* Pp. 247. Beverly Hills, CA: Sage Publication, 1982. $29.95. Paperbound, $14.95.

KRAMER, RALPH M. and HARRY SPECHT, eds. *Readings in Community Organization Practice.* 3rd ed. Pp. iv, 444. Englewood Cliffs, NY: Prentice-Hall, Inc., 1983. Paperbound, no price.

KRITZ, MARY M., ed. *U.S. Immigration and Refugee Policy: Global and Domestic Issues.* Pp. xxi, 415. Lexington, MA: D. C. Heath & Co., 1983. No price.

KRUECKEBERG, DONALD A., ed. *Introduction to Planning History in the United States.* Pp. xiv, 302. New Brunswick, NJ: Center for Urban Policy Research, Rutgers University, 1983. Paperbound, $12.95.

LAUER, ROBERT H. and WARREN H. HANDEL. *Social Psychology: The Theory and Application of Symbolic Interactionism.* 2nd ed. Pp. xi, 372. Englewood Cliffs, NJ: Prentice-Hall, 1983. $21.95.

LEGUM, COLIN, ed. *Crisis and Conflicts in the Middle East: The Changing Strategy, from Iran to Afghanistan.* Pp. 159. New York: Holmes and Meier Publishers, 1982. Paperbound, $12.50.

LEITES, NATHAN. *Soviet Style in War.* Pp. xxvi, 398. New York: Crane, Russak and Company, 1982. $22.50.

LEVINTHAL, CHARLES F. *Introduction to Physiological Psychology.* 2nd ed. Pp. x, 515. Englewood Cliffs, NJ: Prentice-Hall, Inc., 1983. No price.

LEWIS, WILLIAM J. *The Warsaw Pact: Arms, Doctrine and Strategy.* Pp. xii, 471. New York: McGraw-Hill, 1982. $29.95.

LONG, SAMUEL, ed. *Political Science Abstracts: 1981 Annual Supplement.* 3 vols. Pp. 2265. New York: IFI/Plenum, 1982. $375.00.

MARTIN, GARY and JOSEPH PEAR. *Behavior Modification: What It Is and How to Do It.* Pp. xxii, 522. Englewood Cliffs, NJ: Prentice-Hall, Inc., 1983. Paperbound, no price.

MARTINEZ-BRAWLEY, EMILIA E. *Seven Decades of Rural Social Work: From Country Life Commission to Rural Caucus.* Pp. xiv, 275. New York: Praeger, 1982. $23.95.

MAZMANIAN, DANIEL A. and PAUL A. SABATIER. *Implementation and Public Policy.* Pp. 299. Glenview, IL: Scott, Foresman and Company, 1983. Paperbound, $10.95.

McKAY, DAVID H., ed, *Planning and Politics in Western Europe.* Pp. x, 197. New York: St. Martin's Press, 1982. $27.50.

MILES, ROBERT, *Racism and Migrant Labour.* Pp. x, 202. Boston: Routledge and Kegan Paul, 1983. Paperbound, $9.95.

MILLER, ROSALIND S. and HELEN REHR, eds. *Social Work Issues in Health Care.* Pp. xi, 291. Englewood Cliffs, NJ: Prentice-Hall, Inc., 1983. No price.

MILLOR, MANUEL R. *Mexico's Oil: Catalyst for a New Relationship with the U.S.?* Pp. xi, 267. Boulder, CO: Westview Press, 1982. Paperbound, $19.50.

MOMIGLIANO, ARNALDO. *Essays in Ancient and Modern Historiography.* Pp. 387. Middletown, CT: Wesleyan University Press, 1982. Paperbound, no price.

MORELL, DAVID and CHAI-ANAN SAMUDAVANIJA. *Political Conflict in Thailand: Reform, Reaction, Revolution.* Pp. 362. Cambridge, MA: Oelgeschlager, Gunn and Hain, 1981. No price.

MYANT, MARTIN. *Poland: A Crisis for Socialism.* Pp. xvii, 254. London: Lawrence and Wishart, 1982. Distributed by Humanities Press, Atlantic Highlands, NJ. $21.00.

NAGEL, STUART, ERIKA FAIRCHILD, and ANTHONY CHAMPAGNE, eds. *The Political Science of Criminal Justice.* Pp. xv, 288. Springfield, IL: Charles C Thomas, 1983. $29.75.

NEWBY, JAMES E. *Teaching Faculty in Black Colleges and Universities: A Survey of Selected Social Science Disciplines, 1977-1978.* Pp. xvi, 95. Washington, DC: University Press of America, 1982. Paperbound, no price.

NOVOSELOV, SERGEI P., ed. *Problems of the Communist Movement.* Trans. D. Skvirsky. Pp. 336. Moscow: Progress Publishers, 1981. Distributed by Imported Publications, Chicago, IL. Paperbound, $6.00.

O'GORMAN, FRANK. *The Emergence of the British Two-Party System, 1760-1832.* Pp. xi, 132. London: Edward Arnold, 1982. Distributed by Holmes and Meier Publishers, New York. Paperbound, $10.50.

OLSON, WILLIAM C., DAVID S. McLELLAN, and FRED C. SONDERMANN. *The Theory and Practice of International Relations.* 6th ed. Pp. xiv, 401. Englewood Cliffs, NJ: Prentice-Hall, 1983. $14.95.

ORUM, ANTHONY M. *Introduction to Political Sociology,* 2nd ed. Pp. xi, 355. Englewood Cliffs, NJ: Prentice-Hall, 1983. No price.

PALMER, JOHN L. and ISABEL V. SAWHILL, eds. *The Reagan Experiment: An Examination of Economic and Social Policies under the Reagan Administration.* Pp. xvii, 530. Washington, DC: Urban Institute Press, 1982. $29.95. Paperbound, $12.95.

PAREKH, BHIKHU. *Contemporary Political Thinkers.* Pp. x, 219. Baltimore, MD: Johns Hopkins University Press, 1982. $22.50.

PEJOVICH, SVETOZAR, ed. *Philosophical and Economic Foundations of Capitalism.* Pp. xii, 144. Lexington, MA: D. C. Heath & Co., 1983. No price.

PLUNZ, RICHARD, ed. *Design and the Public Good: Selected Writings, 1930-*

1980 by Serge Chermayeff. Pp xxxiv, 414. Cambridge, MA: MIT Press, 1983. $35.00.

POPENOE, DAVID. *Sociology.* 5th ed. Pp. xx, 636. Englewood Cliffs, NJ: Prentice-Hall, 1983. $21.95.

PUNCH, MAURICE, ed. *Control in the Police Organization.* Pp. xvi, 346. Cambridge, MA: MIT Press, 1983. $30.00.

PUYANA DE PALACIOS, ALICIA. *Economic Integration among Unequal Partners.* Pp. xxvi, 405. Elmsford, NY: Pergamon Press Inc., 1982. $40.00.

ROBERTSON, A. H. *Human Rights in the World: An Introducion to the Study of International Protection of Human Rights.* 2nd ed. Pp. viii, 243. New York: St. Martin's Press, 1982. $22.50.

RODGERS, HARRELL R., Jr. *The Cost of Human Neglect: America's Welfare Failure.* Pp. x, 226. Armonk, NY: M. E. Sharpe, 1982. Paperbound, no price.

ROSS, STANLEY R. and THOMAS F. McGANN, eds. *Buenos Aires: 400 Years.* Pp xxii, 192. Austin, TX: University of Texas Press, 1982. $20.00.

ROSSI, PETER H., HOWARD E. FREEMAN, and SONIA R. WRIGHT. *Evaluation: A Systematic Approach.* Pp. 336. Beverly Hills, CA: Sage Publications, 1982. $20.00.

ROSSI, ROBERT J., KEVIN J. GILMARTIN, and CHARLES W. DAYTON. *Agencies Working Together: A Guide to Coordination and Planning.* Pp. 119. Beverly Hills, CA: Sage, 1982. Paperbound, $7.50.

RUBENSTEIN, RICHARD L., ed. *Modernization: The Humanist Response to Its Promise & Problems.* Pp. 393. Washington, DC: Paragon House Publishers, 1982. $24.95.

RUDWICK, ELLIOT. *Race Riots at East St. Louis.* Pp. 300. Champaign, IL: University of Illinois Press, 1982. Paperbound, $9.95.

RYAN, MARY P. *The Empire of the Mother: American Writing about Domesticity, 1830-1860.* Pp. 180. New York: Haworth Press, 1982. $24.95.

SCHACHTER, HINDY LAUER. *Public Agency Communication: Theory and Practice.* Pp. x, 239. Chicago: Nelson-Hall, 1983. $22.95.

SCHIAVONA, GIUSEPPE, ed. *East-West Relations: Proposals for the 1980s.* Pp. xiv, 217. New York: St. Martin's Press, 1982. $32.50.

SCHULZ, EBERHARD et al., eds. *GDR: Foreign Policy.* Pp. xxii, 348. Armonk, NY: M. E. Sharpe, Inc., 1982. $35.00.

SEARS, WILLIAM, M. D. *Creative Parenting: How to Use the New Continuum Concept to Raise Children Successfully from Birth through Adolescence.* Pp. 512. New York: Everest House, 1982. $19.95.

SECORD, PAUL F., ed. *Explaining Human Behavior: Consciousness, Human Action and Social Structure.* Pp. 320. Beverly Hills, CA: Sage Publications, 1982. No Price.

SIEGEL, IRVING H. and EDGAR WEINBERG. *Labor-Management Cooperation: The American Experience.* Pp. xi, 316. Kalamazoo, MI: W. E. Upjohn Institute for Employment Research, 1982. $13.95. Paperbound, $9.95.

SKLARE, MARSHALL, ed. *Understanding American Jewry.* Pp. xiv, 310. New Brunswick, NJ: Transaction Books, 1982. $21.95.

SLANY, WILLIAM Z. et al., eds. *Foreign Relations of the United States 1951.* Vol. V. *The Near East and Africa.* Pp. xxvi, 1497. Washington, DC: Government Printing Office, 1982. No price.

SNOWDEN, LONNIE R., ed. *Reaching the Underserved: Mental Health Needs of Neglected Populations.* Pp. 304. Beverly Hills, CA: Sage, 1982. $25.00. Paperbound, $12.50.

Stanford Central American Action Network, ed. *Revolution in Central America.* Pp. xx, 508. Boulder, CO: Westview Press, 1983. $30.00. Paperbound, $13.95.

STOJANOVĬC, RADMILA, ed. *The Functioning of the Yugoslav Economy.* Pp. ix, 276. Armonk, NY: M. E. Sharpe and Spokesman, Great Britain, 1982. $35.00.

STUART-FOX, MARTIN, ed. *Contemporary Laos: Studies in the Politics and Society of the Lao People's Democratic Republic.* Pp. 345. New York: St. Martin's Press, 1982. No price.

SUMMERSCALE, PETER. *The East European Predicament: Changing Patterns in Poland, Czechoslovakia and Romania.* Pp. vii, 147. New York: St. Martin's Press, 1982. Published for the Royal Institute of International Affairs. $20.00.

SWEENEY, TERRANCE, A., S. J. *Streets of Anger, Streets of Hope: Youth Gangs in East Los Angeles.* Pp. xxiv, 229. Glendale, CA: Great Western Publishing, 1980. Paperbound, $8.95.

TAYLOR, STAN. *The National Front in English Politics.* Pp. xvii, 212. New York: Holmes and Meier Publishers, 1982. $34.50.

TOCH, HANS and GRANT J. DOUGLAS. *Reforming Human Services: Change through Participation.* Pp. 272. Beverly Hills, CA: Sage, 1982. $22.00. Paperbound, $10.95.

TOUVAL, SAADIA. *The Peace Brokers: Mediators in the Arab-Israeli Conflict, 1948-1979.* Pp. xiv, 377. Princeton, NJ: Princeton University Press, 1982. $30.00. Paperbound, $14.50.

United Nations Educational, Scientific and Cultural Organization. *UNESCO Yearbook on Peace and Conflict Studies 1981.* Pp. xiii, 396. Westport, CT: Greenwood Press, 1982. $35.00.

United States Department of State. *United States Chiefs of Mission 1778-1982.* 2nd ed. Pp. 394. Washington, DC: Department of State, 1982. Paperbound, no price.

VALEO, FRANCIS R. and CHARLES E. MORRIS, eds. *The Japanese Diet and the U.S. Congress.* Pp. xii, 212. Boulder, CO: Westview Press, 1983. $12.00.

VEDUNG, EVERT. *Political Reasoning.* Pp. 232. Beverly Hills, CA: Sage, 1982. $22.00.

VOLKOMER, WALTER E. *American Government.* 3rd ed. Pp. x, 418. Englewood Cliffs, NJ: Prentice-Hall, 1983. Paperbound, no price.

WAGENFELD, MORTON O., PAUL V. LEMKAU, and BLAIR JUSTICE, eds. *Public Mental Health: Perspectives and Prospects.* Pp. 320. Beverly Hills, CA: Sage, 1982. $22.00. Paperbound, $10.95.

WARREN, ROLAND L. and LARRY LYON, eds. *New Perspectives on the American Community.* Pp. xiii, 433. Homewood, IL: Dorsey Press, 1983. Paperbound, no price.

WEINTRAUB, SIDNEY and STANLEY R. ROSS. *"Temporary" Alien Workers in the United States: Designing Policy from Fact and Opinion.* Pp. xi, 124. Boulder, CO: Westview Press, 1982. Paperbound, $16.00.

WISER, JAMES L. *Political Philosophy: A History of the Search for Order.* Pp. xi, 419. Englewood Cliffs, NJ: Prentice-Hall, 1983. $22.95.

WOLL, ALLEN L. *The Hollywood Musical Goes to War.* Pp. xii, 186. Chicago: Nelson-Hall, 1983. $19.95. Paperbound, $9.95.

YORK, PHYLLIS and DAVID and TED WACHTEL. *Toughlove.* Pp. 210. Garden City, NY: Doubleday and Company, 1982. $12.95.